Contemporary
American Indian Writing

American Indian Studies

Elizabeth Hoffman Nelson and Malcolm A. Nelson
General Editors

Vol. 6

PETER LANG
New York · Washington, D.C./Baltimore · Boston
Bern · Frankfurt am Main · Berlin · Vienna · Paris

Dee Horne

Contemporary American Indian Writing

Unsettling Literature

PETER LANG
New York · Washington, D.C./Baltimore · Boston
Bern · Frankfurt am Main · Berlin · Vienna · Paris

Library of Congress Cataloguing-in-Publication Data

Horne, Dee.
Contemporary American Indian writing: unsettling literature / Dee Horne.
p.   cm. — (American Indian studies; vol. 6)
Includes bibliographical references and index.
1. American literature—Indian authors—History and criticism.
2. Indians of North America—United States—Intellectual life.
3. American literature—20th century—History and criticism.
4. Indians in literature. I. Title. II. Series.
PS153.I52H67   810.9′897—dc21   98-53141
ISBN 0-8204-4298-4
ISSN 1058-563X

Die Deutsche Bibliothek-CIP-Einheitsaufnahme

Horne, Dee:
Contemporary American Indian writing: unsettling literature / Dee Horne.
–New York; Washington, D.C./Baltimore; Boston; Bern;
Frankfurt am Main; Berlin; Vienna; Paris: Lang.
(American indian studies; Vol. 6)
ISBN 0-8204-4298-4

Cover design by Lisa Dillon
Cover art by Karin Weber

The paper in this book meets the guidelines for permanence and durability
of the Committee on Production Guidelines for Book Longevity
of the Council of Library Resources.

Printed in the United States of America

For Dylan, Kyle, and Peter

Until you can see through the rules, you can only see through the rules.

R. D. Laing *The Politics of Experience*

Acknowledgments

I am greatly indebted to friends and colleagues who have influenced and supported my work. I wish to thank Marika Ainley, Karin Beeler, Heidi Burns, David Dowling, Julia Emberley, Elizabeth Hoffman-Nelson, Jo-Anne Fiske, Ross Leckie, Malcolm Nelson, and Sue Matheson for reading and commenting on this book. Their feedback has been invaluable. Special thanks to Heidi for her excellent editorial assistance and her dedication to this project. I am grateful to Alton Becker, Rosalia Dutra, and John Robert Ross for keeping me informed of their research and for sharing their insights about language. I also thank Margaret Anderson, Jeannette Armstrong, Marcelle Gareau, Donna Goodleaf, Mary-Ellen Kelm, Antonia Mills, and Deanna Nyce for contributing to the dialogue of decolonization. I have learned much from their work and I have enjoyed many wonderful conversations. I am also grateful to Mary-Ellen Skinner and Karin Sleggs for their friendship and support throughout this project. I extend my thanks and appreciation to Karin Sleggs for her conceptual design for the cover.

Parts of chapter two, "To Know the Difference: Mimicry, Satire, and Thomas King's *Green Grass, Running Water*," appeared in *Essays on Canadian Writing* and are reprinted by permission of *Essays on Canadian Writing*, Toronto. Copyright © ECW Press. Parts of chapter three, "Listening to Silences" appeared in *Studies in Canadian Literature*, issue 23.2 (1998), and are reprinted with permission. I have also presented parts of this work at conferences. I delivered a paper entitled "Settler Culture Under Reconstruction" at the Inter-National Regions conference held at the University of Northern British Columbia in October, 1994. This paper draws on parts of the section on Tomson Highway's plays in chapter seven. It was subsequently published in the selected conference proceedings, *Diverse Landscapes: Re-Reading Place Across Cultures in Contemporary Canadian Writing*, and is reprinted here with the permission of UNBC Press.

I am grateful to the University of Northern British Columbia for providing me with several conference travel grants. I have presented some of the material in this book at conferences: International Conference on Narrative Literature (1994), BC Studies (1994), Inter-National Regions (1994), Association for Canadian Studies in Australia and New Zealand (1995), Sense of Place (1995), Crossroads in Cultural Studies (1996), American Culture Association (1996, 1997), and Western Literature Association (1998). I appreciate the warm reception that these audiences gave me.

I thank students at the University of Northern British Columbia for their thoughtful questions and comments. Their insights have contributed to my thinking and understanding of these works. I also gratefully acknowledge the assistance that Cindy Tanner, Joanne Matthews, and the other librarians at the University of Northern British Columbia provided.

I especially want to thank my family for their love, encouragement, and endless support. My companion Peter Thompson has been a thoughtful reader and listener. He knows the difference between colonial and subversive mimicry and values creative hybridity. Our children, Kyle and Dylan, have shared stories and reminded me of the importance of humor and play. This book is dedicated to them.

Contents

Preface

A challenge that many American Indian[1] writers face is to discover ways to write in English, one of the languages of the colonizer, about the colonial relationship and discourse without perpetuating them. Language does not determine or embody culture. However, language and culture are inextricably intertwined. In discussing how discourse extends the linguistic field, Ania Loomba writes: ". . . no utterance is innocent and every utterance tells us something about the world we live in. But equally, the world we live in is only comprehensible to us in its discursive representations" (40). Moreover, language is relational and ideological. For instance, the English language carries traces of the historical practices of colonialism and its discourse. Thus, when an author writes about colonialism in the language of the colonizer it is often difficult (but not impossible) to find ways of discussing these practices without perpetuating the very terms and ideology that underlie colonialism. Given that language and usage are subject to change, writers can subvert the language of the colonizer. This book grew out of my fascination with subversive narrative strategies and the different ways diverse American Indian writers disavow the colonial relationship and discourse. Each of the writers discussed in this book use and also alter the language of the colonizer. Each has different innovative strategies to unsettle the colonial relationship and affirm alternative discourses.

Writing a study of American Indian literature is problematic because it suggests that there is a homogeneous body of literature when there is not. As Thomas King observes, "when we talk about contemporary Native literature, we talk as though we already have a definition for this body of literature when, in fact, we do not. And, when we talk about Native writers, we talk as though we have a process for determining who is a Native writer and who is not, when in fact, we don't" (*All My Relations* x). While there is

no consensus among literary critics about what constitutes
American Indian literature, the question is not whether there is
such a body of literature which is distinctive, but rather who
defines it as such and why. What is at stake is cultural self-
determination. When non-Natives construct the category of
American Indian literature, they are often perceived by American
Indians and others as creating a false homogeneity. Their efforts
are perceived by some American Indian critics as endeavors to
marginalize Native writers—to position them as peripheral to the
eurocentric canon—or to create a sub-canon of select American
Indian writers that excludes many talented writers.

A study devoted to American Indian writers can become a
means of marginalizing them and of perpetuating the colonial
Manichean opposition of us and them. The classification of
American Indian literature can consititute essentialism in which
the literary critic places diverse authors, each with his or her
unique creative vision, into a homogeneous category. Marilyn
Dumont voices the frustrations that Métis and American Indian
writers face in light of others' endeavors to canonize them. The
narrator in Dumont's poem, "Circle the Wagons," points out how
this categorization often perpetuates colonial stereotypes: "There
it is again, the circle, that goddamned circle, as if we thought in
circles, judged things on the merit of their circularity, as if all we
ate was bologna and bannock . . ." (57). Distraught, the narrator
asks: "Is there nothing more than the circle in the deep structure of
native literature?" (57). She later describes the vicious circle she
experiences. Even though the narrator does not want to be
trapped by "the circle," she feels "compelled to incorporate
something circular" into her writing to dispel the stereotype of the
vanishing Indian and to prevent herself from feeling "lost," "a
fading urban Indian caught in all the trappings of Doc Martens,
cappuccinos and foreign films" (57). Dumont, and other authors,
engage in strategic essentialism,[2] in which they position themselves
as American Indian writers to assert cultural differences and to
counter colonial essentializing practices that disavow these
differences.

In considering selected writings by Thomas King, Jeannette
Armstrong, Ruby Slipperjack, Beatrice Culleton, Tomson
Highway, and Lee Maracle, this book examines how these diverse

authors contest the colonial discourse and civilizing mission.[3] Whenever writers attempt to challenge an official discourse while employing the "rules of recognition" (Bhabha *The Location of Culture* 114)[4] of that discourse, there exists a danger that they may fall off the precipice—the chasm between colonial mimicry and subversion of it—they are walking along and become co-opted. The question of access to power, resources, and materials is intricately linked to the question of colonial mimicry and attendant notions of representation and identity. How does one gain access to the resources, positions, and power of settlers without duplicating the very political, social, and economic structures that have marginalized or been denied to American Indians? Or to put it another way, is it possible to mimic elements of settler discourse without becoming a colonial mimic?

Tricksters are often excellent mimics and impersonators. They exemplify change and fluidity. They delight in eluding and transgressing boundaries, conventions, and definitions. Their subversive mimicry offers strategies for writers to dismantle the colonial discourse and its rules of recognition. By partially mimicking colonial rules in different, decolonized contexts, writers can estrange them from colonial authority; the rules undergo a process of transformation wherein they cease to serve colonizers and their discourse.

Like tricksters, the writers addressed in this book elude the binary oppositions of colonizer and colonized and settler attempts to classify, incorporate, and define American Indians. Through trickster mimicry, they partially represent the colonial relationship, while also asserting cultural differences, to re-present the language and rules of recognition of colonial discourse. Their trickster-like narratives contribute to the project of decolonization; they "decolonize our minds" (Césaire *Discourse on Colonialism* 78) and "invent souls" (Césaire qtd. in Fanon's *The Wretched of the Earth* 197).

Drawing on American Indian and eurocentric settler cultures,[5] these narratives resist literary "contamination" (Brydon "The White Inuit Speaks" 191) through strategies of literary infiltration.[6] They bridge cultural differences and exemplify ways of fostering co-existence with differences. Each chapter focuses on different subversive strategies that these writers use to resist colonial mimicry and to challenge and reconfigure the rules of recognition of the dominant society and colonial discourse.

Chapter one provides a theoretical framework for the book in which I differentiate between colonial mimicry and subversive mimicry. I explicate colonial mimicry and demonstrate why it is necessary for colonized writers to resist it. The chapter illustrates how these authors can dance along the precipice of colonial mimicry by creating narrative strategies that subversively mimic aspects of the colonial relationship in order to contest it and propose alternative paradigms.

Chapter two discusses some of the ways that Thomas King uses satire to realize this subversive power and to free his work, and readers' thinking, from an oppressive Manichean opposition. Chapter three examines how Ruby Slipperjack, in *Silent Words*, draws attention to the gap between cultures. She challenges the judgmental binary thinking underlying many colonial attitudes toward silence. By putting the language of colonizers under erasure, Slipperjack writes over the "epistemic violence" (Gayatri Spivak, *Women's Texts* 273) of colonization. At the same time, she uses a strategy of *implicature* to convey and validate silence as part of the continuum of language. Her narrative strategically writes through silence to alter literary expression and to create an alternative discourse which affirms American Indians.

Chapter four explores the relationship between cognition, affect, and stereotypes. *In Search of April Raintree* illustrates how Beatrice Culleton deploys stereotypes to subvert them. In interweaving the narratives of April and Cheryl Raintree, the author presents a paradigm of colonial stereotypic discourse that I analyze within the context of Homi Bhabha's concept of colonial stereotypes. Racism is one of the primary determinants of the reception of this text, yet the text itself is challenging racism through this narrative of colonial stereotypic figuring. The narrative provides a paradigm for recasting colonial impressions.

Chapter five examines Jeannette Armstrong's *Slash*. In drawing on history in her fictional narratives, Armstrong performs an act of rememoration that debunks settler histories. The author displaces settler versions of the past while drawing on and contributing to American Indian social memories. This commemoration leads to rememoration of American Indians, and to the formation of new social memories.

Chapter six examines Lee Maracle's *Ravensong* and the ways in which American Indians can resist colonial shame. Through trickster's song, shame is a means of social reform to teach non-Natives and to bridge cultural differences. Chapter seven further examines tricksters and looks at two of Tomson Highway's plays and a short story by Thomas King. Like Maracle, these two writers adapt trickster figures (Nanabush and Coyote, respectively) from American Indian oral traditions to create post-colonial tricksters that affirm cultural differences and elude colonial dichotomies. The epilogue returns to the theme of dancing along the precipice. It reviews the subversive strategies and discusses how these narratives transform reading practices. It also offers directions for further research.

The subtitle of my book alludes to the ways in which these writers are unsettling (both in the sense of subverting and in the sense of decolonizing) mainstream literature. An underlying premise is that, although American Indians have undergone imperialism and neocolonialism, they are still being colonized. Colonialism refers to the process by which European powers achieved economic, political, and cultural hegemony while imperialism refers to a particular phase of colonialism from the latter part of the nineteenth century to the first part of the twentieth century when the emphasis shifted from territorial conquest to market expansion. The term neocolonialism refers to the change from primarily military and political to economic and cultural means of control (Shohat and Stam 15, 17).

Another central premise of this book is that all cultures, and specifically all literatures, are hybrid. There are particular ramifications that cultural and literary hybridity have for American Indians, namely assimilation and the perpetuation of racism and inequality that arise when one or more cultures attempt to impose their values and beliefs on others. Hybridity can be a problematic term because of the ways in which it has historically been used to rationalize and perpetuate racist theories and discourse, but also because hybridization has often been confused with, and at times disguised as, assimilation.[7] Nonetheless, hybridization need not be assimilation—one culture dominating and taking over another culture—but can be a recognition of the interactions between cultures. In seeing cultures as dynamic and ever changing, I am intrigued by the ways in which ideas travel and, in many cases, are translated within and between societies.

In his linguistic model of hybridity, Mikhail Bakhtin describes how in a hybrid construction an "utterance . . . actually contains mixed within it two utterances, two speech manners, two styles, two 'languages,' two semantic and axiological belief systems" (*The Dialogic Imagination* 304). Bakhtin further explains how even "the same word will belong simultaneously to two languages, two belief systems that intersect in a hybrid construction—and the word has two contradictory meanings, two accents" (305). While Bakhtin is describing how an utterance can contain two belief systems, two languages, I am interested in how the writers addressed in the following pages create dialogic narratives in which American Indians now re-configure settler colonial discourse. Through relational, multi-voiced narratives which allude to the double-voiced colonial discourse without perpetuating it, these narratives articulate how power relations and identities are ever-shifting.

Creative literary hybridity unsettles the authority of the colonizers and their language and discourse. Whereas Bakhtin distinguishes between the process of merging (organic hybrid) and the process of dialogizing (intentional hybrid), I concur with Stuart Hall's observation that these are "two phases of the same movement" ("New Ethnicities" 252). Hybridity is simultaneously "'organically' hegemonizing, creating new spaces, structures, scenes, and 'intentionally' diasporizing, intervening as a form of subversion, translation, transformation" (Young 25). As Young points out, this doubleness in hybridity is significant because otherwise hybridity implies fixed categories (25).

In his discussion of hybridity within the context of the colonial relationship, Homi Bhabha addresses this doubleness. He describes the ambivalence inherent in the colonial presence which is "always ambivalent, split between its appearance as original and authoritative and its articulation as repetition and difference. . . . Such a display of difference produces a mode of authority that is agonistic (rather than antagonistic)" (*Location* 108). I agree with Bhabha that hybridity "unsettles the mimetic or narcissistic demands of colonial power but reimplicates its identifications in strategies of subversion that turn the gaze of the discriminated back upon the eye of power" (*Location* 112).

Bhabha's assertion that "the effect of colonial power is seen to be the *production* of hybridization" has important ramifications for colonized writers because the "ambivalence at the source of traditional discourses on authority enables a form of subversion, founded on the undecidability that turns the discursive conditions of dominance into the grounds of intervention" (*Location* 112). American Indian authors can augment this ambivalent space "so that other 'denied' knowledges enter upon the dominant discourse and estrange the basis of its authority—its rules of recognition" (*Location* 114).

Elaborating on his concept of hybridity, Bhabha describes how it includes diverse forms of counter-authority, a "third space," which can intervene to create:

> . . . the hybrid moment of political change. Here the transformational value of change lies in the re-articulation, or translation, of elements that are *neither the One . . . nor the Other . . . but something else besides*, which contests the terms and territories of both. (*Location* 28)

Through subversive mimicry, the writers discussed in the following pages move toward this third position of political change because they challenge the colonial discourse without perpetuating it. Their hybrid narratives offer readers the opportunity to participate in a productive transformation where we "move towards a genuine affirmation of multiple forms of native 'difference'" and "achieve a genuinely transformative and interventionist criticism of post-colonial reality" (Ashcroft, Griffiths, and Tiffin 180).

Creative hybrid texts are productive of meaning (reforming society by re-formulating it within the text); they are not simply reflective or expressive of existing reality. Critical reception that involves a colonial mimetic reading of post-colonial texts often serves to incorporate these texts into the dominant discourse. Such colonial mimetic readings gloss over the distinctiveness of these texts and lose sight of their subversive characteristics by ignoring the ways in which these texts go against the colonial grain (Bhabha "Representation" 95–96). In order to avoid such misreadings, readers need to be cognizant of the ways the text re-forms society. Creative hybrid texts, as I have defined them here, partially represent or repeat the colonial discourse to contest and re-present it. Estranged from their source of authority, the rules become suspect, and often comic.

In addressing the problems of colonial mimicry and examining creative literary hybridity in which writers employ subversive strategies, this book addresses Ashcroft, Griffiths, and Tiffin's contention that Canada "has not generated corresponding theories of literary hybridity to replace the nationalistic approach" by which it attempts to assert its difference from British or American cultures (36). This book builds on cultural studies, post-colonial and narrative theories as well as studies of American Indian literature in English in North America. There are several studies that focus on contemporary American Indian writings, but few examine in detail the "counter-discourses" (Tiffin "Postcolonial Literatures" 17) that operate in these works.

Julia Emberley's *Thresholds of Difference* (1993) investigates how the writings of American Indian women in Canada exemplify hybridity and resist universalizing theories and practices. Terry Goldie's *Fear and Temptation* exposes the ideological factors that led to similar cultural constructions of the indigene, and processes of indigenization, in Canada, Australia, and New Zealand while Louis Owens' *Other Destinies: Understanding the American Indian Novel* (1992) examines questions of identity and illustrates how contemporary American Indian writers deconstruct western constructions of American Indians as others. Thomas King, Cheryl Calver, and Helen Hoy's collection, *The Native in Literature: Canadian and Comparative Perspectives* (1987), provides essays on western constructions of the Native as well as on the influences of oral traditions in American Indian writings. *Smoothing the Ground* and *Recovering the Word* include essays on American Indian oral traditions. Several of the essays examine the challenges of translation and discuss how American Indian writers adapt oral traditions to print.

Arnold E. Davidson's *Coyote Country: Fictions of the Canadian West* (1994) looks at how writers in Canada use parody and other strategies to challenge the genre of the Western and to offer cross-cultural paradigms of the West. *Narrative Chance: Postmodern Discourse on Native American Literatures* (1989), edited by Gerald Vizenor, illustrates how the postmodern condition "is not literature on trial but a liberation of tribal stories" (xii). Vizenor's chapter on trickster discourse in this collection has proven invaluable.

Native Writers and Canadian Writing (1990; co-published with *Canadian Literature*) includes articles on contemporary American Indian writers that generated ideas for my writing. Margery Fee's "Upsetting Fake Ideas: Jeannette Armstrong's *Slash* and Beatrice Culleton's *April Raintree*" and Barbara Godard's "The Politics of Representation: Some Native Canadian Women Writers" examine counter-hegemonic strategies while Margaret Atwood's "A Double-Bladed Knife: Subversive Laughter in Two Stories by Thomas King" illustrates how humor can unsettle and heal readers. Noel Elizabeth Currie's "Jeannette Armstrong & the Colonial Legacy" examines how *Slash* reveals the underlying racism, sexism, and classism behind colonialism, while Basil Johnston's "One Generation from Extinction" reminds readers of the effects of colonialism and provides a stimulating discussion of the importance of cultural survival for American Indians.[8]

Literary hybridity is a subject that many writers and critics have touched on in their forays in the field, but few have focused on the possibilities that hybridity offers for writers as well as for readers. While *Contemporary American Indian Writing* will be of particular interest to scholars of American Indian literature, it will also appeal to readers interested in hybrid strategies that do not sublate differences.

Most of the writers discussed in this book have indicated that they are primarily writing for American Indians, although they also recognize that their audience will include non-Native readers. As a non-Native reader who lacks the cultural contexts and experiential knowledge that these authors draw on, I am interested in understanding how the subversive strategies they employ can create not only a double movement of re-presentation and representation but also dialogues in which settlers may participate in the process of decolonization. I examine what these texts may teach readers about diverse American Indian world views. Specifically, this book investigates how these hybrid narratives unsettle settler society and its colonial discourse.

Many American Indian academics and individuals often perceive the work of non-Native scholars and critics as suspect.

Ever cognizant of this perception, I acknowledge and work within the parameters of a reader who is a product, and a part, of the societies that have colonized and oppressed American Indians. I am well aware that I can escape neither my own eurocentric aesthetics nor my own cultural values. Rather than trying to ignore or work around these limitations, I have chosen to acknowledge them. In no way do I wish to appropriate this literature. If such appropriation is evident, it is unintended and the fault is mine alone.

The following pages examine texts that employ diverse trickster-like strategies that unsettle colonial discourse. In focusing on the different subversive strategies that these authors use in their writing, this book enters a dialogue which other critics and readers will necessarily revise and extend in different directions. While this book has discussed how and why it is necessary to subvert colonial mimicry, more analysis of colonial mimicry and its ramifications would benefit those interested in decolonization. By understanding and interrogating colonial mimicry, writers and readers can construct strategies to deconstruct it. The interrelationships between subversive mimicry and irony, parody, and satire also offer opportunities for further research and investigation.

My selection of authors is by no means exhaustive. There are numerous American Indian writers and many more strategies of subversion than I have discussed here. Although I have focused on what settlers can learn from American Indian literature, there is an increasing amount of writing on this literature by American Indian authors. Many of these writers are actively engaged in ongoing cultural projects in which they support new, upcoming writers and their works. Many are also involved in community projects that support American Indian cultural diversity while also providing opportunities for writers and artists from different American Indian communities to share their cultures. Studies of American Indian literature written by American Indians have offered, and will continue to provide, further insights into these and other narratives. I hope that this book will provide the impetus for further studies of American Indian literature and of subversive mimicry.

Chapter One

Dancing along the Precipice

> So what is this tickling at the heels to which Kafka's all too human ape
> would refer us all too apish humans to? I call it the mimetic faculty, the
> nature that culture uses to create second nature, the faculty to copy,
> imitate, make models, explore difference, yield into and become Other.
>
> Michael Taussig *Mimesis and Alterity* xiii

When N. Scott Momaday's novel, *House Made of Dawn* (1968),
was awarded the Pulitzer Prize for fiction, a member of the
Pulitzer jury commented that "an award to its author might be
considered a recognition of 'the arrival on the American literary
scene of a matured, sophisticated literary artist from the original
Americas'" (qtd. in Owens 90). Significantly, the juror did not
perceive Momaday's work as the arrival on the American Indian
literary scene, but incorporated Momaday into the "American
literary scene." Instead of recognizing how Momaday and his
work build on existing traditions of American Indian writers like
Matthews, McNickle, Mourning Dove, or others, the juror's
comments reveal a colonial perception that colonized writers need
"to imitate the discourse of the cultural center—Euramerica—"
well enough to be "accepted, perhaps canonized" (Owens 90).

The reception of Momaday's work is one indication of the
ways in which the dominant society invalidates colonized writers
and their works. Colonizers privilege writing and experiences that
conform to the rules of recognition of the dominant society. The
prejudices and power imbalance in the colonial relationship are
evident in the ways in which "only certain categories of experience
are capable of being rendered as 'literature'" (Ashcroft, Griffiths,
and Tiffin 88). Colonized writers face a double bind. If their
writing conforms to these rules of recognition, then their work is

either dismissed as inauthentic, an imitation, and they are often dismissed as colonial mimics, or their work is incorporated into the canon, and they are acknowledged as mastering the dominant discourse. Both forms of critical reception reveal prejudices underlying the dominant society's privileging of writing which consign post-colonial writers to "a world of mimicry and imitation"; they are "forced to write about material which lies at one remove from the significant experiences of the post-colonial world" (Ashcroft, Griffiths, and Tiffin 88). If their work operates outside the colonial rules of recognition and works within alternative rules and cultural traditions, then colonial critics often dismiss it as marginal because it is outside the eurocentric canon. Louis Owens describes the options available to American Indian authors: "Confronted with the authoritative privileged voice of European America, the Indian resorts to subversion or often falls silent" (8). When authors, like Momaday, write within the colonial rules of recognition while simultaneously contesting these rules, they often find that their subversive strategies are either unnoticed or overlooked in efforts to sublate cultural differences and incorporate the work within the existing western canon.

Mimicry is often linked to mimesis which refers to how cultures structure representations of their perceptions of reality. Mimetic representations are problematic given that all acts of representation are socially constructed. What makes mimetic studies particularly problematic in colonial contexts is that literary representations often reflect and re-inscribe eurocentric views of the world and dismiss alternative representations and ways of seeing the world. Edward Said, Homi Bhabha, and Michael Taussig discuss how mimesis has often served colonial discourse.[1] In describing mimesis as "the nature culture uses to create second nature," Taussig rightly perceives how this second nature is "foundering and highly unstable" (252). He describes how "now the self is inscribed in the Alter that the self needs to define itself against" (252). Mimesis has the potential to be subversive, however. Interactions in which the mimetic reflections of the West are depicted by those who have been altered can create "mimetic excess—*mimetic self-awareness, mimesis turned on itself*, on its colonial endowment" (Taussig 252; emphasis added). Said critiques essentialism which is characteristic of colonial discourse and illustrates how the apparent stability of this discourse is threatened not only by forces that challenge it but also by the internal inconsistencies within colonial discourse itself. Bhabha distinguishes between mimesis, which is an apparently homogeneous system of representation, and mimicry which articulates the desire for a "reformed, recognizable Other, *as a subject of a difference that is almost the same, but not quite*" (*Location* 86). Mimicry destabilizes and calls into question the homogenizing impulses of the dominant society. In their desire to fix identity and to define themselves against reformed "others" who are encouraged to emulate—to become like, colonizers—but are never quite the same, colonizers create a "discourse of mimicry" that is "constructed around an ambivalence" (*Location* 86): "mimicry emerges as the representation of a difference that is itself a process of disavowal" (86).

Bhabha's observation that "mimicry emerges as one of the most elusive and effective strategies of colonial power and knowledge" (*Location* 85) is an accurate description of the emphasis of the *colonial* mimic. All representation is re-presentation. However, colonial mimics are more concerned with repeating than with re-presenting colonizers, whereas subversive mimics critically represent colonizers and their discourse to re-present them. The colonial mimic can never exactly repeat the colonizer because of the power imbalance and the constructed difference between colonizer and colonized which is the basis for the colonial relationship. The colonial assumption of superiority is, as Said discusses in his analysis of Western relations with the Orient, a "flexible positional superiority" which puts the colonizer in a "whole series of possible relationships" with the colonized without ever relinquishing the "relative upper hand" (Said *Orientalism* 7). The colonial mimic who attempts to repeat colonizers is actually engaged in a re-presentation of them wherein the colonial mimic is still disavowed as other, as different from the colonizer. Bhabha's discussion of mimicry is an analysis of colonial mimicry; he does not consider how writers might deploy other modes of mimicry which are not colonial. He acknowledges that the "ambivalence of mimicry" suggests that the "colonial culture is potentially and strategically an insurgent counter-appeal" (*Location* 91), but he does not address how colonized people might use this ambivalence to create modes of mimicry to contest colonial power and knowledge and, more importantly, to subvert the colonial relationship. In noting how "mimicry is always produced at the site of interdiction" and is a form of colonial discourse that is "uttered between the lines and as such both against the rules and within them" (*Location* 89), Bhabha focuses on the ways in which colonizers often speak "in a tongue that is forked" (*Location* 85), but does not examine how colonized writers might deploy irony, "forked tongues," to challenge the authority of colonial discourse.

Subversive modes of mimicry allow writers to partially represent the colonial discourse without perpetuating it. Often, subversive mimicry employs irony which, as Linda Hutcheon observes, can be a "rhetorical strategy for working within existing discourses and contesting them at the same time" ("Circling the Downspout of Empire" 154). She describes the "trope of irony as a doubled or split discourse" which has "the potential to subvert from within" (154). Colonized writers create a "split discourse" in which they partially mimic colonizers and the colonial discourse to challenge and re-present colonial rules of recognition. While it would be useful to provide an extensive discussion of the various modes of mimicry, this book investigates two modes: colonial mimicry and subversive mimicry and will examine how mimicry, in its subversive mode, is an effective counter strategy to the colonial enterprise.

Mimicry

The *Oxford English Dictionary* defines mimicry as "the action, practice, or art of mimicking or closely imitating, either in sport or otherwise, the manner, gesture, speech or mode of action of persons, or the superficial characteristics of a thing" (1799). As previously discussed, mimicry is often linked to mimesis, which refers to representations of reality, but while mimesis refers to representation mimicry can be better appreciated as the act or art of re-presentation. It calls attention to itself in ways that a representation does not.

Mimicry is imitation, but no imitation is ever exact. While the mimic may desire to become like another, the mimic can never be the other.[2] Instead, all mimicry involves a re-presentation of that which is being imitated. It involves a simultaneous process of displaying similarities and differences. The mimic strives to resemble that which is being imitated, but in imitating the other, the mimic reveals—either knowingly or unknowingly—his/her differences. In his discussion of mimicry, Walter Benjamin remarks on human beings' "capacity for producing similarities" and argues that this "gift of seeing resemblances is nothing other than a rudiment of the powerful compulsion in former times to become and behave like something else" (*Reflections* 333). Although mimicry signals this desire to become like another, it also continually frustrates it. It is a process of partial repetition in which the mimic's efforts to repeat—"to become and behave like something else"—contain traces of difference that simultaneously signal the ways in which the mimic is unlike, dissimilar to, something else. In the colonial relationship, the colonized who attempts to mimic the colonizer—to become like the colonizer—is always reminded by the colonizer of his/her differences.

Mimicry is a response to a pre-existing object or person. It always implies a relationship between the mimic and that which is being mimicked. This relationship signals an unequal power relationship in which one person (or group) performs the role of the model and the other performs, or is constructed to be, the imitator. Frequently, the target of the mimicry is constructed as primary—as the master, origin, or original—and the mimic is constructed as secondary—as the copy, the one who re-presents the original referent.[3]

In the colonial relationship, colonizers assume the role of models (of authors of authority) and construct the colonized as those in need of remodeling, of "civilizing." Colonizers construct themselves to be the origin and original and the colonized as secondary, or derivative to justify their assumed position of authority, of mastery. Settlers attempt to justify the occupation of the colonizeds' territory and to disavow territorial claims that the colonized possess. If colonizers were to acknowledge that their discourse is neither inherently superior nor original, then the bipolarization of the colonial relationship and the legitimacy of the colonizers' claims to power, which includes occupation of the colonizers' territory, would be called into question. Colonial mimicry refers to the process wherein colonizers encourage the colonized to partially imitate them while they, the colonizers, perpetuate the eurocentric colonial assumption of superiority. As part of their civilizing mission, settlers encourage colonial mimicry in their efforts to facilitate the process of assimilation.

The civilizing mission involves a process of simultaneously constructing similarity and difference. The colonized may only participate in a partial repetition because colonizers, if they are to remain colonizers, differentiate themselves from the colonized to maintain power and authority over them. While they want the colonized to imitate them—to become the same as them and assimilate into settler society—they also maintain difference: "the same but not quite, the same but not white" (Bhabha *Location* 89). Settlers encourage the colonized to mimic their culture and discourse, to assimilate into settler society. When colonizers force—either through legislation or other means—the colonized to use settler discourse, they disavow existing cultural differences in the name of their constructed difference, of civilizing. Witness the repeated efforts by settlers to suppress American Indian cultures. In 1884, for instance, the Canadian government outlawed the potlatch, a significant social, political, and economic institution of Pacific Northcoast Indians. Perceiving totem poles to be objects of heathen worship, missionaries often destroyed or removed totem poles from the communities. Although Parliament repealed the laws against the potlatch and land claims organization in 1951, the devastating effects of these repressive laws still remain with American Indians today.

The experience of some American Indians in residential schools where they have been required to speak English, and not allowed to speak their own language(s), is another example.[4] The colonial subtext is that American Indians can learn to speak English and be like settlers—to become civilized—but they are still deemed inferior. While the colonized may learn the settlers' language, history, discourse, and rules of recognition, they continue to be disavowed as long as they either accept or participate in the underlying structural power imbalance.

The eurocentric assumption of superiority continues to inform the dominant society as it validates its cultural adaptation (as evidence of progress and innovation) while simultaneously invalidating the cultural adaptation of diverse American Indians as "aping the white man" and indicating their "loss of culture and rights" (Tennant 15). In the civilizing mission, settlers encourage American Indians to assimilate—to become like, but not the same as, them—while simultaneously disavowing American Indians because of their differences. At the same time the dominant society disavows and denies aboriginal rights to Indians who have assimilated on the basis of their similarities. This double bind is evident in two "complementary" settler views that undermine aboriginal rights: "The first denies aboriginal rights on the grounds that Indians were in the beginning too different from Whites. The second view denies aboriginal rights on the grounds that Indians have now become too similar to Whites" (Tennant 15).

Settler appropriation of American Indian cultures endangers the efforts of diverse peoples to assert their aboriginal right to self-determination. Settlers may disavow the diversity of American Indian cultures by suggesting that the characteristics they have selected are representative of all American Indians. Settlers who expect an American Indian person to speak for, or represent, all American Indians also reveal their stereotypical constructions of American Indians as homogeneous. In Thomas King's short story, "A Seat in the Garden," Red Matthews (Joe Hovaugh's friend) comments to the three Indians he meets in the garden "I'll bet you guys know just about everything there is to know about Indians" (88).[5] The "first Indian" articulates the need to recognize cultural differences when he replies, "Jimmy and Frank are Nootka and I'm Cree" (89).

Some settlers invoke authenticity as a means to invalidate American Indians. Wendy Rose describes how as "an Indian, I am rendered 'unreal'" (413) because she does not fit settler concepts of what an "Indian" should be. She criticizes those settlers who expect her to "negate the reality of my—and my people's— existence in favor of a script developed within the fantasies of our oppressors" (W. Rose 413). Thomas King satirizes settler constructions of the authentic Indian in many of his works. In *Green Grass, Running Water*, Portland changes his name and dons a prosthetic nose that makes him look like a clown in an effort to accommodate a Hollywood director who does not think he looks Indian enough (129). In King's short story, "Joe the Painter," Joe asks the Indians who perform in his pageant to wear wigs because they do not "look like Indians" (*One Good Story* 110).

Those settlers who appropriate selective aspects of American Indians to disavow differences often engage in a form of cultural imperialism in which the underlying assumption is that all human beings are the same. Wendy Rose writes: "Rather than taking pride in their own deeply rooted ethnicity, most Euroamericans feel duty-bound to sublimate it" (410). She observes that "even the most avowedly progressive Euroamericans seem to want a Disney-ish world in which everyone is a different shade of the same thing" (410).

While some writers and critics argue that all writing is a form of appropriation and that it is a writer's prerogative to borrow material wherever she/he sees fit, others acknowledge that appropriation may have negative consequences, but argue that they can use material from different cultures as long as they are responsible and their research is accurate. Still others argue that all cultural appropriation is wrong and believe that writers should only write about their own culture. Underlying the appropriation debate lies the fear, by some settlers, that American Indians are "'staking a claim' as the sole interpreters of Indian cultures" (W. Rose 415). The issue is not whether or not non-Indians can write about American Indians, but rather how and why they do: "We accept as given that whites have as much prerogative to write and speak about us and our cultures as we have to write and speak about them and theirs. The question is how this is done and, to some extent, why it is done" (W. Rose 416). Ultimately, it is a question of "integrity and intent" (W. Rose 416). For Rose, there is "a world of difference" between non-Native writers who write about American Indians and those who claim they have "become 'an Indian'"; between those who articulate that their writing reflects their perceptions and those who perpetrate "the fraud of having been appointed 'mediums' of Indian culture"; and between those who "rely for their information upon actual native sources" and those who "simply invent them" (416).

In her discussion of "white shamanism," Rose describes how writers like Lynn Andrews, Carlos Castenada, and Hyemeyohsts Storm selectively appropriate and re-contextualize American Indian material. In so doing, they distort and misrepresent American Indians and their cultures.[6] In his short story, "Totem

Poles," Thomas King critiques settler appropriation. The story satirizes those settlers who have taken totem poles out of their cultural contexts and their attempts to turn totem poles, and by implication American Indians, into objects—cultural artifacts. The story describes how the totem poles talk back and refuse, like American Indians, to be silenced, contained, "protected," or ignored. The story is a humorous indictment of various settler policies and tactics to deal with what settlers have constructed as the "Indian problem."[7] King satirizes colonial assumptions of superiority which imply that "non-Indians always (inherently) know more about Indians than Indians themselves" (W. Rose 406).

Colonized people experience both fear and desire and a tension between self-preservation and self-destruction. They may desire to imitate the colonizer to gain access to the power, resources, and privileges that the colonizer wields. At the same time, colonized people fear this call to mimicry because colonial mimicry risks self-effacement. There is the danger that by participating—either fully or partially—in the colonizers' rules, the colonized will perpetuate the colonial relationship that they seek to undo. Colonized writers who write in English need to be wary of the dangers of incorporation, of duplicating colonial discourse or creating other forms of oppression.

Chinua Achebe believes that writers should be able to make the English language "bear the burden" of their experiences, whereas Ngugi wa Thiong'o disagrees with Achebe.[8] In *Decolonising the Mind*, he argues that it is imperative that writers write in their own language and refuse to write in English. He believes African writers have a responsibility to reject the language(s) of those who have colonized them. He discusses how language is intricately tied to cultural identity: "The choice of language and the use to which language is put is central to a people's definition of themselves in relation to their natural and social environment" (4).[9] The latter position is untenable for those American Indian authors who never learned the language of their ancestors or who have lost their ancestral language due to experiences at residential schools or other factors. Access to publishers and to a wide distribution of readers is important to all writers, but particularly important to American Indian authors who have often been marginalized or excluded from mainstream publishing houses. But American Indian writers who choose to submit work to large publishing houses to access the larger distribution and readership face the danger of colonial mimicry. If writers mimic the codes and conventions of the dominant society, then they are in danger of becoming inducted into the mainstream. As Wendy Rose explains, "Ours is always the balancing act between selling and selling out" (413). Another recourse is to submit work to one of the presses that either is owned and operated by American Indian people or is committed to American Indian Literature.

A major disadvantage for American Indian writers is that they have often been alienated from their culture(s), and writing in English—the language of the dominant power and discourse— exacerbates this. Some concepts are distorted when translated while others are untranslatable. Language is also one of the main tools that settler society uses to indoctrinate the colonized subject. Correct, standard English (capital E) is validated and any deviations from this—speaking "Indian," use of the vernacular, or hybridized speech—is often not only invalidated as inauthentic, "incorrect" but also, in the colonial discourse, equated with inferiority. Language becomes a representation and further codification and inscription of value judgments and of power imbalances. Those who deviate from the "correct" usage are devalued and marginalized. The extreme effect of this destructive process occurs when the marginalized subject is shamed into silence, into a position of negation and absence.

When colonizers employ mimicry as a means of control and education, they encourage the colonized to imitate the colonial discourse without allowing them to articulate their cultural differences. All imitation, to some extent, requires resemblance, familiarity, if it is to be recognized. Colonized writers can dance along this precipice by presenting their ideas within existing traditions, some familiar terrain for readers, while also articulating their differences and defamiliarizing those aspects of familiar terrain which undermine or disavow their differences. Writers partially mimic to ensure that their work is recognized; the challenge is to affiliate with existing literary traditions without succumbing to filiation, to servile forms of subordination in which their work is perceived to be a pale imitation, an inferior copy.

In colonial mimicry, the guise of affiliation is marked by filiation; subsequently, affiliation is always on the colonizers' terms—terms that perpetuate the colonial relationship and continue to inscribe the colonized as other. In this respect, Gayatri Spivak's perception that the subaltern cannot speak because they are trapped by the very "epistemic violence" they seek to contest holds true.[10]

Ralph Singh, the protagonist in V. S. Naipaul's *The Mimic Men*, exemplifies the colonial mimic who attempts to affiliate with the dominant society by a dangerous practice of filiation. He perceives the colonizers as real and feigns a pretense of being real. Performing the role of colonial puppet, Ralph exemplifies the colonial mimic who comes to view himself through the lens of the colonizer: "We pretended to be real, to be learning, to be preparing ourselves for life, we mimic men of the New World, one unknown corner of it, with all its reminders of the corruption that came so quickly to the new" (Naipaul 146). Naipaul delineates the dangers of pretenses of affiliation that are rooted in filial practices and illustrates how filiation is doomed to failure. Filiation leads to Ralph's loss of confidence and perpetuates his position of powerlessness. In being filial and subservient, he is corrupted by the process of colonial mimicry and his differences continue to be disavowed.

Colonial mimics internalize colonialism and learn to see themselves, either wholly or partially, through the lens of settlers. They are caught betwixt and between cultures that disavow them. By internalizing settler values and stereotypes, colonial mimics participate in their own self-effacement. The colonial mimic who desires to become like the settler is often categorized as an "apple" (red on the outside, but white on the inside). April Raintree, for instance, in Beatrice Culleton's *In Search of April Raintree* exemplifies the "apple." Cheryl, her sister, believes that April has sold out and denied her own culture while the settler family April marries into continues to exclude and disavow her on the grounds that she is Métis. When she lives with a foster family, her foster sister jeeringly refers to her as "ape" and reminds both, April and readers, of what Michael Taussig has described as "the felt relation of the civilizing process to savagery, to aping" (xiv).

Colonized people simultaneously desire and fear the power of the colonizer. Since the colonial enterprise often disguises its exploitative purpose as a civilizing mission, colonizers try to impose their language because this is a tool with which they can implant their rules of recognition. Herein lies the ambivalence of the colonial relationship; in imposing their language, colonizers are giving the colonized the key to entry in the dominant discourse. When the colonized engage with the dominant discourse, by writing in English for instance, they can either be incorporated or can change the rules of recognition and alter the language of the dominant power so that it expresses their reality. In this way, they call into question the basic assumptions upon which the colonial relationship—the difference established between colonizer and colonized—is based.

American Indian writers who write in english[11] always risk walking the precipice of colonial mimicry as they strive to sell their writing without selling out. Given that colonial mimicry is a significant tactic that colonizers employ to impose their authority and rules on the colonized, it is important for writers to challenge it. They may use subversive mimicry—in which they partially repeat aspects of colonial discourse to re-configure it—to contest colonial mimicry.

In subversive mimicry, the writer emphasizes the guise, not the filiation, and the writer affiliates by referencing this pattern of filiation that colonizers seek to engender in colonized people without participating in it. From the perspective of colonizers, "filiation gives rise not only to conflict but is driven by a desire to exterminate what has been engendered" (Said *The World, the Text and the Critic* 118). Those institutions which preserve the process of filiation also "protect filiation by instituting affiliation, that is, a joining together of people in a nongenealogical, nonprocreative but social unity" (Said *World* 118). The "unresolved tension . . . not only between uniqueness and repetition, but also between filiation and affiliation as instances of repetition" (Said *World* 119) offers opportunities for intervention.

Through subversive mimicry, American Indian writers can adopt the guise of affiliation (of appearing to write within the colonial discourse and colonizers' language) to unmask, to exterminate, the colonial pattern of filiation that the colonial relationship engenders. As the following chapters discuss, writers who employ subversive mimicry do not participate in filiation but present the dangers of guises of filiation. While filiation is driven by a desire to exterminate that which has been engendered it is also true that colonized people whom colonizers have constructed as filial also desire to exterminate this engendering—to reject the colonizer and their discourse—in their bid for autonomy and independence. Writers who employ subversive mimicry can challenge colonial filiation while simultaneously forging alternative forms of affiliation. These alternative forms do not reproduce filiation in the affiliative structure, but instead create a "transition from a failed idea or possibility of filiation to a kind of compensatory order that . . . provides men and women with a new form of relationship, which I have been calling affiliation but which is also a new system" (Said *World* 19).

Two Modes of Mimicry

In colonial mimicry, the mimic imitates to become like another while in subversive modes of mimicry the mimic imitates to critique another. While the colonial mimic imitates colonizers in an effort to access, take on, their power, the subversive mimic engages in partial repetitions of colonial discourse to contest its authority.[12] In challenging the authority of the model or referent underlying the mimicry, the subversive mimic, unlike the colonial mimic, is self-aware. Although both colonial and subversive mimics may desire the powers and privileges of the colonizer, writers who deploy subversive mimicry do not replicate the structures or ideologies underlying the colonizer's power. Instead, the subversive mimic critically interrogates those elements which he/she imitates while simultaneously asserting his/her differences, whereas the colonial mimic often loses sight of his/her differences in efforts to become like the colonizer. The subversive mimic does not want to become like the colonizer, but rather delights in differences and strategically displays them by turning the gaze of colonizers back upon themselves. For instance, in "The Halfbreed Parade," Marilyn Dumont re-invents the stereotype of the Métis as object and inverts the stereotype by re-positioning settlers and Métis so that settlers are depicted in terms of the very stereotypes that they apply to Métis people. She ironically challenges the "white judges," the colonizers, who construct Métis people as objects in a parade. Settlers are now the objects who are being gazed upon as is evident when the prairie transforms into a float where "the only thing missing was a mariache band/and a crowd of pilgrims stretching/miles down the gravel road/which offered passage to our grand mansion" (M. Dumont 16). In a clever inversion, the white judges are now spectators as well as part of the spectacle which they have constructed.

Through this inversion strategy, Dumont not only deconstructs the colonial stereotypes but also challenges the authority of settlers. She encourages readers to question settler constructions of Métis while at the same time replacing these stereotypical constructions with a vision that positions settlers as others, as objects. Dumont presents the objects being mimicked (colonizers and colonial discourse) and mimics their disavowal, in which they construct Métis as objects in a parade, back upon settlers so that now settlers are the objects in a parade which the Métis watch. To borrow Taussig's words, "The very mimicry corrodes the alterity" (*Mimesis* 8) because Dumont has now made settlers part of the object of study; she has made settler readers alter to themselves. Those readers who take offense at this construct may well ask why this is different from settler constructions of Métis as objects. In so asking, they interrogate colonial assumptions and stereotypes. Instead of replicating the colonial relationship, subversive mimicry gives a refracted reflection in which colonizers may see images of themselves through the eyes of the colonized. The re-presented image of the colonizer and the colonial relationship has been altered and, in some cases, informed by previously denied colonial knowledges and rules of recognition.

History, as Michel Foucault observed, "has the form of a war rather than that of a language: relations of power, not relations of meaning" (*Power/Knowledge* 114). When American Indian writers seek to challenge colonial history, to talk back to these relations of power, by entering into a dialogue with it, they need to be wary of becoming trapped by the very colonial discourse which they seek to contest. Any attempt to define difference in relation to the colonial relationship is precarious because, as Ernesto Laclau has observed, ". . . if the oppressed is defined by its difference from the oppressor, such a difference is an essential component of the identity of the oppressed. But in that case, the latter cannot assert its identity without asserting that of the oppressor as well"(101–2).

Any discussion of contemporary American Indian literature within a binary framework simplifies the complexities of cultural interactions and exchanges and risks perpetuating imbalances of power. While Frantz Fanon's description of the colonial relationship as a "Manichean" one in which colonizers construct a binary opposition of us and them points to the power struggle operating in the colonial relationship, it does not address the ways in which power relationships are ever shifting and exhibit "a wide spectrum of complex relationalities of domination, subordination, and collaboration" (Shohat and Stam 343). As Richard Terdiman has pointed out, "no discourse is ever a monologue . . . . Its assertions, its tone, its rhetoric . . . always presuppose a horizon of competing, contrary utterances against which it asserts its own energies" (36).

American Indian writers can enter into a dialogue with the colonial discourse without perpetuating its rules of recognition by creating a multi-voiced discourse that illustrates the "complex relationalities" of power. Mikhail Bakhtin defines hybridization as "a mixture of two social languages within the limits of a single utterance, an encounter, within the arena of an utterance, between two different linguistic consciousnesses, separated from one another by an epoch, by social differentiation or by some other factor" (358). He discusses how writers can create multi-accented texts which include a "double-accented, double styled hybrid construction" (*The Dialogic Imagination* 304). He defines a "hybrid construction" as one in which an utterance "actually contains mixed within it two utterances, two speech manners, two styles, two 'languages,' two semantic and axiological belief systems" (304). He further explains how even "the same word will belong simultaneously to two languages, two belief systems that intersect in a hybrid construction—and the word has two contradictory meanings, two accents" (305). Bakhtin is describing how language can contain two belief systems. His description of hybridity implies two coherent identities which are now mixed, whereas creative hybridity, as I am defining the term, articulates fluid shifting identities. Through creative hybrid narratives, writers can articulate cultural differences while at the same time fostering other dialogues between settler and American Indian narratives. While colonial history has shown a rather slanted dialogue that reflects, and reinforces, a power relationship that favors the colonizer, writers can create a multi-voiced discourse which includes a "double-voiced" (Bakhtin 324) one.[13] The binarism that Fanon discusses in his description of the colonial relationship as a "Manichean world" is but one, out of many, relations of power. By including, without privileging, this double-voice, writers can challenge the colonial discourse and the civilizing mission without participating in its rules of recognition. The embedded double-voice articulates cultural differences while simultaneously re-presenting and contesting this binarism.

By viewing subversive mimicry as a dialogue, a contestation as well as a re-imagination of existing power relations, writers can experiment with dialogic narrative practices that challenge the colonial notion that contact between cultures is a one-way process—the imposition of one culture over another. Instead, such narrative practices foreground contact between different cultures as ongoing processes of cultural exchanges. Dialogic narrative strategies enable writers to present exchanges in which cultural differences remain heterogeneous while at the same time mapping out a terrain in which readers can bridge, not eliminate, cultural differences.

Since power relationships are ever shifting, American Indian authors can present multiple positions while still addressing the power imbalance evident in the colonial relationship between colonizer and colonized. In Leslie Marmon Silko's *Ceremony*, for instance, the author illustrates how the colonized can define community to resist settlers. Tayo's, the Laguna protagonist's, social identity consists of multiple communities and ever shifting affiliations which he constantly has to negotiate. Silko presents a paradigm of liberation that is a hybrid "third space": "the cutting edge of translation and negotiation, the *in-between* space—that carries the burden of the meaning of culture" (Bhabha *Location* 38). She illustrates how aboriginal people empower themselves through their processes of self-determination.

Silko constructs a collective identity of Indianness that recognizes and respects tribal cultural differences while simultaneously forging a collective Indian consciousness. The collective Indian "we" includes all tribes as well as mixed bloods like Tayo, Betonie, Descheeney, and the Mexican dancer. According to Tayo, this collective consciousness is evident in traditional American Indian ways in which there exists an "old sensitivity . . . when the people shared a single clan name and they told each other who they were . . . the people shared the same consciousness" (68). Silko differentiates between Indian consciousness which validates community and colonizers who validate individualism: "Christianity separated the people from themselves; it tried to crush the single clan name, encouraging each person to stand alone" (68). Betonie counters eurocentric settler values of private property and ownership with his perception of the web of creation in which all strands are necessary and no strand can be broken without upsetting the balance. He reminds Tayo, "They only fool themselves when they think it [Mount Taylor] is theirs. The deeds and the papers don't mean anything. It is the people who belong to the mountain" (128).

In a strategic maneuver, Silko resists colonial constructions of Indians as others by arguing that settlers are a product of the witchery which Indians created. This is not merely a simple reversal of the civilizing mission; instead, Indians empower themselves by claiming primary origin and responsibility for themselves, and for evil, of which settlers are only one product.[14] In claiming that they are the originators of the witchery, Indian peoples assert the primacy of their claims to the land; hence, they resist the colonizers' construction of themselves as original. By ascribing the witchery to Indians (132), Betonie suggests that those American Indians like Harley, Leroy, Pinkie, and Emo who blame others only participate in self-destruction, perpetuating cycles of retribution. As Betonie explains to Tayo, binary oppositions are simplistic: "'Nothing is that simple,' he said, 'you don't write off all the white people, just like you don't trust all the Indians'" (128). Silko suggests that Indians can liberate themselves by changing their position so that they do not define their identity within a colonial binary structure.[15] In so doing, they resist the colonial power structure and the rules and apparatus by which it operates. For instance, Tayo refrains from killing Emo because he now recognizes that if he does, then he will have completed the "deadly ritual" of the witchery.

Silko avoids replicating the binarism in the colonial relationship by forging multiple positions that operate on several co-existing, ever-changing levels of affiliation, or strands of the web. An international identity complements, rather than competes with, local tribal identities. While this paradigm is primarily a liberatory, empowering strategy for Indian peoples to own their processes of cultural self-determination, it also serves as a model of social responsibility from which all human beings can benefit.

At the end of the novel, the web of affiliations widens when Silko alludes to the witchery that is destroying the planet. In describing the threat of nuclear holocaust and extinction, she points toward the construction of a necessary inclusive identity in which "human beings were one clan again, united by the fate the destroyers planned for all of them, for all living things; united by a circle of death" (246). Yet even this more inclusive vision can never fully escape the paradox inherent in collective identity. An international Indian consciousness excludes those who are not Indian. A Laguna collective excludes those who are not Laguna. The novel addresses this exclusivity by suggesting that one affiliation need not exclude or preclude others; Tayo can be Laguna and Indian and Emo can be Laguna and a member of the American Army. Silko negotiates new spaces, akin to Bhabha's concept of a "third space" (*Location* 38), in which multiple, shifting positions and affiliations are represented. At the same time, she contests the imbalance in the colonial relationship by foregrounding both Laguna identity and a constructed collective identity of Indian people, so that now their narratives inform settler ones.

American Indian writers can resist literary "contamination" (Brydon "The White Inuit Speaks" 191)—the imposition of settler narratives over American Indian ones—by deploying a strategy of literary infiltration. Re-presentations of diverse American Indian narratives infiltrate settler ones, so that readers can no longer read settler narratives in the same way without remembering how the writer has altered them. In this way, they call into question the basic assumptions upon which the colonial relationship—the difference established between colonizer and colonized—is based. Previously denied knowledges now estrange the basis of the authority of the dominant discourse by infiltrating the values and rules of recognition of diverse American Indians into the dominant discourse.

Mikhail Bakhtin describes how

> What is realized in the novel is the process of coming to know one's own language as it is perceived in someone else's language, coming to know one's own belief system in someone else's system. There takes place within the novel an ideological translation of another's language, and an overcoming of its otherness—an otherness that is only contingent, external, illusory. (365)

Bakhtin is discussing the novel in the context of a linguistic model. The following chapters illustrate how colonized writers can perform an "ideological translation" of the colonizer's language and discourse by transforming the language so that the narrative becomes the process not of "coming to know one's own language as it is perceived in someone else's language" (Bakhtin 365) which is a form of assimilation, but rather of translating the language so that it bears the burden of the colonized person's experiences. By infiltrating their rules of recognition into the colonizer's discourse, they estrange the authority of that discourse. They also provide a paradigm in which colonizers and their language may be assimilated into American Indian discourses. Eurocentric grand narratives are "transcontextualized" (Hutcheon in *Rethinking Bakhtin* 89), re-configured in light of American Indian narratives, so that colonizers may understand their colonial language and discourse as it is perceived through the lens of the colonized.

Readers are often unfamiliar with the cultural terrains of American Indians. This lack of familiarity and knowledge of diverse American Indian rules of recognition creates a blind spot, a gap wherein much of the subtext and intertextual references escape detection. The "double-voiced discourse" embedded in the multi-voiced narrative can articulate cultural differences while at the same time enabling settler readers to imagine the effects of colonization from the perspective of the colonized. As Gary Saul Morson explains, in his elaboration of Bakhtin's idea: "The audience of a double-voiced word is therefore meant to hear both a version of the original utterance as the embodiment of its speaker's point of view (or 'semantic position') and the second speaker's evaluation of that utterance from a different point of view" (Morson qtd. in Gates 50).

Subversive mimicry that employs a "double-voiced discourse" becomes, as Taussig has written in his description of the mimetic faculty, "the faculty to copy, imitate, make models, explore difference, yield into and become Other" (Taussig xiii). While it is not possible to become another, it is possible to "become Other"; settlers may momentarily see themselves as the ones now being othered.

For instance, Thomas King's short story, "Joe the Painter," plays on settler stereotypes and creates an ironic twist that requires those readers who hold stereotypical views of American Indians as savages to re-examine history in light of violence perpetrated by colonizers. King creates a lens in which settlers can recognize their stereotypical assumptions and the ways in which these assumptions often serve as a justification for oppression. He illustrates how colonial stereotypes often validate colonial versions of history which, this story suggests, whitewash historical events. By juxtaposing settler and American Indian narratives, King places responsibility on readers for acknowledging their underlying cultural assumptions not only about diverse American Indians but also about settler narratives being read.

King contests colonial history, and the eurocentric stereotypes that underlie it, by creating a dialogue between colonizers and colonized in which he subversively mimics and re-deploys elements of the civilizing mission to contest it. The story is about Joe Ghoti, whose primary characteristic is his honesty. In actuality, everything Ghoti tells is suspect as he spins his tall tale. As an act of civic duty and pride, Joe writes and performs a pageant for the town's centennial celebration. He plans to recount the town's origins, and assures the narrator that his pageant will be based on historical documents. The narrator and readers are led to believe that Joe will tell a colonial history because he plans to tell about how Matthew Larson "the lumber magnate" (105) settled the community.

King subversively mimics the colonial view of North America as a "blank, empty continent" that needed to be discovered and mapped by settlers who would "civilize" the "savages." Joe tells the narrator that when Larson arrived in 1863, there was "Nothing here then but the salt flats and the bay and the trees and some Indians" (105). He later tells the audience that the pageant will illustrate how Larson "came to Sequoia County in 1863 and sculptured a town out of a barren wilderness" (112). Joe's script also mimics aspects of the civilizing mission in which settlers attempt to convert American Indians to Christianity. Upon meeting Chief Redbird on Deer Island, Larson gives him "a couple of iron kettles and a Bible" (112).

King satirizes how settlers invoked the civilizing mission to justify their claims to the land. At the end of the second act, Larson and his men claim that the land "belonged to them" (113) while, in the third act, Larson justifies his slaughter of the Indians on Deer Island by claiming that it is "God's work" and he is bringing "the light of civilization to this dark land" (115). King mimics the rhetoric of the civilizing mission only to subvert it by placing the words in the mouth of Larson just as he is about to massacre the Indians. By enacting the savagery of settlers, honest Joe unwittingly reveals their hypocrisy and the discrepancy between their rhetoric and practice. Larson's justification of his use of violence is ironic when, just after he has massacred the Indians, he says "I abhor the taking of a human life but civilization needs a strong arm to open the frontier" (116).

King sets up a trap in which he snares those readers who have colonial assumptions in their own discourse. Readers who hold such assumptions will presuppose that history will show how the settlers are massacred by the "savage" Indians. The narrative plays on these and other colonial expectations. When Joe initially relates his plans for a pageant to the narrator, he tells him that the Deer Island Massacre occurred on the night of March 31 in 1863 (105), "but Larson survived and built the town" (106). Joe adds: "It's all history. You can't muck around with history. It ain't always the way we'd like it to be but there it is. Can't change it" (106). This statement is ironic because it points to the ways in which settlers have rewritten historical events and because Joe, in choosing to adhere to actual events, tells a history that contests settler authority. Readers who maintain colonial stereotypes of the "savage Indian" often fail to remember that honest Joe is speaking. They do not expect Joe to tell how settlers perpetrated acts of violence against the Indians.

Readers who hold colonial stereotypes will experience a shock of recognition. If they persist in viewing Indians as "savages," then they will expect a massacre of settlers by the Indians. By detailing how the Indians were massacred by the settlers, Joe (and King) holds up a mirror in which readers see the savagery and violence of the colonizers. This mirroring effect is not unlike the mirror in Virginia Woolf's *Between the Acts* where a mirror is held up for the audience to view itself (135). Subversive mimicry partially mirrors/represents aspects of colonizers and their discourse and also refracts these images.[16] Readers who view the distortion may question colonial discourse and history. Those readers who perceive the mirror image but are unable, or unwilling, to recognize the distortion may, like the Mayor in the story, disqualify the pageant on the grounds that "it wasn't apppprooooopriate!" (*One Good Story* 117). King unsettles the colonial relationship by using humor as a "subversive weapon" in which he ambushes the reader (Atwood 244).

He effectively resists literary "contamination" (Brydon "White Inuit" 191)—the imposition of settler narratives over American Indian ones—by deploying a strategy of literary infiltration. Joe's re-presentation of history foregrounds the untold American Indian histories and the "unspeakable thoughts, unspoken" (Morrison *Beloved* 199). We can no longer read settler history without remembering this story, and the way it calls into question "official histories" and the colonial stereotypes which inform them. Previously denied knowledge now estranges the basis of the authority of the dominant discourse by infiltrating the values and rules of recognition of American Indians into settler discourse.[17] While King mimics settlers and their discourse in his presentation of Joe and Larson and his followers, he subverts colonial mimicry by having Joe perform a pageant that changes the rules of recognition. Dancing along the precipice of colonial mimicry, King constructs a con/text that presents settler histories in a different context.

Affiliative Relations

In subverting the colonial constructions of American Indians as other/object, writers can re-present the colonized as empowered subjects and contest the constructed difference between colonizer and colonized which the colonial relationship implies. In the colonial relationship, colonizers have historically situated themselves as the models and have encouraged American Indians to partially mimic them. In deploying mimicry as a subversive strategy, writers can contest this relationship and position American Indians as models from whom settlers are encouraged to learn while simultaneously alluding to, and challenging, settler efforts to encourage colonial mimicry and foster assimilation. For instance, in "Joe the Painter," King subverts colonial constructions of American Indians as other/object. He re-presents them as empowered subjects and contests the constructed difference between colonizer and colonized which the colonial relationship implies. This new rule of recognition—American Indians as subjects—transforms the colonial filiative relationship to an affiliative one. The acquisition of this new rule shifts "structures of attitude and reference" (Said *Culture and Imperialism* 52) and facilitates non-Indian collaboration in the decolonization process.

While each author discussed in this book has a different experience of colonialism, all of them articulate how American Indians are still being colonized. Each resists "literary colonialism" (Owens 23)—efforts by non-Indians to define, co-opt or incorporate American Indians and their writings within a colonial framework and discourse. In challenging colonial inventions, each writer envisions alternatives in which American Indians are not seen in relation to colonizers but in terms of decolonized relations which are ever-shifting.

They employ diverse strategies to dance along the precipice of colonial mimicry all the while referencing it, by alluding to the dangers of being subsumed by the dominant society. Instead of fearing and/or desiring the colonizer, they celebrate their differences and assert agency. Their narrative strategies, which often draw on trickster discourse, challenge cultural norms and boundaries and present alternative visions in which American Indians are no longer positioned as alter, as colonizers' constructed others.

While these different dances along the colonial precipice are survival strategies in which these writers resist the colonial relationship, their respective narratives are not merely acts of resistance in which they only react to the colonial hand that history has dealt them. In creating creative hybrid works that draw on and support diverse American Indians and oral traditions while challenging the hierarchical imbalances of power underlying the colonial relationship, each writer takes issue with the ways in which settler society has attempted to define American Indians, specifically within eurocentric epistemologies. Their writing unsettles the colonial relationship while simultaneously engaging readers in transcultural dialogues. Each partially mimics aspects of the civilizing mission and colonial discourse while at the same time re-presenting them to give readers paradigms for decolonization. By selectively adapting elements from diverse American Indian and settler cultures, they create literature that articulates and affirms cultural differences.

Chapter Two

To Know the Difference

... you would have
to be colonial to know the difference,
to know the pain of history words contain,
....

Derek Walcott *The Star-Apple Kingdom* 12

Assumptions are a dangerous thing.

Thomas King "Godzilla vs. Post-Colonial" 10

In section six, entitled "The Sailor Sings Back to the Casuarinas," of "The Schooner Flight," Saint Lucian writer Derek Walcott alludes to the ways in which language often reflects the "pain" of colonial history. In his poem, Walcott poignantly describes how colonizers in the West Indies have often imposed their language and words on those they have colonized. The narrator in the poem describes the dangers of colonial mimicry, of seeing oneself through the lens of the colonizer, when he warns: "'. . . and we,/if we live by the names our masters please,/by careful mimicry might become men'" (*The Star-Apple Kingdom* 12).

In their civilizing mission, colonizers encourage colonized people to partially mimic them; however, those who see themselves and their lives through the lens of the colonizer may come to believe that their experiences are inauthentic. They may come to see, as Walcott's narrator explains, casuarinas as "classic trees" and, in so doing, they become like casuarinas that "bend like cypresses" (*The Star-Apple Kingdom* 12). Since there are no classic trees in the West Indies, the reference alludes to the ways in which colonizers attempt to impose their cultural and geographical landscapes on those they colonize. The narrator, in Walcott's poem, describes the civilizing mission and the precipice of colonial mimicry in the context of the West Indies. He points out the necessity of knowing the difference between colonial mimicry and self-definition (casuarinas are not cypresses). Walcott, through his narrator, captures the pain of history, whereas Cherokee/Greek/German writer Thomas King uses humor to convey the "pain of history words contain" (Walcott *The Star-Apple Kingdom* 12). King employs parody and satire to illustrate the difference between colonial mimicry and self-determination in *Green Grass, Running Water* (1993).[1] He subversively mimics aspects of the colonial discourse and its civilizing mission to re-present it in a hybrid American Indian context. In so doing, he subverts colonial rules of recognition and the underlying "dangerous" ("Godzilla vs. Post-Colonial" 10) assumptions with which his characters and readers are familiar.

In light of his comments in "Godzilla vs. Post-Colonial," King might well object to a post-colonial analysis that examines how his work resists colonial mimicry. In this article, he rejects the term *post-colonial* because it "reeks of unabashed ethnocentrism and well-meaning dismissal" and "assumes that the starting point for that discussion is the advent of Europeans in North America" (11). King argues that "the idea of post-colonial writing effectively cuts us off from our traditions, traditions that were in place before colonialism . . . , traditions which have come down to us through our cultures in spite of colonization, and it supposes that contemporary Native writing is largely a construct of oppression" (12). This limited definition of post-colonialism ignores the ways in which post-colonial analysis not only critically interrogates the colonial relationship but also posits the possibility of moving beyond colonialism. King's use of the phrase "in spite of" only underscores colonialism's critical relevance. While colonialism is certainly neither the starting point for American Indians nor the yardstick by which their writing is measured, it continues to have an impact on them. In *Green Grass, Running Water*, King illustrates how colonialism is still a part of American Indian experience but, in positioning his work within a hybrid American Indian context, he subverts the authority of colonial discourse.

Creating a Hybrid (Con)text

Green Grass, Running Water exhibits many of the characteristics of a postmodern novel, but readers who interpret it solely in the context of eurocentric literary forms often do not acknowledge the diverse American Indian cultural traditions that also inform King's work. Readers can learn about these "other forms of practice" (Krupat *The Turn to the Native* 36) by paying attention to the contexts which King provides in his work.

For instance, while *Green Grass, Running Water* is a postmodern novel it is also a more complex version of the "story cycle"—"a form that's very prominent in Native oral literature" (King qtd. in Rooke 64)—that King used in *Medicine River*. The multi-voiced "story cycle" (King qtd. in Rooke 64) includes and critiques the double-voiced discourse of colonialism. Amidst the webbed stories, there are three threads. There is a love triangle between Alberta Frank, a university history professor, Lionel, who sells televisions for Bill Bursum, and Charlie, who works for Duplessis (the engineering firm that is responsible for a dam project in the community of Blossom). The second thread is Eli Stands Alone's endeavor to stop the flow of the dam and protect his mother's house and his community while the third thread involves four Indian elders and Coyote, all tricksters (*bricoleurs*), who attempt to fix a world that is bent. Interspersed with these plots are frequent tellings and re-tellings of origin tales in which King creates comic interplays between American Indian and non-Indian stories and re-contextualizes the latter within the former cosmology.

The structure of *Green Grass, Running Water* affirms the importance of living in balance with the natural world. Each of the four sections has an illustration of grass and water followed by Cherokee scripts which allude to the four directions and four seasons: part one is East, Red; part two is South, White; part three is West, Black; part four is North, Blue.[2]

King parodies the Bible and linear eurocentric grand narratives by re-contextualizing them in this American Indian context. Alluding to the gospels, the first section is "according to the Lone Ranger" (6), the second is "according to Ishmael" (88), the third is "according to Robinson Crusoe" (193), and the fourth is "according to Hawkeye" (274). In a parody of Genesis, part One (East, Red) relates how First Woman[3] and Ahdamn leave the

Garden of Eden and First Woman later metamorphoses into the Lone Ranger. Part Two (South, White) parodies the biblical account of the Fall when Changing Woman falls out of Sky World into Old Coyote and encounters not an ark, but a white canoe filled with poop. Like First Woman, she resists Christian patriarchal rules; she leaves Noah behind and later transforms into Ishmael. Part Three (West, Black) foreshadows the storm that eventually occurs and relates how Thought Woman, who later metamorphoses into Robinson Crusoe, travels from the river into the sky and then into the ocean. Throughout the book there are repeated allusions to *The Mysterious Warrior* (157), a movie that King invents. As the title suggests, the movie parodies Hollywood westerns that stereotype and exoticize American Indians. In part three, the four Indians alter the movie (184) so that the Indians win. In part four (North, Blue), Old Woman underscores the discrepancy between Young Man Walking on Water's (an allusion to Jesus Christ) rhetoric and actions when she comments that he acts as though he had "no relations" (292). The New Testament is repositioned within American Indian origin tales in which Old Woman, who later transforms into Hawkeye, falls through a hole into Sky. It appears that all the stories have been resolved: Lionel attends the sun dance, Alberta is pregnant (King parodies the Immaculate Conception here when Coyote takes credit for her pregnancy), Charlie re-connects with Portland, his father, the dam breaks—liberating the water—and Coyote apologizes. However, King subverts the expectations of those readers who desire closure and reminds them that, like Creation of which stories are a part, the process is ongoing. The story begins, again.

The multiple stories and voices both within and between chapters decenter any single authoritative perspective. There is not one story, but there are many stories which are begun repeatedly in an attempt to set the world straight. The numerous intratextual references, such as the instance when the Lone Ranger tells the other Indians that they have already done that on the "Top of page eleven" (196), remind us of the constructed nature of all stories. The intertextual references suggest that all stories carry traces of other stories. At the same time, these diverse stories are variations on a theme. The narrator informs Coyote: "It's all the same story" (125). Underlying each of these different tellings and re-tellings of origin tales is the "same story" of colonization—of colonizers' repeated attempts to define and contain American Indians and to disavow their agency.

King positions his work within an American Indian context that includes settlers but rejects their colonial assumption of superiority. His narrative strategy is akin to Leslie Marmon Silko's in *Ceremony*. Silko disempowers colonizers and foregrounds the agency of American Indians by describing how settlers are just one aspect of the witchery which Indian peoples created. Similarly King informs readers that Indians, and tricksters (specifically, Coyote's sleeping), created colonizers who are but one, among many, mistakes that Coyote makes which have bent the world. *Green Grass, Running Water* opens with a scene in which the narrator informs us that "Coyote was there, but Coyote was asleep" (1). Coyote's noisy Dog dream is loosed upon the world and proves to be "a contrary" because it "has everything backward"; hence, the dog dream becomes "that God" (2). This transformation, and reversal (God to Dog), renders the Christian God a backward dog, a contrary, which is contextualized in a hybrid American Indian epistemology. Likewise, the colonial history and colonizers' stories related in the work are only one part of numerous versions of the origin of the world. When the Lone Ranger attempts to relate the origin story in Genesis, Ishmael reminds him (and readers) that it is not only "the wrong story" but one that "comes later" (10).

While this might seem to be a parodic inversion, it soon becomes apparent that King's strategy is neither a simplistic reversal in which one set of colonial stereotypes is replaced by others nor merely a counter-discourse in which American Indians are now foregrounded and settlers are constructed as others. Instead of engaging in colonial binary oppositions, King creates "contrapuntal" (Said *Culture and Imperialism* 51, 66–67) stories in which all things (even colonizers) are interconnected. At the same time the work offers a paradigm of creative hybridity in which American Indian and non-Indian epistemologies interconnect and co-exist without domination. King offers readers a world in which "all cultures are involved in one another; none is single and pure, all are hybrid, heterogenous, extraordinarily differentiated, and unmonolithic" (Said *Culture* xxv).

In adapting oral storytelling techniques to print, King offers readers an example of "interfusional literature" which he defines as those parts of American Indian literature that blend "oral literature and written literature" ("Godzilla" 13).[4] In interfusional literature, the "patterns, metaphors, structures as well as the themes and characters come primarily from oral literature" ("Godzilla" 13). The author creates an "oral voice" and uses an "oral syntax that . . . encourages readers to read the stories out loud" ("Godzilla" 13). In this way, prose can re-create "at once the storyteller and the performance" ("Godzilla" 13). In oral stories the audience plays a crucial role in the story and its telling because "a great deal of the story is believed to be inside the listener; the storyteller's role is to draw the story out of the listener" (Silko "Language and Literature" 84). Although King can not duplicate the oral performance of stories, he approximates it. He "draw[s] the story" out of readers by satirizing colonial assumptions with which they are familiar. This re-creation of oral storytelling performances in a written text becomes an "invented tradition" (Krupat *Turn* 37). Like Louise Erdrich, Leslie Marmon Silko, and other contemporary American Indian writers who approximate oral storytelling in their writing, King is both inventing a new form and altering the oral storytelling traditions that inform his work.

Some Elders have argued that stories should not be written because they are removed from their cultural contexts and in danger of being appropriated. Others have argued that the stories need to be written to preserve them. Still others argue that oral traditions cannot be written; once they are written, they cease to be oral. King meets these concerns by creating a fictional hybrid American Indian context that draws on, and combines, diverse American Indian traditions—traditions that include settlers and eurocentric narratives.

Although he writes "both Native and non-Native material," King points out that when he does his Native material he is "writing particularly for a Native community" (qtd. in Rooke 72–73). This does not mean that he has "a specific community in mind" (qtd. in Rooke 72–73), but it does suggest that in positioning himself as a "Native writer" he takes on "responsibilities and obligations" (qtd. in Rooke 72–73). He is careful not to "tell too much about the Native community" (qtd. in Rooke 74) and creates "those silences in part . . . to place closure on those prying eyes" (qtd. in Rooke 74). For instance, he does not relate precise details about the sun dance. At the same time, King believes that these silences also provide "the Native community with that sense of being on the inside" (qtd. in Rooke 74).

By re-presenting settler stories/histories within American Indian contexts, King unsettles them. The Cherokee script at the beginning of each section and the allusion to the water divination ceremony estrange readers unfamiliar with Cherokee; they now experience what it feels like to be displaced. The frequent intertextual references also encourage readers to educate themselves while the satiric undermining of colonial stereotypes encourages those who hold colonial assumptions to re-educate themselves.

In American Indian oral stories, humor not only entertains the audience but often also facilitates social reform. Likewise, in King's text, humor serves to "unmask and disarm [colonial] history, to expose the hidden agendas of historiography and . . . return it to the realm of story" (Blaeser in *Native American Perspectives* 39). By creating characters who are able to laugh at colonial discourse, as well as at themselves, King gives the appearance of being evenhanded—of wielding a "double-bladed knife" (Atwood 244) that critiques both American Indian and settler cultures. His knife does not cut both ways, however. His trickster-Coyote humor is directed primarily at settlers and at American Indians who have internalized colonialism. Characters like Lionel, Charlie Looking Bear, Portland Looking Bear, and Eli Stands Alone become the target of King's knife only when they act like colonial mimics.

In this respect, King's work is polemical, yet it is tempered by humor and a non-directive approach. According to King, "polemical" literature is concerned with the "clash of Native and non-Native cultures or with the championing of Native values over non-Native values" ("Godzilla" 13). It charts "the imposition of non-Native expectations and insistences (political, social, scientific) on Native communities and the methods of resistance employed by Native people in order to maintain both their communities and cultures" ("Godzilla" 13). *Green Grass, Running*

Water does not engage in colonial binary oppositions or champion American Indian values over settler ones; however, there is an implied polemic. By positioning the work within an American Indian context, King affirms American Indians. The re-telling of non-Native stories in this context alludes to the clash of American Indian and settler cultures and challenges colonial stereotypes and assumptions.

For instance, the title of *Green Grass, Running Water* satirically alludes to the United States government's phrase that they would uphold their treaties with American Indians "as long as the grass is green and the waters run."[5] In mimicking the rhetoric of the United States government in the title of his work, King re-configures this aspect of colonial discourse and undermines its rules of recognition. These words now take on new meanings for readers who interpret them in light of settler historical practices. The interplay between what the words say and the historical practices that readers recall, articulates the discrepancy between that rhetoric and that practice. This non-directive approach is in keeping with American Indian oral storytelling traditions. Lee Maracle explains: "When our orators get up to tell a story, there is no explanation, no set-up to guide the listener—just the poetic terseness of the dilemma is presented" (*Sojourner's Truth* 12). In this tradition of oral stories, the storyteller engages listeners who "are drawn into the dilemma and are expected at some point in their lives to actively work themselves out of it" (*Sojourner's Truth* 12).

King provides a trickster mirror that re-presents settlers and colonial discourse in order to critique them. This mirror, contrary to Bhabha's view that hybridity "has no such perspective of depth or truth" (175), does become a vehicle of truth-telling through distortion, and the distortion is in the eyes of settler readers. As Jonathan Swift explains, satire is "a sort of glass wherein beholders do generally discover everybody's face but their own, which is the chief reason for that kind of reception it meets in the world, and that so very few are offended with it" (qtd. in Cuddon 827).

The etymology of the word *satire* goes back to the Greek satyr plays, associated with Dionysus, the Greek god of wine, as well as with tragedies. The word also leads back to the Latin *satura*, "which primarily means 'full,' and then comes to mean 'a mixture full of different things'" and "medleys" (Highet 231, 232). According to Northrop Frye, the "chief distinction between irony and satire is that satire is *militant irony*" (223; emphasis added). He delineates the comic effect of satire:

> Hence satire is irony which is structurally close to the comic: the comic struggle of two societies, one normal and the other absurd, is reflected in its double focus of morality and fantasy. . . . Two things, then, are essential to satire; one is wit or humor founded on fantasy or a sense of the grotesque or absurd, the other is an object of attack. (224)

Frye is only partially correct when he writes that to "attack anything, writer and audience must agree on its undesirability" (224), because American Indian writers can, through subversive satire, prey on settler blindness to their prejudices and construct a text wherein they laugh precisely because they fail to see that they are the object of attack. Settlers who are aware of how King plays on colonial assumptions realize that, in laughing at the text, they are really laughing at themselves. In effect, King plays the part of Coyote, the trickster.[6]

What apparently begins as a tale told *to* Coyote becomes a tale told *on* Coyote and *on* us. As a trickster, Coyote can be both creative and destructive; she/he causes the earthquake that causes Eli Stands Alone's death, yet also liberates the river.[7] However, Coyote, like the settler, is often self-centered and naïve about the ways of the world and fails to think through the implications of his/her actions. Like settlers, Coyote is constantly making mistakes, bending the world.

That the four Indians in *Green Grass, Running Water* are also trickster figures is evident from their actions, their old ages, and their ability to change genders and identities. Doctor Hovaugh (a satiric allusion to Jehovah), for instance, claims that the Indians are male, whereas Babo Jones tells the police that they are female (45). Unlike Coyote, who has much in common with settler readers, these four trickster figures exemplify creative hybridity— subversive mimicry that is not assimilation. The tricksters, like King, appropriate what they want from settler and American Indian cultures. Disguising themselves in settler garb and identities, they set out to critique and undo settler exploitation of American Indians.[8]

In critiquing colonization, King targets the cultural icons of patriarchal settler society. He critiques its materialism and capitalism, and he illustrates the four ideological pillars—Christianity, progress/technology, stereotypes of indigenous peoples, and history—that settler society attempts to impose on American Indians to transform them into colonial mimics.[9] He uses satire to mock these ideological pillars, and, in critiquing them, he reveals them to be fraudulent and destructive.

Christianity, in its pursuit of the "civilizing mission," has played a crucial role in the formation of mimics and in the exploitation of American Indians. In depicting First Woman as a non-mimic and Ahdamn as a mimic—a miniature God—King mocks patriarchal Christianity. The re-telling of the story of Adam and Eve in the Garden of Eden in this American Indian context challenges the Christian view of Eve as the first woman and questions the concept of original sin. First Woman is a rebel who not only critiques settler Christianity but also refuses to play the part of the mimic. As First Woman points out, the paradisal garden is "boring" (33) and restrictive.

Adam, here, becomes Ahdamn. The emphasis on the expletive is derogatory and serves to delegitimize Adam. His name also alludes to the dam, itself an emblem of settler exploitation. King satirizes the eurocentric emphasis on possession, private property and ownership, as well as the need to catalogue and classify American Indians in attempts to transform them into artifacts. Like God, who needs to own everything in the garden (33), Ahdamn insists on naming everything. Adam's authority is further undercut by Ahdamn who, in misnaming everything, is unable to see things for what they are (33). Ahdamn's vision has become clouded by materialism; he thinks Elk is a microwave oven, Bear is a garage sale, Cedar Tree is a telephone book, and Old Coyote is a cheeseburger (33). Bear's suggestion that Ahdamn needs "some glasses" (33) humorously underscores the fact that Ahdamn's vision is blurred.

King reveals the patriarchal nature of Christianity when he juxtaposes God and his pronouncement that there is only one world with American Indian origin stories of two worlds—Sky World and Water World. God is egotistical, controlling, and rude. Coyote remarks: "This dog has no manners" (2). In contrast, grandmother Turtle reminds us to "mind your relations" (32). Coyote, partially performing the role of settler so that settler readers may better view themselves, wants a garden. When grandmother Turtle argues that is the last thing we need, Old Coyote (like settlers) says: "A garden is a good thing. Trust me" (32). Old Coyote's comment alerts readers to be on their guard. Western concepts of individualism, private property, and ownership co-exist with American Indian concepts of community in which relations and relationships are valued.

Seen in the context of American Indian spiritual traditions, Christianity, with its Christian rules, is a self-serving religion, and God is a materialist who is fond of the possessive pronoun and of naming/possessing everything (individual as opposed to communal ownership): "And just so we keep things straight, says that GOD, this is my world and this is my garden" (56).[10]

God is often angry, patriarchal, and vindictive, and he falls flat next to the perceptiveness of First Woman, Changing Woman, Thought Woman, and Old Woman—the tricksters who metamorphose into the Lone Ranger, Ishmael, Robinson Crusoe, and Hawkeye, respectively. The destructiveness of patriarchal Christianity is evident in the portrait of its male God, who is authoritarian, imperious, and an advocate of individualism (as long as the individual is white). In contrast, the American Indian women are considerate and benevolent and validate sharing and the community.

The retelling of the flood and Noah's ark satirically re-presents Noah's ark as a "canoe" that is filled with "poop" (122). Like Timothy Findley's portrait of him in *Not Wanted on the Voyage*, Noah in *Green Grass, Running Water* excludes and destroys those who either dissent or do not serve his needs. His perspective, like that of Findley's Noah, "mimics the binarist 'Manichean' view that Frantz Fanon assigns to the European colonizers" (Donaldson 36). That Noah throws his wife overboard further reinforces the hypocrisy or discrepancy between the "Christian rules" and the practice.

The exclusivity of Christianity and its discourse is evident in the "Christian rules" and falls short in the context of the inclusive approach of American Indian spirituality. God refuses, for example, to share food in his garden, and emphatically states:

"There are rules" (57). Noah's "rules" are sexist and sanction his selfishness and lechery: "The first rule is Thou Shalt Have Big Breasts" (125). The sexism and exclusivity of Christian rules underlie settler culture and the way in which it deploys them to fashion colonial mimics. Noah abandons Changing Woman because she will not comply with his rules. Borrowing the words that Noah uses in Findley's novel, he says: "I am a Christian man. This is a Christian journey. And if you can't follow our Christian rules, then you're not wanted on the voyage" (125).

Similarly, Christ (renamed Young Man Walking on Water) has rules that exclude women and emphasize individualism (291). His patriarchal behavior is evident in his refusal to allow Old Woman to aid him; when she does, he invalidates her actions. That she perceives the authoritarian and exclusionary nature of Christianity is evident in her suggestion that Christ's disciples are merely his "deputies," "subalterns," or "proofreaders"—subordinates whose sole function is to serve him (292). Young Man Walking On Water unwittingly confirms this view when he defines the function of his disciples as that of adoring followers who will "love me and follow me around" (292).

The opposition between settlers who exploit natural resources for commercial profit and those who are excluded and exploited is evident when Changing Woman meets Ahab in search of Moby-Dick. Ahab represents a vengeful Christian, and his hunt for the great white whale (like the Grand Baleen dam) symbolizes the imperialism of settler culture. Echoing Findley's Noah, Ahab argues that it is a "Christian world" where "we only kill things that are useful or things we don't like" (163).

Changing Woman satirically undermines the primacy of white settlers when she informs Ahab that he is mistaken; Moby-Dick is in fact Moby-Jane, the great black whale. King alludes to colonial binary oppositions: Dick and Jane readers; Black and White; male and female, and the sexism and racism underlying colonization and its civilizing mission. Unlike Ahab, Changing Woman perceives how all things are interconnected. Ahab's response to this resistance to his patriarchal world view is to throw everyone who disagrees with him overboard. His authoritarianism pales in relation to Changing Woman's consensus decision making. She refuses to comply with Ahab's authoritarian dictates and jumps overboard into the water where she swims with Moby-Jane.[11]

King ridicules settler culture and its need to invent the imaginary Indian, a colonial mimic constructed in the settler image to serve settler interests. In *The White Man's Indian: Images of the American Indian from Columbus to the Present*, Robert Berkhofer describes the construction of the imaginary Indian:

> Since the original inhabitants of the Western Hemisphere neither called themselves by a single term nor understood themselves as a collectivity, the idea and the image of the Indian must be a White conception. Native Americans were and are real, but the *Indian* was a White invention .... (3)

Those who do not comply are, according to settler culture, impediments and must be assimilated or annihilated. Dr. Hovaugh's attempts to convince John to sign death certificates for the four missing Indians (even though he has no evidence of their demise) (39) parodies settler efforts to deny the existence of, and exterminate, American Indians and their cultures.

Settler society denies American Indians self-identification and self-determination. As with all the other settler figures in the text, Gabriel (alluding to the archangel) cannot accept Thought Woman as she is, but renames and recasts her into his preconceived image; she is, he insists, the Virgin Mary. Likewise, when Latisha once tried to explain the sun dance to her non-Native friend, her friend could not understand, but could only imagine it within the context of Christianity (307). Robinson Crusoe, with his Western need to reclassify everything as either good or bad points, wants to recast Thought Woman as Friday because, "as a civilized white man, it has been difficult not having someone of color around whom I could educate and protect" (245). Similarly, when Old Woman comes across "Nathaniel Bumppo, Post-Colonial Wilderness Guide and Outfitter" (327), he mistakes Old Woman for Chingachgook, his Indian "friend" whom he wants to kill.

By constructing stereotypes of the indigene (and of women), settler society attempts to consolidate and contain the Other. Through this construction, settler society manufactures colonial mimics who consent. The repeated references to John Wayne, Hollywood westerns, and romantic western novels ridicule the media and their stereotyped caricatures that serve to trivialize and domesticate American Indians. Settler figures of authority are reduced to cartoon caricatures. For example, Lionel converses with two hotel men called Tom and Gerry and two policemen named Chip and Dale (52).

By transforming diverse individuals into imaginary Indians, settler society establishes and maintains the Manichean opposition wherein Others are perceived as dehumanized objects that cannot emulate the settlers completely because they are *"the same but not quite"* (Bhabha "Of Mimicry" 130). In the western that Eli reads, for instance, the American Indian character has no specific name; he is only a "Mysterious Warrior" (137).[12]

The caricature of Natty Bumppo and Natty's idea of Indian "gifts" further subversively mimics settler stereotypes of the imaginary Indian. Alluding to the concept of the Indian giver as a cheat, a person who does not conform to white expectations or rules, King calls this racist concept into question and encourages us to reconsider it. As an icon of settler culture, Natty is emblematic of the "Manichean allegory" operating in settler culture and discourse. Abdul JanMohamed describes this as

> . . . a field of diverse yet interchangeable oppositions between white and black, good and evil, superiority and inferiority, civilization and savagery, intelligence and emotion, rationality and sensuality, self and Other, subject and object. (63)

According to Natty, renamed "Nasty Bumppo," Indians have a "keen sense of smell" (327) and other characteristics of the "noble savage," and are set in opposition to the "superiority" of the "civilized" settler:

> Indians can run fast. Indians can endure pain. Indians have quick reflexes. Indians don't talk much. Indians have good eyesight. Indians have agile bodies. These are all Indian gifts, says Nasty Bumppo.

> Interesting, says Old Woman. Whites are patient. Whites are spiritual. Whites are cognitive. Whites are philosophical. Whites are sophisticated. Whites are sensitive. These are all white gifts, says Nasty Bumppo. (327–28)

Settler society constructs this opposition to depict, as Old Woman perceives, whites as "superior" and Indians as "inferior" (328) and to justify its exploitation of American Indians. Given this colonial relationship, Coyote asks: "Who would want to be an Indian?" (329).

Whenever there is a discrepancy between reality and its constructed view of American Indians, settler society manipulates reality to suit its construction. In transforming American Indians into cultural artifacts and commodities, Hollywood movies and westerns are debilitating in their romanticized images of the indigene and the "noble savage." Westerns, as either films or novels, reconstruct history—itself a fictional construction insofar as settler versions of American Indian histories reflect settler perspectives and interests—to glorify settler expansion and exploitation. As Latisha observes, "if the Indians won, it probably wouldn't be a Western" (161).

Portland (who can only obtain parts in B westerns) and his son, Charlie, have to grunt when they work as parking attendants in Hollywood because doing so conforms to settler expectations and the constructed image of American Indians as "savages" (174). Portland wears a fake nose because he is not "Indian" enough, and he changes his name from Portland Looking Bear to Iron Eyes Screeching Eagles (127).

The purpose of transforming diverse peoples into cultural artifacts, into museum pieces, is not only to dehumanize but also to disempower them. In King's text, however, those settlers who try to appropriate American Indian cultures to exploit them—to make them serve settler interests and conform to the settler world view—are disempowered. For instance, the Blossom community does not allow either the Michigan tourist (who claims he does not know the sun dance is sacred) or George Morningstar (who knows it is a sacred ceremony and intends to sell his photographs to a New Age journal) to take illicit photographs of the sun dance.

By juxtaposing Eli's western novel with his flashback about his former partner, Karen, and her desire to attend another sun dance, King critiques another facet of settler appropriation of American Indians—the "wannabe Indian." In telling her friends about the sun dance, Karen transforms it into a cultural artifact. When she first sees the tepees on the horizon, she romanticizes American Indians, perceiving the tepees as a journey into a past world and time. She is incapable of acknowledging that the tepees, and their inhabitants, exist in the present. This form of cultural appropriation, while perhaps more an indication of Karen's naïveté and ignorance than of deliberate malice, is just as destructive as the appropriation of rituals and religious ceremonies to suppress, or annihilate, American Indians and their cultures.

In a satiric twist on settler appropriation, the four Indian tricksters appropriate the names of settlers who, in turn, have appropriated "Indians." As Old Woman says, Hawkeye "sounds like a name for a white person who wants to be an Indian" (329). Hawkeye is one version of James Fenimore Cooper's Natty Bumppo in his group of novels, *Leather Stocking Tales*, so named after the deerskin leggings that Natty wears. Natty is a pioneer scout who exemplifies the "wannabe" Indian stereotype. All four of the settler characters whom the Indians appropriate exemplify "rugged" individualism. As pioneers isolated from society, they are colonialists/imperialists who tame/conquer what settler society perceives as "savages" in the "frontier wilderness." Robinson Crusoe, Ishmael, and the Lone Ranger symbolize settlers whose relationship with the "noble savage" is that of patriarchal Europeans on a civilizing mission. All four have American Indian accomplices who symbolize the noble savage: Lone Ranger-Tonto, Robinson Crusoe-Friday, Ishmael-Queequeg, and Hawkeye/Natty -Chingachgook. By re-presenting these settler literary characters as a community of Indian Elders/tricksters that sets out to fix the world, King satirizes these settler icons and suggests that the values they represent have contributed to the mistakes settlers have made. Ironically, the four Indians are more compassionate and sane than the society that incarcerates them.[13]

King also satirizes settler values of progress and technology and settler exploitation of the environment. Settler efforts to master/tame the environment, like their attempts to contain American Indians, women, and all people of color prove futile. Their technology also repeatedly backfires. Sifton assures Eli that his engineering firm can contain/restrain the flowing water, even though Eli warns him that the dam has "stress fractures" (115). The name of the dam, the Grand Baleen (Great Whale), alludes to the whales which settlers exploited as well as to the dam controversy over the Great Whale River which flows into Hudson's Bay.[14] The dam symbolizes settler society and its oppressive tactics; just as the dam holds back the river (which, after prolonged damming, will die), so settler society restrains and attempts to annihilate American Indians. The numerous references to excrement (the dam reminds Eli of a "toilet" (115), toilets overflow in the Dead Dog Café, Amos drives his truck into an outhouse and the white canoe is filled with poop) underscore the hypocrisy and false promises of colonizers and their various forms of pollution. By killing the river and all the cottonwood and elm trees (60, 311), the dam, and other settler exploitation of the environment, results in a world where the grass is no longer green and the waters no longer run.

Settler society invokes progress and technology in efforts to exclude and exploit others. The word *progress* is ethnocentric and eurocentric in its implications of advancement, superiority, civilization; it is a means for settler society to delineate further its "Manichean world" (Fanon *The Wretched of the Earth* 41). Discussing treaty rights with Eli, Clifford Sifton, the engineer of the dam, observes that "the government . . . made promises it never intended to keep" (117). His name alludes to the Canadian Minister of the Interior during Laurier's government (1896–1905) who was responsible for bringing settlers to the west of Canada and promised free land to prospective farmers. The allusion to Minister Sifton reiterates the recurring refrain of broken promises. Government officials like Sifton and companies like Duplessis (a reference to the premier of Quebec from 1936–1960) only care about making a profit, not about keeping promises. Sifton tells Eli that "those treaties aren't worth a damn" (119). He reveals the underlying premise of the extermination of American Indians when he adds: "Government only made them for convenience. Who'd of guessed that there would still be Indians kicking around in the twentieth century" (119). The assumption is that colonized American Indians cannot completely mimic the settler because they are, in the settler's eyes, inferior and therefore incapable of progress.

In contrast to this stereotype, the stereotype of the "noble savage" is often invoked by settlers who are dissatisfied with their own culture and romanticize American Indians. Underlying the stereotype of the "noble savage" is the assumption that "savages" are "noble" precisely because they have existed in a state of nature/innocence and have escaped industrial society. When describing Eli and other American Indians who have become mimics and been assimilated into settler industrial society, Sifton says, "you guys aren't real Indians anyway. I mean, you drive cars, watch television, go to hockey games" (119).

Bill Bursum fails to understand why Lionel and Eli (who embody mimic men insofar as they are assimilated American Indians and therefore, in Bursum's eyes, are not "really Indians anymore") become "testy" about the term "Indians" (156). He is not only unaware of his racism but also perceives himself as non-racist solely because he "had lived with Indians all his life"; he believes that his business dealings with the community are evidence of his fair-mindedness (224). Blind to his own paternalism and sexism, Bursum is unable to comprehend that labels/names are a form of categorization and that some labels reflect and perpetuate the racism and sexism in the settler language and discourse. He refuses, for example, to respect Minnie's wish to be referred to as "Ms. Smith" (156).

Green Grass, Running Water satirizes the paternalist and expansionist projects of the Bursums of this world. Bursum's name alludes to the Bursum Bill proposed in Congress in 1922. If passed, the bill would have opened Pueblo lands to euramerican settlement.[15] Bursum's map, constructed out of television sets, is of Canada and the United States but, significantly, it excludes Blossom. His model for his advertising idea is Machiavelli's *The Prince*—a text on power and the art of manipulation. The map provides Bursum with the illusion of "being in control" (109). He believes: "Power and control . . . [are] outside the range of the Indian imagination" (109). His statement is ironic in the context of the four Indians' subsequent tampering with his televisions. Bursum repeatedly stabs the remote control (267) to no avail. He is unable to control *The Mysterious Warrior*, the movie which the four Indians have revised; hundreds of soldiers now disappear and the empowered Indians shoot back.

Christianity and history are stories that settlers construct to justify exploitation of others. King re-presents settler history when Christopher Columbus' three ships—the Pinta, the Niña, and the Santa María—that sailed in 1492 to North America are transformed into the cars—the Pinto, the Nissan, and the Carmen Ghia—that the four Indians later "sailed" (337) onto Parliament Lake and "float[ed] into the dam just as the earthquake began"

(346). By naming Portland's fellow actors after explorers: C. B. Cologne[16] and his wife Isabella, Frankie Drake, Johnny Cabot, Sammy Hearne, and Henry Cortez, King links political exploration with popular culture to suggest that both are forms of cultural appropriation and exploitation. The racism underlying imperialism is evident when the Pequod, Ahab's whaling ship, which symbolizes imperialist exploitation, is equated with the Pequots, the American Indians, whom settlers annihilated.

That First Woman, Changing Woman, Thought Woman, and Old Woman are always captured by soldiers and sent to Florida where they are imprisoned in Fort Marion not only serves as a structurally unifying device within these segments but also comically retells the history lesson that Alberta gives to her class. The American army's campaign in 1874 to force the southern Plains tribes onto reservations exemplifies the racist policy of containment, and ultimately extermination, of American Indians.

The recurring emphasis on soldiers, and border guards elsewhere in the text, suggests that settlers still practice a wardship colonial system of administration and policies. Dr. Joseph Hovaugh and his hospital attempt to confine the four Indians, but they escape; Sick Children's Hospital attempts to keep Lionel in the hospital, but he escapes; soldiers attempt to capture First Woman, Thought Woman, Changing Woman, and Old Woman and imprison them in Fort Marion, but they escape. The underlying objective of these paternalistic practices is to eliminate American Indians and their cultures, or at least to contain them. Border guards, for example, confiscate Amos Frank's sun dance outfits. When they are finally returned, the outfits have been desecrated (215). Gabriel, when he meets Thought Woman, acts like a border guard; he gives her the wrong card, his identification as a member of the Canadian Security and Intelligence Service. He also pulls out the wrong paper, which is, significantly, the White Paper (225).[17]

In their civilizing mission, colonizers present colonial versions of history which often deny or trivialize the histories of the colonized ("the pain of history words contain"). If the colonized see the world through the colonizers' lens, they may come to forget or be ignorant of their own history. For instance, Coyote (who is aligned with settlers insofar as both Coyote and settlers have misguided vision) claims that the narrator does not know the story of *Moby-Dick*. The narrator tells Coyote: "You haven't been reading your history" (164). In an effort to re-educate Coyote, the narrator explains: "It's English colonists who destroyed the Pequot" (164).

Throughout the text, King retells and re-presents the settler history of Fort Marion and the imprisonment of the Plains tribe, because First Woman, Changing Woman, Thought Woman, and Old Woman transform themselves, respectively, into the Lone Ranger, Ishmael, Robinson Crusoe, and Hawkeye and escape, leaving Fort Marion and settler oppression behind. Frequent retelling ensures that this history of oppression is not forgotten, and also reminds us that all tellings are cultural constructions that are subject to revision.

The characterizations of Lionel, Charlie, Eli, and Portland point to the ways settler culture manufactures "mimic men."[18] There are four central characters who, at times, succumb to colonial mimicry—Eli, Charlie, Lionel, and Portland, and four main female characters—Norma, Alberta, Latisha, and Babo who are not colonial mimics.[19] As Norma constantly tells Lionel, his uncle Eli exemplifies an American Indian who has "gone white." Eli left the reserve and moved to Toronto, where he married Karen, a white woman, and became a university professor, specifically a professor of English. In Toronto he never wants to look back to the reserve. He is reluctant to take Karen to another sun dance because he wants to distance himself from the reserve. He describes himself in terms of a "wannabe" white when he compares himself to Thoreau and to Grey Owl, who was a white, "wannabe" Indian (238). Similarly, Lionel's mentor is John Wayne—"Not the actor, but the character. Not the man, but the hero" (202)—a cultural icon of settler society.

Charlie and Lionel have both worked for Bursum and mimic his consumerism. Although Charlie leaves Bursum, he remains a product of Bursum's tutelage because he works as a lawyer for Duplessis, the company that is building the Grand Baleen Dam. Both Alberta and Lionel perceive Charlie as "sleazy," as someone who is selling out his band; however, Charlie describes himself as "slick" (99). Whereas "sleazy" implies selling out, "slick" suggests mastering the game. American Indian individuals, like Charlie, who attempt to master the game of colonial mimicry, lose their souls and become, by definition, sleazy.

Lionel, although not sleazy, is another mimic who has made "three mistakes" (25) in his life and, until the end of the text, lacks the courage to develop his potential. He plans to go to university, but never does; instead, he remains trapped in his job working for Bursum. Like Eli, he avoids his family and his obligations to his relations in pursuit of capital gain. King underscores Lionel's role as mimic man by giving him a history of former employment with the Department of Indian Affairs. Lionel equates advancement, progress, with abandoning the reserve and his "Indianness."

Charlie's father, Portland, is also a mimic who denies his identity and his culture to "progress" in settler culture. He not only emulates settler values but also physically transforms himself to comply with settler expectations and stereotypes. Portland's mimicry is a form of prostitution as is evident in his pornographic dance with Pocahontas, during which a cowboy dancer runs on stage and defeats the Indian (175–76). In changing his name and his nose, Portland loses himself and unwittingly becomes a tragic caricature—an imaginary Indian.

In contrast to these mimic men, the women not only refuse to assimilate but also subvert settler culture. Alberta's last name is, appropriately, Frank. She resists gender stereotypes in her decision to have a child without marrying and in her conviction that, "apart from no men in her life, two was the safest number" (37).[20] While Eli teaches English and subversive settler texts like "Bartleby the Scrivener," Alberta teaches and re-presents history from an American Indian perspective. For example, she describes the actions of the American army in 1874 as a "campaign of destruction" (14), and she encourages her apathetic students[21] to think about "the people" who drew the Plains Indian ledger art and "the world in which they lived" (16).

Latisha manipulates settler stereotypes as an advertising ploy by calling her restaurant the Dead Dog Café (another allusion to Coyote's Dream). Preying on settler expectations and perceptions of American Indians as "savages," she disguises hamburger as "dog meat" (92). She regularly attends the sun dance and confronts George Morningstar, her abusive former spouse, reminding him that he cannot take photographs at a sun dance.

Babo is also not a mimic, but serves as a counterpart to Doctor Hovaugh. Her name alludes to Captain Cereno's devoted black servant in Herman Melville's short story "Benito Cereno." In this gothic tale of white masters and black revenge, the slaves rebel, enslave Cereno and slaughter their master. Unlike Hovaugh, Babo Jones can perceive the actions of the four Indians and always observes, "isn't that the trick" (200). When Hovaugh rhetorically asks if her "ancestors were slaves," she disagrees and differentiates between being "slaves" and being "enslaved" (261). Unlike Lionel, Charlie, Eli, and Portland, Babo realizes that there are "All sorts of slaves in the world" and that servitude can take many forms: "Drugs, television, junk food, religion, cars, sex, power, cigarettes, money—" (261).

Norma, unlike her brother Eli and her nephew Lionel, values her American Indian culture and her relations.[22] She chastises both Eli and Lionel, for becoming mimic men and turning their backs on their identity and their relations. She always has a tepee at the sun dance, and it is she who organizes the rest of her relations, after the dam bursts, to rebuild her mother's/Eli's cabin.

That none of the mimics is a woman suggests that feminism is a force with which to resist colonial mimicry. Paula Gunn Allen argues that "traditional tribal lifestyles are more often gynocratic than not, and they are never patriarchal" (*The Sacred Hoop* 2). In *Green Grass, Running Water*, women repeatedly reject the "social fictions" of patriarchal discourse and "Christian rules" chorused by God, Noah, Ahab, A. A. Gabriel (Archangel Gabriel), Dr. Hovaugh, George Morningstar, Bursum, and others. Alberta, Babo, Latisha, and Norma are powerful as well as empowering characters who frequently give evidence of their ability to resist sexist stereotypes. Likewise, First Woman resists God's patriarchal dictates, his "Christian rules" (57), and leaves the garden; Changing Woman resists Noah's (123) and Ahab's rules (164) and "dives into the water" (164); and Thought Woman resists A. A. Gabriel and Robinson Crusoe's Manichean lists and "dives into the ocean" (246).

King juxtaposes this American Indian validation of women as creative and powerful with patriarchal views of women as procreators, as vessels to serve men. Like racism, sexism is just another form of slavery. Noah, for instance, repeatedly tells Changing Woman that it is "time for procreating" (124), but she resists his advances. Similarly, A. A. Gabriel wants Thought Woman to procreate and refuses to acknowledge or respect her refusal to comply:

> So, says A. A. Gabriel, you really mean yes, right? No, says Thought Woman. But that's the wrong answer, says A. A. Gabriel. Let's try this again. Let's not, says Thought Woman, and that one gets back into the water. (227)

By diving into the water, Thought Woman cleanses and purifies herself of settler rules. Paula Gunn Allen explains: "Among medicine people it is well known that immersing oneself in water will enable one to ward off dissolution" (*The Sacred Hoop* 24).

Thought Woman also embodies original, creative thinking which A. A. Gabriel, Noah, Ahab, and those who follow their rules lack. In *The Sacred Hoop*, Gunn Allen explains how original thinking is transformative:

> A strong attitude integrally connects the power of Original Thinking or Creation Thinking to the power of mothering. That power is not so much the power to give birth, as we have noted, but the power to make, to create, to transform. Ritual, as noted elsewhere, means transforming something from one state or condition to another, and that ability is inherent in the action of mothering. (29)

The women in *Green Grass, Running Water* are often transmitters of culture and exhibit their power "to make, to create, to transform" (Gunn Allen *The Sacred Hoop* 29). For example, Norma frequently advises her nephew, Lionel. She reminds him of his similarity to Eli and encourages him to return home and attend the sun dance. She advises him about how he might improve his relationship with Alberta and, as mentioned earlier, she warns him not to become a mimic man like his uncle Eli. The women resist the attempts by others to classify them as inferior or incompetent.

Norma, Latisha, Alberta, and Babo, as well as the four male/female Indian tricksters, transform the mimic men. They teach the men to value who they are and to reject colonial mimicry. Eli returns to his mother's log cabin and resists the dam project. Eli's name alludes to Eli in the Bible who stands alone and ignores the prophecy about the downfall of his house. Eli's name and his injunctions which impede progress on the dam also recall Elijah Harper and the role he played in the Meech Lake Accord in 1987.[23]

Both Charlie and Lionel, in vying for Alberta's love, come to appreciate their culture. Charlie eventually loses his job when Duplessis no longer needs a token "Indian" lawyer, and he reunites with his father. Lionel, owing to the assistance of the four Indians, has his moment of courage when he confronts George Morningstar. He decides to take responsibility for his life and to leave his job at Bursum's. He reunites with his relations and participates in the sun dance. Portland, owing to the four Indians, has his moment of triumph when he is transformed into the chief who leads the Indians to victory in the revised movie. Owing, too, to the four Indians and Coyote, the water is finally liberated from the dam. Through trickster mimicry, King rejects colonial rules and enables readers to laugh at settlers and their mistakes. His multi-voiced narrative includes, yet re-presents, settlers and colonial narratives. By re-configuring colonial histories/stories within an American Indian context, he foregrounds the agency of American Indians and estranges colonial rules from their sources of authority. Resisting closure, *Green Grass, Running Water* reminds readers that attempts to fix the world and the dialogue of decolonization are ongoing.

"Only Stories"

King rejects a definitive solution, a single history/(his)story or Truth. There is no one "right" solution, but rather many different voices. The open ending implies that the story will be retold repeatedly and there are multiple world views and discourses. As the narrator reminds Coyote and readers: "There are no truths, ... Only stories" (326).

King demonstrates that he "knows the difference" between creative hybridity and colonial mimicry. He sculpts a space in which readers can look in this trickster mirror and perceive their own unique faces reflected. In seeing American Indians as individuals, rather than as constructed "Indians," settler readers collaborate in the decolonization process and learn other ways of seeing. American Indian stories/histories now infiltrate settler ones so that readers can no longer read these settler narratives without remembering how King has re-contextualized them. Through intertextual references, he transforms and translates the colonial referents to which he alludes. In reconfiguring the Bible within American Indian contexts, for instance, King encourages readers to re-consider how settlers have employed the Bible in the service of the civilizing mission. In so doing, he expands our vision so that we no longer read the Bible in the same way.

Green Grass, Running Water not only satirizes settler culture and colonial mimics but also imaginatively re-presents an alternative discourse—one that is neither patriarchal nor capitalistic (with the underlying and self-perpetuating ideas of progress, individualism, and consumerism). In this fictional hybrid world made up of diverse American Indian perspectives, men and women are equal; relations are important; community, sharing, and consideration are valued; ceremonies, dreams, and visions are not only prophetic but also redemptive and healing; and tricksters attempt to unbend what has been bent.

Chapter Three

Listening to Silences

Well, when you don't understand the language, all the voices sound the same, don't they?

Ruby Slipperjack *Silent Words* 159

In time I learned how to listen to those stories, how to see beyond their casual appearance. To say that they contained lessons would be wrong; instead, they crystallized various scenarios within which some choices would clearly be wise and others inappropriate. The ultimate choice, however, would always be mine.

Rupert Ross *Dancing With A Ghost* xviii-ix

The silent language of physical metaphor is a story in itself.

Lee Maracle *Sojourner's Truth* 12–13

At the TELLING IT conference in Vancouver, British Columbia in November 1988, Jeannette Armstrong described the challenge of writing across a cultural gap. The chasm between cultures is an open space—an absence that is also a negation, an abyss into which much of the situational context of her culture and language disappears (*Telling It* 27). In *Silent Words* (1992), Ruby Slipperjack addresses this challenge. She writes through the silence/silencing of colonization to speak about, and resist, the effects of the "epistemic violence" (Gayatri Spivak *Women's Texts* 273) of colonization. She transforms the language of the colonizer so that it becomes a different language, one that not only speaks about violence/silence but also challenges binary oppositions and alters colonial frames of reference.[1] Slipperjack transforms the language so that it conveys the Ojibway traditions and experiences of her fictional community and its inhabitants.

In an interview with Hartmut Lutz, Ruby Slipperjack discusses the difficulty she faces writing in another language: "If I could speak Indian, I could tell you exactly what I am trying to say" (205). In her discussion of her first novel *Honour the Sun* (1987), Slipperjack expresses some things "like a shrug of the shoulder, that can mean so much," by attempting to parallel them, "use English words" and "devise situations where the English language would fit, still keeping the Native content intact" (qtd. in Lutz 206). In attempting to "get the flavour" of what she would "say in the Native language," her main concern is to ensure that "the feeling comes across" in English (qtd. in Lutz 206).

This parallelism strategy, also evident in *Silent Words* (1992), initially appears to exemplify colonial mimicry; the writer rethinks her experience in English rather than altering the language so that English speaking readers re-think their experience. What prevents Slipperjack's work from falling into the trap of colonial mimicry is her determination to convey "the feeling between the sentences":

> As long as I can see the feeling, then I can still understand it, because it is not just words. If the feeling is not there, then it is worthless. In the stories I have to have that feeling between the sentences. If it is not there, then I have lost something. (Slipperjack qtd. in Lutz 210)

In this way, Slipperjack conveys the unspoken silences of her characters' experiences and their feelings in the meaning "between the lines" (Lutz 205).

Further, she calls into question the language of the colonizers, thereby eluding the problem of colonial mimicry. She endeavors to re-form the English language. For instance, regional dialect and colloquial language express cultural differences and also affirm Ojibway variants of English. The author re-configures colonial language and discourse and re-presents English so that, in *Silent Words*, the language expresses the silent words of a fictional Ojibway community in Northern Ontario.

The plot revolves around Danny Lynx, an adolescent, and his experiences. Alienated from his family and his community, he runs away from home. During his travels, Danny forms relationships with diverse American Indians and learns to validate his Ojibway culture. He begins to understand the First Nations expression, "all my relations,"[2] and his father later reminds him that his Ojibway community is "like one big family" (244). Although Slipperjack uses the first person point of view, she emphasizes the group (Danny's Ojibway community) rather than the individual. As Danny later discovers, he has never really been lost. He has always been a part of his Ojibway community; when he later returns home he discovers that relatives and friends have helped him throughout his journey.

Within this Ojibway context, Slipperjack conveys the multiple meanings of silences. Danny's silences signal not only his loss of his language but also, at times, his loss for words. The narrative alludes to the ways in which colonizers have attempted to silence American Indians generally and this fictional Ojibway community specifically. Slipperjack illustrates how Danny and others have become estranged from their language and suggests that other aspects of Ojibway culture must fill this gap. One of these is pedagogy. Danny undergoes a learning process in which he acquires experiential knowledge and realizes the value of sharing and community. Even though Slipperjack depicts some of the impacts of colonization, she focuses on the daily activities of Ojibway and other First Nations people, not on the colonial relationship. In this way, the narrative affirms First Nations and offers readers an alternative discourse and a pedagogy of silences.

The challenge of trying to express a language of silences[3] (unspoken silent words) in print (silent words) is that the writer who attempts to write these silences often falls into the trap of writing about them; the writer tells about, instead of shows, a language of silences. Initially, it appears that there is a discrepancy between the message (validating oral traditions) and the medium (print). Paradoxically, Slipperjack foregrounds the importance of silence in Ojibway oral traditions yet uses words to write about it. The means and mode of production, specifically writing in English, appear to be inconsistent with the message (affirmation of Ojibway oral traditions). The author writes about the importance of experiential knowledge, yet she is writing a book. She illustrates the importance of speaking "Indian" (30), yet she writes in English. She points out the necessity of paying attention to oral traditions and the wisdom of elders, yet she chooses to express this through the medium of print. Upon closer examination, however, it becomes apparent that there is no discrepancy between the message and the medium. Slipperjack avoids being didactic because she uses a non-directive, pedagogical approach that is evident in many American Indian cultures. The implied silent words of Ojibway traditions and of the characters' feelings and memories are a discourse uttered "between the lines" (Lutz 205). These implied words put the silent words of print under erasure; readers have to start "reading and understanding between the lines" (Slipperjack qtd. in Lutz 205).

Slipperjack creates a hybrid form of writing in which she writes in English to critique the written as well as the spoken English of colonizers, yet uses *implicature* to foreground Ojibway pedagogy. Further, she conveys Ojibway traditions not only through but also between the silent words of print. I am using *implicature* to refer to the implied meanings, the unspoken words and feelings between the lines of print. I am also drawing on Adam Jaworski's definition in which he writes that *implicature* is the "unsaid elements of the utterance" (Jaworski 79). In *Silent Words* the unsaid utterances often include unsaid, but implied, Ojibway traditions. While Slipperjack is careful not to describe sacred rituals and ceremonies, she uses *implicature* to allude to them. *Implicature* enables the author to convey Ojibway traditions not only through but also between the silent words of print. This strategy draws attention to the gap between cultures and also affirms Ojibway cultural traditions. Moreover, *implicature* encourages readers to pay attention not only to what is said but also to what is left unsaid.

By titling her novel *Silent Words* (1992), the author puts her novel under erasure. Literally, the title refers to the transition from orality to literacy; the silent words convey the silence inherent in the practices of reading and writing. Metaphorically, the title alludes to the "epistemic violence" (Gayatri Spivak *Women's Texts* 273) of colonization, and the ways in which American Indians and their words have often been silenced. At the same time, the title foregrounds the importance of silence in oral traditions in which silence is not the absence of speech, but part of the continuum of communication.

As Ortega y Gasset observes, "each language represents a different equation between manifestations and silences. Each people leaves some things unsaid in order to be able to say others" (246). Some cultures have greater tolerance for silence and may value it more than those societies in which people expect talk to occur when they interact. In *Silent Words*, for instance, the lack of an immediate verbal reply to a statement does not threaten Ol' Jim or Old Woman Indian or impede the communication process. According to Adam Jaworski, there is a larger degree of tolerance for silence in American Indian communities than in settler society (47, 55–56). The ways in which people use and interpret silence is culturally specific, however.

In the course of history, there have been instances when colonizers have legitimized speech over silence and other forms of non-verbal communication. Definitions which posit silence as the absence of speech are essentialist and culturally biased because they erroneously imply that speech is presence and silence is absence. However, silence is not in opposition to speech, but part of the continuum of language; silence and speech are complementary forms of communication.[4] If "speech consists above all in silences" (Ortega y Gasset 246), then it is equally true that the absence of speech does not imply the absence of communication. Even "absolute motionlessness is itself a powerful gesture" (Ong 68). Further, the interpretation of speech often relies heavily on the nonverbal component of communication (Jaworski 46) and how a person interprets a message "may equally depend on the understanding of both the said and the unsaid elements of the utterance (*implicature*)" (79). Not all types of silence are communicative, but for those that are "the actual interpretation of someone's silence takes place only when the communication process is expected or perceived to be taking place" (Jaworski 34). Even then, individuals may interpret or misinterpret silences or non-verbal gestures and expressions. Cultural differences can further complicate the communication process. For example, in some settler cultures direct eye contact is a sign of honesty, assertiveness, and empowerment. The person who avoids eye contact is often seen as evasive. In Ojibway and Cree cultures, on the other hand, those who use direct eye contact are considered rude. In order to "send messages of attention and respect," the person refuses "to look anyone in the eye" (Ross 4).

American Indians are not homogeneous; hence, attitudes

toward silence vary from community to community as well as within each community. Each has its own cultural traditions and customs which define the uses of silence (Ruoff 8). Nevertheless, for many American Indians "the power of the word" is coupled with "the power of silence" (Ruoff 8). Walter Ong argues that, for oral cultures, words are closely tied in with the event and words themselves are events, whereas, in typographic cultures, there is a distancing between the word and the event, phenomenon, condition or activity that it signifies (32–33). Ong describes how "oral peoples . . . consider words to have magical potency" (32). Further, this is linked to "their sense of the word as necessarily spoken, sounded, and hence power-driven"(32). Since words are "power-driven," it is important to think through one's words carefully and to know when to speak and when to remain silent. Okanagan writer Jeannette Armstrong writes:

> One of the central instructions to my people is to practice quietness, to listen and speak only if you know the full meaning of what you say. It is said that you cannot call your words back once they are uttered and so you are responsible for all which results from your words. It is said that, for those reasons, it is best to prepare very seriously and carefully to make public contributions. (*The Native Creative Process* 90)

Leslie Marmon Silko also describes the importance of thinking through one's words before speaking because, once told, stories/words cannot be called back (*Ceremony* 138). In *Silent Words* Danny initially needs to tell his story, but later learns how to decipher and communicate through the silent words of Ojibway traditions.

Slipperjack subverts the silence/violence of colonial oppression through Danny, and his telling of his story. He has been doubly silenced. Settler society refuses to acknowledge his presence as a subject with agency. Settlers often perceive Danny as an object that is relegated to a position of alterity and inferiority. For instance Tom, Danny's friend, resorts to stereotypical name calling to disempower Danny: "Why should I shut up? I don't need a stupid Injun telling me to shut up!" (9). Moreover, Danny's family also silences him in a denial of abuse. Initially, his father neglects and silences him. His father is unable, and unwilling, to listen when Danny attempts to tell him about Sarah's, his stepmother's, abuse. His father, for example, refuses to hear when Danny attempts to tell him the truth about his stepmother's abusive actions and duplicitous words. When Danny tells his father about the times that Sarah has hit him, his father "believed her" and "yelled" at him "never to tell stories about her again" (5). According to Danny, "that really hurt. Dad picked her side" (5). It is important to note, here, that Danny's father suffers from his partner's deception as well as the colonization of First Nations by settler society.

Danny learns that how a listener interprets a speaker's words largely depends on whom a listener perceives to be legitimate as well as what the listener wants to hear. In another instance, a vendor on a train insists that Danny pay for candy that a fellow passenger has already paid for and given to him. Although the vendor knows Danny does not owe him money, he discredits the boy (22). The vendor's abuse of his position of power reveals his racism, his colonial assumptions of superiority.

The act of speaking the unspoken liberates Danny from his former silence. In telling about the violence he has survived, Danny says that "it felt so good to tell a grandfather [Ol' Jim] my problems" (95). Within this narrative, there are embedded re-tellings (both in the sense of telling his story repeatedly and in the sense of revising his story). What Danny tells and how much he reveals to each person depends on his relationship with his audience. He often retreats into silence when asked about his family or his scars. His silence signals to the speaker that this is a taboo subject and indicates Danny's reluctance to speak about his past and reveal his identity (78, 120, 190). Eventually, Danny subverts the "epistemic violence" and silencing effects of colonization by learning a language of silences (unspoken silent words) that enables him to experience personal, familial, and cultural reintegration.

At the beginning of his journey, however, Danny exemplifies the colonial mimic because he views the world through the lens of colonizers and has become alienated from his Ojibway culture. That Danny's father initially is unable to listen to his son attests to the ways in which he, too, has been silenced by colonization. Like Billy and others in the community, Danny and his father experience the dispossession and fragmentation that is a product of colonial mimicry.

Colonial mimicry warps subject formation because it creates a "double bind."[5] Settler society encourages Danny and his community to assimilate, but then disavows them. For Danny's father, Billy, and other members of this Ojibway community, town represents settler society and the negative effects of its assimilation process. For example, Danny's father was healthy when he was trapping, but becomes unhealthy when he moves into town. Billy does paperwork in town because he can no longer make a living trapping (189). Danny's father, Billy, and others in this community have been dispossessed and have experienced social and personal alienation as well as spiritual impoverishment. In attempting to emulate settler society, as represented by the move from their trapline to town, Danny and his family adopt the lifestyle and language of colonizers. In so doing, they become estranged from their Ojibway language and culture.

Equally destructive, and central to the book, is the implied silence that is the loss of American Indian languages. Slipperjack writes in English, not Ojibway, and Danny frequently speaks in English. Although he can speak Ojibway, he rarely does. For example, when other First Nations children ask him why he does not speak Ojibway, he replies: "Yeah, I just haven't had much practice talking it, but I can understand pretty good!" (30). He then asks them: "Why don't you speak English?" Clearly, Danny exemplifies a generation of young First Nations who have lost much of their language and other parts of their culture.

Slipperjack subverts this loss of language by making this silence—the absence of Ojibway language—speak. In addition, silences articulate the gaps between settlers and American Indians, language and meaning, feelings and words, and the world and human apprehension of it. Slipperjack not only writes through the silencing of colonization, she also writes silences; she foregrounds a language of silences (unspoken words) which communicates.

Silence is multifaceted and can signify diverse meanings. In his journey, Danny experiences many faces of silence: abuse, loss, death, reluctance, anticipation, closure, meditation, sacredness, acceptance, dismissal, love, memories, avoidance of conflict (and other face saving strategies), anger, fear, shame, humiliation, embarrassment, taboo or inappropriate behavior, misunderstanding, or liberation. Silence allows for ambiguity and points to the slippage between language and meaning.[6]

At the same time, given the ambiguity of silence and the subjectivity of interpretation, it is not surprising that silence can lead to miscommunication and confusion. Relating the story through Danny's words, the author draws attention to how his interpretations, and misinterpretations, of words and gestures reflect his perceptions, psychological state, and frame of reference. In this way, Slipperjack suggests that communication is not just what and how something is said or communicated, but relies on the perceptions and receptivity of the listener. Danny is not always accurately decoding the message that is communicated. Estranged from his Ojibway culture, he often misinterprets the silences of others.

Conflicting cultural frames of reference can contribute to miscommunication. For example, when Danny asks Bobby why he does not just buy a spoon instead of carving one, Danny is met with "a deep silence as if they were waiting to see what Bobby would do" (32). Danny's cultural frame of reference, here, is that of an assimilated person who has become reliant on store bought goods, whereas Bobby's frame of reference is that of an unassimilated, self-reliant person who validates his First Nations culture by practicing it. Bobby communicates this to Danny through his non-verbal body language and actions. Danny observes how "Bobby just glanced at me, shrugged, and resumed his careful work" (32). In another instance, Danny asks Ol' Jim what the wolf had been waiting for but Ol' Jim does not answer immediately. Danny fears that Ol' Jim has not "heard" (118). In both cases, silence signals the cultural gaps between the two speakers and, as I discuss later, encourages Danny to modify his behavior.

More often than not, Danny is unable to decipher the cultural contextual codes and misconstrues silence as an indication of dismissal; he fears he is being ignored. In most cases the listener is paying attention and his/her silence signifies a response which Danny is not always immediately able to interpret. When Danny first encounters Mrs. Old Woman Indian he interprets her silence as a refusal to acknowledge him:

> She just ignored me. She wouldn't even look at me. . . . She continued
> walking for another long while before she glanced at me again. This time
> she had no expression. It was as if I wasn't even there. . . . She wasn't
> even listening. (48)

Danny does not know how to deal with her lack of expression,
and is still looking for guidance and direction. His response to her
non-verbal gestures reflect more about him than about Mrs. Old
Woman Indian. That Danny fears he has not been heard reminds
Danny, and readers, of the way in which his family and settler
society have marginalized him in the past. Similarly, Danny is
quick to interpret Old Man Indian's silence as an indication that
he has not been heard: "The old man never said very much. . . . I
tried talking to him once but he didn't answer me. Maybe he
didn't hear me" (53). Danny's interpretation of Old Man Indian's
silence may also be a face saving strategy. He assumes that he has
not been heard instead of considering the possibility that he has
not learned how to listen to silence. His interpretations, and
misinterpretations, of words and gestures reflect his colonial
frame of reference; he has not yet remembered how to decipher
Ojibway cultural codes and contextual cues. In most instances,
however, the listener has heard and his/her silence signifies a
response, which Danny is not always immediately able to
interpret.

Given the many facets, and ambiguity, of silence the question
arises: how can individuals decipher meaning when silence is
subject to such diverse interpretations? The answer lies in context
rather than text. The subjective perceptions of the individual to
whom one is communicating as well as the context influence how
one reads or interprets a situation: "The greater contextual effects,
the greater the relevance" (Sperber and Wilson 119). However,
one's frame of reference also influences how and what one sees. In
the earlier situation with the vendor, Danny interprets the
vendor's words accurately because he understands the racist
context in which they are spoken. With Old Woman Indian, on the
other hand, Danny repeatedly misinterprets her silences because
he has yet to understand the context. In order to learn how to
decode silences, Danny undergoes a process of reframing; he pays
more attention to context and reconnects with his Ojibway culture
and community.

Instead of telling the reader and Danny what specific silences mean, the author configures contextual situations in which Danny and readers arrive at their own conclusions. Further, Danny and readers learn to interpret silences in light of ever shifting contexts. For example, consider Ol' Jim's story of the beaten dog that was shot after it killed its abusive master. Danny interprets this story in light of his present and experience. He thinks Ol' Jim is just rambling off in his memory world again. Ol' Jim's story also reminds him of his past encounter with the wolf pup on the beach (114–15). Readers interpret this story in light of this particular situation, and in relation to the whole narrative. This tale reinforces the story of settler oppression of First Nations, and of the abuse that Danny experienced at home. It also foreshadows the end of the text when Danny, still scarred and scared, misinterprets the situation and accidentally shoots his father. In order to illustrate pedagogy—Danny's experiential learning—through the medium of a written text, Slipperjack resorts to a descriptive, allusive style in which she conveys much non-verbal communication through situational contexts and by playing on the ambiguity and multi-faceted nature of silence.

Re-framing the Picture

Drawing on artistic principles of foregrounding, nuance, spatial placement, perspective, hue, and tone, Slipperjack avoids didacticism and signals the importance of context. Even her painting on the cover of *Silent Words* illustrates the importance of learning how to decode visual stimuli.[7] For example, the title and Slipperjack's cover illustration of the novel frame the silent words and inform how we read the text. The picture is framed by a blue border with red right angles. Next to a placid lake, there is an unpopulated sandy beach with Jack pines, birch, and other trees in the background. The painting is realistic and resembles a photograph. What is immediately apparent is the tranquillity and solitude—the silence—of this wilderness scene. This representational picture of Nature is evocative, requiring the viewers to draw on their feelings and memories. At a first glance, the picture appears to convey stillness. Upon closer inspection, movement is apparent. The wind is side shore, as is evident from the ripples perpendicular to the shore. The sand shows evidence of tracks (like traces of language), but there are no human footprints. How much or how little viewers see is dependent on their ability to decipher the signs in the natural world—cloud formations, ripples, reflections in the water, tracks in the sand, and the movement and direction of bending trees. The curve along the beach highlights the border between land and water. By placing it slightly off center, Slipperjack draws readers into the picture so that they, too, can see how environment offers a language of silences. Slipperjack explains: "Everything is tied with nature. . . . They may be just rocks to you, but . . . these are things that we know the land by. . . . The land, rocks, trees are part of our history, a part of us" (qtd. in Lutz 207).

Ol' Jim, through his example, teaches Danny to become more attuned to his environment. He demonstrates the inadequacy of spoken and written words, and suggests that we need to learn how to listen—to pay attention to the world around us and to our inner feelings, thoughts, and memories. From him, Danny learns that words can become a source of meaningless distraction—white noise. Ol' Jim also teaches Danny how to cultivate his senses and feelings to raise his level of awareness. When they reach a clearing, he asks Danny to "tell me what you see" (123). Danny interprets the word "see" literally and relies on visual clues instead of using all of his senses and faculties to decipher the signs. He is unable to make deductions from his observations because he is only partially aware; his vision is limited. Ol' Jim is silent, but "rolled his eyes in exasperation" (123). This gesture is a signal for Danny to heighten his awareness and to deduce signs of former human habitation (123). Ol' Jim later draws Danny's attention to the fact that he relies too much on visual stimuli: "You are getting better at noticing things, but let your eyes tell you all of what they see" (143).[8]

Through non-verbal communication, Ol' Jim encourages Danny to cultivate his awareness, to expand his language. Unlike verbal language, the language of silences is non-intrusive, non-directive, and non-authoritarian. Ol' Jim often does not tell Danny how to interpret these lessons, but allows him to discover their meaning for himself. For instance, Ol' Jim indicates the importance of knowing how to read the signs in the natural world when he tells Danny, "You rush too much, you know that? . . . You should take

time to look around and remember how things are, son. Would
you remember how we got here if you had to do the trip all over
again without me?" (129). Danny's impatience impedes
awareness, and both awareness and memory are essential to
survival. American Indian languages, oral traditions, and histories
are passed from one generation to the next through social and
individual memories. As Ol' Jim demonstrates, Elders play a
pedagogical role because they educate the young through their
stories, lives, and actions; thus, this process of rememoration
contributes to the survival of American Indians (143–44).

Throughout the narrative, Slipperjack illustrates the complex
web between memory, history, and land. As she points out to
Lutz, land is central to American Indians because it is their history
(Lutz 207); land is an integral part of their stories, lifestyle,
traditions, and culture(s) generally.

Memory also plays an integral role in subject formation. The
past influences and shapes the present and the present modifies
how the individual interprets the past. In the concluding passage
of the novel, Slipperjack employs silence as a metaphor for a
language of feelings and memories that document Danny's history.
He explains: "You can't escape the silent words of your memory.
They grow on you, layer after layer, year after year, documenting
you from beginning to end, from the core to the surface. I built my
cabin with silent words" (250).

Instead of falling into the trap of writing about silence and
being didactic, Slipperjack uses metaphor and imagery to write a
language of silences. Silence as a state can be conceptualized
metaphorically as a container, whereas an act(ivity) of silence can
be conceptualized metaphorically as a substance (Lakoff and
Johnson 30). It is useful to consider the example of the difference
between a play and a pantomime. In a play silence is
conceptualized as an activity and can be treated as a substance,
whereas in pantomime silence is "a state in which their
performance takes place," and thus is "a *container* that provides a
wider frame for the viewing of a show" (Jaworski 146–47). In
Slipperjack's novel, silent words are concrete, non-analytical
events, but they also convey unspoken words, psychological, and
spiritual states. For instance, Danny learns to listen to the voices
of ancestors at the sandcliff when Ol' Jim does not answer him;

instead, Ol' Jim's silence allows him to experience fear and respect for the dead (172–73).

Just as Ol' Jim is a pedagogical influence for Danny so is Old Man Indian. He also teaches Danny the importance of the land— the importance of not showing disrespect for Nature by poisoning the environment (56). In explaining the need for people to respect and listen to Nature, Old Man Indian informs Danny that people who do not hear or see this are "stone deaf an bline" (56). He criticizes those that "'ab gibin up da honour dat was gibin to you by da Creator!" and says: "It is da people you 'ab not forgodden!" (57). Old Man Indian teaches Danny that all human beings are part of the web of creation and, like "da leaf," follow the natural cycle from birth to death (59). Here, and throughout the text, dialect validates Ojibway variants and offers an alternative discourse, one that writes over colonial language and foregrounds Danny's Ojibway culture.

In depicting Danny's journey, Slipperjack offers readers a pedagogical alternative to patriarchal, directive pedagogies. Silence is a pedagogical tool that allows the sender of the message the freedom to deliver it in a non-directive, non-didactic way and allows the recipient of the message to interpret it in their own way and in their own time. In this respect, silence enables Ol' Jim and others to teach Danny about his culture without being didactic. For instance, when Danny asks Ol' Jim why Henry will not talk to him, Ol' Jim advises him to be patient and then "said no more" (201). Danny perceives this silence as Ol' Jim's closure of this conversation and shifted attention: "He seemed deep in thought about something" (201). While Ol' Jim has closed the conversation with his silence, the implied message is that Danny must digest the information in his own time and deal with the situation in his own way.

Silences facilitate Danny's modification of his assimilated behavior. In the earlier example that I cited when Danny asks one of his new acquaintances why he does not speak English, the boy just looks at Danny and "shrugged" and then asks: "Why?" (30). Danny realizes that he does not "have an answer for that" and tells his new acquaintances his name in Ojibway. Only then do they "relax" and listen to him (30). In this example, the boy's gesture contextualizes and frames the boy's question and indicates how Danny should interpret it. Danny does not know how to reply to the question and interprets the shrug and the question as a disavowal of English; hence, he replies in Ojibway. Similarly, Old Man Indian's silence serves as a cue for Danny to speak in Ojibway (48).

During the time he spends with Mr. Old Man and Mrs. Old Woman Indian, Danny begins to learn how to communicate without using words: "I shrugged hopelessly and she [Mrs. Old Woman Indian] smiled and looked away. I just did it! I mean talking not in words but by actions" (60). Through silences, Ol' Jim also encourages Danny to modify his assimilated behavior. For instance, when Danny speaks to him in English, Ol' Jim pretends not to hear and Danny switches to Ojibway (116). His experience with Ol' Jim also plays a central role in his subject formation and reintegration with his Ojibway culture. Ol' Jim teaches Danny the importance of sharing and community: "Boy, when you come home, you don't just find yourself, you already got yourself! What you find are all the people who love you!" When he returns to visit Mr. Old Man and Mrs. Old Woman Indian, Danny realizes that the non-verbal communication of "silent words" of warmth and love are "the little things I had almost forgotten" (193).

Non-verbal gestures and silences can also create a safety net that allows the recipient of the message to save face. When Danny is staying with Charlie's family, for instance, he learns to recognize the inappropriateness of his words and the judgmental and accusatory tone underlying his English words. The situation is defused when Billy's mother, "smiled and shrugged at me" (45). Danny can pay attention to the reprimand without losing face because he is still made to feel welcome and accepted. Consequently, he does not respond with anger or denial; instead, he accepts Billy's reprimand and modifies his behavior: "Well, I guess I have to watch what I say from now on. And I guess she's right, I can't act like I'm at home in someone else's home" (45).

In an example that I cited earlier, Danny asks Ol' Jim why the wolf waited. When Ol' Jim does not answer immediately, Danny fears that the older man has not "heard." Ol' Jim finally explains that the wolf "probably knows you from somewhere and waited to see if you knew. You obviously did not" (118). Danny still does not understand that the wolf is his protector because he has not yet learned to validate spirituality. His vision is limited; his assimilated eyes can only see the wolf as a potential predator. Ol' Jim's silence encourages Danny to modify his behavior. Ol' Jim refuses to elaborate and remains so "very quiet" that Danny "wondered if I had offended him or something. I decided to keep my mouth shut and make myself useful" (118). When Danny later overhears the men talking about how the wolves are Danny's protectors he begins to understand (222). Here, and throughout the story, Ol' Jim's actions and his frequent slips into his "memory world" (117) are silent words that communicate.

Ol' Jim usually has a non-directive, experiential pedagogical approach, but on those rare occasions when he does direct Danny he discreetly tempers the lessons with humor. When Danny sets his first rabbit snare, Ol' Jim comments: "That is kind of a hard decision to ask a rabbit to make. To stretch or duck under. I think I would decide to duck under if I was a rabbit" (136). Ol' Jim is telling Danny that his snare is too high off the ground; thus, he teaches Danny to put it lower. By taking the point of view of the rabbit, he also teaches Danny to visualize his prey in order to trap it. Likewise, Ol' Jim does not chastise Danny for his prank on Hog, but merely comments: "I think that snake borrowed two legs from somewhere" (170). He subtly communicates that he knows Danny is responsible for the prank while at the same time remaining non-judgmental; moreover, he communicates his acceptance that Danny had reasons for taking the actions that he did.

Silence often is a motivational trigger for Danny that reminds him to pay attention and take responsibility for his actions. For instance, Danny hears a noise behind him and sees Ol' Jim walking back to camp. Danny briefly wonders: "Why didn't he say anything?" but then takes the initiative and decides to check his snares (140). He begins to incorporate the knowledge and skills Ol' Jim has given him and to recognize when he has made a mistake without any cues from Ol' Jim. Through his silences, Ol' Jim teaches Danny the importance of self-reliance, of not wasting words and of speaking with words only when necessary. Danny learns "not to ask stupid questions because he [Ol' Jim] just pretended he didn't hear me anyway" (97).

At other times, silences signify sacred places and respect.

Through his example, Ol' Jim teaches Danny to cultivate awareness and expand his vision. Ol' Jim's silences as well as his stories about the Memegwesiwag (97–98), the Magic Rock (118–19), the Medicine Man and sacred rocks (156–57), and the sand cliff old burial site (172) facilitate Danny's rememoration of Ojibway spirituality.[9]

Silences can be ambiguous or they can be a powerful form of communication that raise the awareness of the sender and/or the recipient. The receiver of the message has to pay close attention not to words, but to body language, gestures, feelings, intuition, and situational context. When such communication is successful and no longer ambiguous, then the communication that takes place is on a deeper level. It can signify a spiritual communion in which both parties are synchronous and words are no longer necessary.

One way recipients can disambiguate silent messages is by learning to see not just with their eyes, but to use all their senses to perceive signs and the interrelationships between them. Silences often foreground the inadequacy of spoken and written words, and suggest that Danny needs to learn how to listen—to pay attention to the world around him and to his inner feelings, thoughts, and memories. Unlike verbal language, the language of silences is non-intrusive, non-directive, and non-authoritarian. Non-verbal communicative silence consists of gestures, feelings, and actions that, to use an old cliché, speak louder than words. Talk is often depicted as intrusive and insensitive, whereas silences, in many situations, encourage Danny to heighten his powers of observation and perception.

Silence can indicate a sacred ritual in which much can be left unsaid because "religious language is highly ritualized and low in the content of new information" (Jaworski 47). As previously mentioned, social customs, and traditions define the uses of silences. After Old Man Indian's story about how "We are da chi'en of da Eart" (56), there "was silence for a long time as he refilled his pipe and pointed it to the four directions with each puff of smoke" (56). Ol' Jim is also silent when performing rituals. Silence is "the dimension in which ordinary and extraordinary events take their proper places" and, in American Indian oral traditions, "silence is the sanctuary of sound. Words are wholly alive in the hold of silence; there they are sacred" (Momaday "The

Native Voice" 7).

For many Ojibway people, there are "two different realities" that are "concurrent and simultaneous as well as impinging upon one another constantly" (J. Dumont 79). This vision is a "'total way of seeing' which encompasses the essential elements of ordinary reality and seeks out the all-important manifestations of non-ordinary reality" (J. Dumont 79). In challenging settler notions of "progress" and colonial assumptions of superiority, Slipperjack suggests, to borrow Dennis Tedlock's words, that "we have lost sight of one whole dimension" (Tedlock and Tedlock xx). Ol' Jim describes how many American Indians have, through assimilation, become alienated from their spirituality; they have lost the "level of thought and knowledge to be able to see and talk" with the Memegwesiwag (97).

Initially, Danny talks too much and his vision is limited. The Old Woman Indian advises him to develop a new kind of vision: "Use your eyes an feel inside you wat da udder is feelin. Dat way, dere is no need for words. Your ears are for 'earin all da udder tings 'round you" (60). The next day, Danny observes: "No one said a word, but we said a lot. I was learning" (61). Whereas Danny earlier equated words with deception, oppression, and prejudice when he was silenced at home, he discovers in the course of this healing journey how to speak through silence; he voices the colonial violence/silencing he endured and communicates in silent words. Through silences, not words, Danny heightens his awareness of both "ordinary" and "non-ordinary" reality and cultivates a holotropic vision.[10] The more he learns to pay attention with his whole being, the less important words become.

Different Voices/Voicing Differences

Listening to birds sing, Ol' Jim comments that "when you don't understand the language, all the voices sound the same, don't they?" (159). Within the context of the situation, Ol' Jim's words refer to the need for individuals to cultivate awareness so they can decipher the signs of the natural world (and, in this case, the birds' songs). As Danny has learned, each sound contains information if the individual is paying enough attention to decipher the codes (139). For Danny, words have acquired an expanded meaning; they are no longer solely equated with speech and writing, but refer to audible and silent signs throughout the natural world.

Ol' Jim's comment about language also has particular resonance for readers. Those who do not understand the language—in this case, the Ojibway language as well as the language of silences (the silent words of Ojibway traditions)— may make the mistake of thinking that all American Indian voices sound the same. Danny's dilemma with his father and his dilemma as an Ojibway contending with settler society further point to a central problem that the narrative frequently foregrounds: how do you speak to those who do not want to listen? The narrative addresses this question by subverting the silence/violence of colonialism through Danny, and his telling of his story. Through *implicature*, Slipperjack offers readers opportunities to cultivate awareness and to be attune to cultural differences.

Focusing on "the gap between the words" and feelings, *implicature* enables readers to pay attention not only to what is said but also to what is left unsaid. *Implicature* can also effectively displace readers by drawing attention to the gaps in their knowledge and understanding. In such instances, the implied meanings that elude readers may well give them insight into the displacement that diverse American Indians experience. Confronted by their own cultural gap (their cultural differences and their unfamiliarity with Danny's Ojibway culture), readers negotiate meanings, confront their assumptions, and deconstruct their reading strategies.

Understandably, the contextual knowledge of Ojibway readers familiar with northern Ontario will be richer than that of readers unfamiliar with the region, and its cultural codes:

> There are sometimes words that mean something specific to that region. So, when you are writing something, the Native person from this region that you are from will read this passage and they will understand exactly what you are trying to say because they have understood the *implied meaning*, and all of a sudden, they are just cracking up laughing, because you would have to be from that region before you could understand what the big joke is! (Slipperjack qtd. in Lutz 206–7; emphasis added)

However, *implicature* enables readers unfamiliar with this region and Ojibway culture "to associate with that world without being encouraged to feel a part of it" (King "Godzilla" 14).

In his discussion of "associational literature,"[11] which he defines as the body of literature created by contemporary Native writers, Thomas King remarks: "For the non-Native reader, this literature provides a limited and particular access to a Native world, allowing the reader to associate with that world without being encouraged to feel a part of it" ("Godzilla" 14). In *Silent Words*, readers who are not American Indian can derive many, but not all, of the implied meanings from the contexts of the words and the situations. American Indian readers familiar with Northern Ontario and Ojibway cultural traditions can draw on this knowledge as well as their cultural codes, social memory, and personal experience. They can derive meaning not only from the situational context but also from their own unique cultural contexts and experiences. For the American Indian reader, as Thomas King points out, "associational literature helps to remind us [American Indians] of the continuing values of our cultures" ("Godzilla" 14).

Slipperjack affirms Ojibway traditions and eludes the danger that writing in English may pose—namely, colonial mimicry—because she reconfigures and expands the contextual meanings of silent (unspoken as well as printed) words. She writes in english[12] without becoming entrapped in the language of the colonizer. Through a strategy of erasure, she draws attention to some of the ways that colonizers have used silence as a political tool to oppress, marginalize, and disavow American Indians. Further, the narrative offers an alternative discourse that writes over the language of colonizers and foregrounds Danny's Ojibway language and oral traditions. In working through the silence and silencing that he initially experienced, Danny learns a different language of silences that heals him. He has learned that *listen* is an anagram for *silent*. Having learned how to listen, he is capable of decoding the silent words in the environment and the silent spaces between spoken words. Ultimately, in crossing cultural gaps, *Silent Words* voices the gap between words and seeing and writes over colonial violence/silence to speak.

Chapter Four

Stereotypography

For the stereotype is at once a substitute and a shadow.

Homi Bhabha *The Location of Culture* 82

In their respective efforts to achieve self-determination and self-government, American Indian and Métis peoples often contend with ways in which colonizers attempt to construct and define identity for them. Stuart Hall has only articulated part of the process of identity formation when he observes that "identities are constructed through, not outside, difference" and that "it is only through the relation to the Other, the relation to what it is not, to precisely what it lacks . . . that the 'positive' meaning of any term—and thus its 'identity'—can be constructed" (*Questions of Identity* 4–5). Hall's comments point to the exclusionary practices that colonizers use to deny the colonized access to power. Although colonized people may define themselves by what they lack (by what they are not), they may also simultaneously define themselves by what they share.

Beatrice Culleton's (née Mosonier) *In Search of April Raintree* (1983, revised and reissued in 1984 as *April Raintree*) foregrounds the question of identity.[1] Culleton describes the dispossession of April and Cheryl Raintree, two Métis sisters. The Children's Aid Society separates them from their natural parents and places them in foster homes. April's early memories of her parents' alcoholism and poverty as well as her negative experiences in foster homes contribute to her rejection of her Métis identity. In an endeavor to access the privileges of the dominant society, she attempts to "pass" for a "white." While April denies her American Indian ancestry, Cheryl validates hers. Unlike April, Cheryl's experiences in foster homes are not negative. Mrs. MacAdams, one of Cheryl's foster mothers, encourages her to learn about, and take pride in, her Métis heritage (45). Cheryl has little recollection of her parents and, in the absence of accurate information, re-imagines and romanticizes them. When she later meets her father, she becomes disillusioned and begins to see American Indians and Métis people through the lens of the colonizer. Following the path of her mother, Cheryl commits suicide. Angered by the societal inequities that contributed to Cheryl's "vanishing" and faced with raising Cheryl's son, April no longer tries to deny who she is but affirms her Métis identity. In illustrating how April embraces metonymic colonial stereotypes and Cheryl cultivates metaphoric ones, Culleton's text abrogates colonial stereotypical discourse and presents a paradigm for counterstereotyping.

Culleton maps the stereotypography of colonial discourse to "work through many fake ideas" (Fee 170) and "upset stereotypes of Native peoples" (Damm 95). In coining the term stereotypography, I am alluding to the etymology of stereotype. Derived from the Greek words *stereos* which means form or solid, and *typos* which means to make an impression or model, the original meaning of stereotype refers to a metal printing plate cast from a mould. Culleton represents metaphoric and metonymic colonial stereotypes to re-cast stereotypical colonial discourse.

Cases of Metonymy and Metaphor

In their colonial discourse, colonizers define colonized people as others by deploying both metaphoric and metonymic stereotypes to construct sameness and difference simultaneously.[2] Colonizers construct metaphoric stereotypes in which they encourage the colonized to be the same as they are, yet disavow the differences of the colonized. Colonizers also construct metonymic stereotypes in which individuals are constructed as representative of a collective other in which the colonized are constructed as the same because of their difference. Colonizers deploy metonymic stereotypes to make the colonized cognizant of what they lack—or how they differ from colonizers. Both metaphoric and metonymic stereotypes illuminate the inclusionary and exclusionary processes implicit in identity politics.

Colonial stereotypes are "cases of metonymy" (Lakoff 79), but they are also cases of metaphor in which colonizers make generalizations and false correlations to disempower colonized people.[3] Stereotypes are the "major discursive strategy" of colonial discourse, "a form of knowledge and identification that vacillates between what is always 'in place,' already known, and something that must be anxiously repeated" (Bhabha *Location* 66). They exemplify the constructed ambivalence whereby otherness is constituted as "the object of desire and derision, articulation of difference contained within the fantasy of origin and identity" (Bhabha *Location* 67).[4]

Colonizers deploy metaphors to construct colonized people as similar, yet they also employ metonyms to negate individuality and subsume individuals (and differences between individuals) into collective categories of otherness in which differences become the mark of sameness. A metonymic stereotype, for instance, is evident when Mrs. DeRosier, April's second foster mother, sees April as representative of all "half-breeds." This constructed sameness is simultaneously conflated with a collective difference which colonizers invoke to differentiate themselves from those they colonize and to justify the colonial relationship.

Metaphoric stereotypes establish a comparison in which individual differences are subsumed into a generalized collective in which the colonized share attributes with each other and with colonizers. At the same time, colonizers disavow this constructed similarity to settlers by asserting difference. The "noble warrior" is like the colonizer, yet is *"almost the same but not quite,"* or as Bhabha adds in underscoring the racism, *"almost the same but not white"* (*Location* 89).

Jean-Jacques Rousseau's "noble savage" is another example of a metaphoric "narcissistic object-choice" (*Location* 77). Colonizers see a metaphoric image like themselves, but it is an image that they have constructed. The "savage" is "noble" because the colonizer situates the "savage" in a state of presumed natural innocence. Settlers naturalize their constructed values (civilization)—values "which, conversely, established 'savagery', 'native', 'primitive', as their antitheses and as the object of a reforming zeal" (Ashcroft, Griffiths, and Tiffin 3). When they construct the colonized as "noble savages," they imagine the colonized (like themselves) as "noble," yet also disavow the colonized with the negative term "savages." The overall concept of the "noble savage" as the individual living in a state of innocence in Nature is an imaginative reconstruction of the colonizer in an Edenic existence. Ironically, this image also implies that the colonizer no longer exists in a state of innocence, but lives in a state of corrupt civilization. In this respect, the ambivalence of the colonizer's constructed image carries a message— unacknowledged by the colonizer—that the colonized may deploy to subvert colonizers and their stereotypical discourse.

Just as colonizers construct an image partially like themselves (noble), they simultaneously see an other, a lack, which is unlike themselves that threatens them. The "metonymic figuring of lack" (Bhabha *Location* 77) consists of stereotypes that direct particular, specific insults while the "metaphoric masking" (Bhabha *Location* 77) consists of more general socially constructed images.

In Culleton's novel, "the Native girl syndrome" (66–67) is a metonymic image that settler society constructs to justify the status quo and to rationalize racism and prejudice toward Métis and American Indians. Mrs. Semple, the social worker, does not connect the effects of this syndrome, in which she blames the "Native girl," with the colonization process; however, the colonial metonymic figuring of lack is evident in her contention that all Native girls end up in jail or on Skid Row (67).

Settlers perceive Native girls as others marked by difference (a lack) that threatens settlers and justifies their aggressive stance.[5] For example, Mrs. Semple's stereotyping of Native girls is a justification for her fear of them. The underlying implication of her speech is that settlers must keep these girls in check to prevent them from returning to what colonizers construe as a savage, uncivilized state. Settler society constructs illusory correlations[6] to disavow the differences of colonized Métis and American Indian subjects. Colonizers delineate difference while at the same time generalizing individuals into a collective other. This constructed difference, "distinctiveness," is then aligned with negative attributes (Bhabha's metonymic figuring of a lack) to establish an illusory correlation that justifies and legitimizes settler society's racist treatment of Métis and American Indians.

"Distinctiveness-based" illusory correlations are relevant to the "initial formation of stereotypic beliefs, whereas expectancy-based illusory correlations pertain to mechanisms by which existing stereotypes become self-perpetuating and resistant to change" (Hamilton, Stroessner, and Mackie 45). For instance, Mrs. Semple's "Native girl syndrome" speech reveals her "distinctiveness-based illusory correlations." She assumes that girls who are Native are therefore bad and destined to become degenerates. April's rapists reveal their "distinctiveness-based illusory correlation" when they make the equation that because April is "Indian" she is a "little whore" (143). One says, "these squaws really dig this kind of action. They play hard to get and all the time they love it" (143). Mrs. DeRosier falsely equates Métis with dirt, "I know you half-breeds, you love to wallow in filth" (39). Culleton depicts these illusory correlations, but refrains from evaluating them. Instead, she challenges the underlying colonial relationship by examining the "processes of *subjectification* made possible (and plausible) through stereotypical discourse" (Bhabha *Location* 67).

Culleton problematizes concepts of identity as constructing sameness (a unity, fixed identity) and identity as asserting differences (a dispersed, unfixed identity) in her depiction of the routes that April and Cheryl initially take. At different points in the novel, each sister denies parts of her identity and internalizes the binary oppositions in colonial stereotypical discourse. April is a colonial mimic who attempts to validate her "white" ancestry in her efforts to assimilate while Cheryl embodies the person who validates her American Indian ancestry and asserts her differences.

Throughout much of the novel, April exemplifies the stereotype of the colonial mimic. To wit, her younger sister nicknames her "Apple"[7] and her foster sister disparagingly calls her "Ape" (50). As a colonial mimic, she tries "to pass for a white person" (49) in her desire to conceal her Métis identity. Inheriting her "part Irish and part Ojibway" mother's pale skin, April is determined to "live just like a real white person," but fears her sister will betray her racial identity: "How was I going to pass for a white person when I had a Métis sister?" (49). This question is telling because it reveals how she denies her Métis heritage and differentiates herself from her sister. April fails to understand the underlying power imbalances that are at the root of racial discrimination; instead, she erroneously equates racism with skin color.[8] She pities "poor Cheryl" who "would never be able to disguise her brown skin as just a tan" (49). April attempts to dissociate publicly from her sister, and from other Métis and American Indians, in an endeavor to associate with settlers.

In identifying with settlers, she perceives and disparages Métis as others—as different from herself (111). She plays with white school children and later, only dates white men. Her desire to mimic settlers is evident in her efforts to re-make herself. She reads fashion magazines and a book on etiquette (100). She considers changing the spelling of her name from Raintree to Raintry because she believes Raintry might pass for an Irish name (49). She later revels in her married name, April Radcliff, again erroneously believing that she has been accepted by settlers (110).

Until the final pages of the text, she embodies the ambivalence inherent in the colonial relationship. She attempts to assimilate, but Mrs. Semple, Mrs. DeRosier and her children, Mrs. Radcliff and other members of settler society repeatedly disavow her; they continue to perceive her as other. In her efforts to assimilate, April engages in "expectancy-based illusory correlations" (Hamilton, Stroessner, and Mackie 45) that perpetuate, rather than displace, existing colonial stereotypes. She expects all "Indians" and Métis to become degenerate "gutter creatures" because she never challenges existing colonial stereotypes. Instead, she internalizes settler stereotypes and dissociates herself from Métis and American Indians. According to April, "Indians" and Métis are "inclined to be alcoholics" because "they were a weak people" who are "put down more than anyone else" because "they deserve it" (49):

> Being a half-breed meant being poor and dirty. It meant being weak and having to drink. It meant being ugly and stupid. It meant living off white people. And giving your children to white people to look after. (49)

When Cheryl tells April about Louis Riel, April is disinterested. She has only read settler versions of history and has internalized colonial discourse and stereotypes. Whereas Cheryl reads Métis books which Mrs. MacAdams gives her to affirm her ancestry, April is relieved that no one in her class knew of her heritage when they read about "that period in Canadian history"

(45). She perceives settler oppression of Métis and American Indians as justifiable. Métis and American Indians are, she believes, inferior "savages" who deserve to be annihilated:

> I knew all about Riel. He was a rebel who had been hanged for treason. Worse, he had been a crazy half-breed. I had learned about his folly in history. Also, I had read about the Indians and the various methods of tortures they had put the missionaries through. No wonder they were known as savages. So, anything to do with Indians, I despised. And here I was supposed to be part-Indian. (44–45)

When Cheryl points out that "there are just as many white people out there who are in the same state" (114–15), April reveals her persistent stereotypes—stereotypes that continue in the face of contrary information:

> I don't remember the white ones, I only remember the drunk natives. It seems to me the majority of natives are gutter-creatures and only a minority of whites are like that. I think that's the difference. (115)

April consistently reveals her illusory correlations. She erroneously equates: looking white with being white; being white with being wealthy; and being wealthy with being happy. As a young child, she perceives "two different groups of children" (15). She sees "the brown-skinned children who looked like Cheryl" as "dirty-looking and dressed in real raggedy clothes," whereas she sees the"white-skinned" children whom she envies as "clean and fresh" and imagines that "they were very rich and lived in big, beautiful houses" (15). April mistakenly believes that if she assimilates into settler "white" society, then she "wouldn't have to live like this" for the rest of her life (85).

April has adopted the colonial discourse and its stereotypes without understanding how she is perpetuating her own alterity and alienation. She does not understand the power relationships which underlie colonial constructions of settler superiority. It is not enough for her to choose assimilation and to act "white"; settler society does not perceive her as "white." Initially, she is often "torn in different directions" (53). Instead of interrogating and modifying her colonial beliefs, she perceives Cheryl and Mrs. MacAdams as exceptions: "For sure, she [Cheryl] would never turn out to be like the rest of the Métis people. She and maybe Mrs. MacAdams were special people" (49). In internalizing colonialism, April participates in her own oppression. Later, when she shares a house with Cheryl, she oppresses her sister. Cheryl accuses her of being Cheryl's "keeper" and "a bigot" against her "own people" (193).

Blind to her own prejudice, April does not perceive the ambivalence that arises from the "perceived value conflict between egalitarianism and individualism" (Fiske and Ruscher 240). She believes that everyone is created equal and that it is up to individuals to develop their potential and opportunities. Consistent with this line of thinking is April's belief that Métis and American Indians deserve to be poor, "gutter creatures" because they have not developed their opportunities. Cheryl, on the other hand, rejects this argument.[9] She sees egalitarianism as an ideal, not a reality. In a world where everyone is not treated equally, so-called success is a matter of "luck" and "opportunities" (120) rather than a reflection of one's ability.

Rejecting colonial mimicry and assimilation, Cheryl frequently articulates and validates her American Indian ancestry. Unlike April, Cheryl initially sees "all the possibilities that we have" (167). Whereas April often passively accepts colonial stereotypes, Cheryl, for much of the text, actively rejects and resists them. Unlike April, Cheryl initially does not passively accept metonymic stereotypic insults, but turns them back on the settler. For instance, Cheryl resists Maggie DeRosier's attempt to treat her like a slave (55). Similarly, Cheryl stands by her beliefs and refuses to retract her Métis version of history, even though the principal threatens to strap her (58). She often challenges the legitimacy and accuracy of metonymic colonial stereotypes and perceives how they justify and perpetuate the status quo: "all you white people can do is teach a bunch of lies to cover your own tracks" (57). At this point, she is unaware that her words betray her own stereotypes.

Through her words and her actions, Cheryl often directs attention to April's stereotypes and prejudice. She criticizes April's determination to pass herself off as white. She warns April that Bob Radcliff (April's fiancée) will not accept April as part of settler society, but will only perceive her as a "half-breed" (109–10). Cheryl also chastises April for her hypocritical double standards. She is contemptuous of April's pity for her because it stems from April's stance of superiority. She reminds her sister that marrying Bob Radcliff to climb the social ladder is just another form of prostitution (197). She accuses April of seeing "through white man's eyes" (115) and perceives April's strategy of avoidance as a defensive self-justifying posture in which she hides behind her "fancy surroundings" and judges "a people" she does not even know (118).

In an effort to educate her sister, Cheryl takes April to the Native Friendship Center and to an Indian pow wow. At the Friendship Center, April has her temporary "mystical spiritual experience"; the Elder, Thunderbird Woman, "had seen something in me that was special, something that was deserving of her respect" (175). April has yet to understand that the Elder woman is "hailing" her as "part of a generation," not as an individual (Fee 172). When she later sees Cheryl's son (who represents the future generation), April understands and validates her Métis identity. When April and Cheryl participate in the Indian pow wow at Roseau River, Cheryl reminds April that "the Indian blood runs through your veins" and "to deny that, you deny a basic part of yourself. You'll never be satisfied until you can accept that fact" (167).

Cheryl realizes that resistance often necessitates deconstructing settler discourse and history as well as re-presenting it. She resists colonial stereotypes by presenting an alternative discourse in which American Indians and Métis are not constructed as others, but are individuals who share a collective colonial identity. Proud of her Métis identity, Cheryl sees the importance of telling Métis history to counter settler versions of history. Riel is not a "crazy" "rebel," but an admirable freedom fighter (75). In her "White Man" essay, Cheryl deploys stereotypes to counter colonial ones and to critique settler notions of progress. When she warns that "if Indian wisdom dies, you, White Man, will not be far behind" (170), she engages in a strategic essentialism in which she constructs a homogeneous Indian identity ("Indian wisdom"). Her alterNative discourse of American Indian and Métis perspectives of colonization challenges settler alter/Native histories that position American Indians and Métis as others.[10]

Cheryl's versions of Métis and American Indian history are equally flawed on two counts. First, she re-presents a romanticized history in which Riel is a heroic freedom fighter. Second, she still perceives history entirely in relation to the colonial structure. In this respect, Cheryl's historical accounts and her metaphoric images elsewhere in the text fail to deconstruct or displace colonial stereotypes because she is merely reversing, rather than re-visioning, the structural basis of the colonial relationship.

While April undergoes a process of selective amnesia in which she attempts to eradicate her past—and her feelings of abandonment by her parents—Cheryl undergoes a process of selective re-construction in which she attempts to create a past that she barely remembers. April's flaw is that she accepts and perpetuates metonymic colonial stereotypes (of lack) in her desire to mimic settlers, whereas Cheryl's flaw is that she fights metonymic stereotypes (of lack) with metaphoric colonial images in her desire to validate her identity. She resists the stereotype of the "savage" with another colonial stereotypical image of "nobility."

Cheryl romanticizes and glorifies the Métis. She dreams of returning to an idyllic pre-contact past and living "like olden day Indians":

> We'd have dogs and horses and we'd make friends with the wild animals. We'd go fishing and hunting, grow our own garden and chop our wood for winter. And we wouldn't meet people who were always trying to put us down. We'd be so happy. (91)

April fosters Cheryl's illusions about her parents by telling her half-truths in a misguided attempt to protect her. Unaware of the reality of her parents' lives, Cheryl exoticizes her parents in her desire to maintain her affiliations and loyalties toward them.

She visualizes her father as a "strong man" who "would have been a chief or a *warrior* in the olden days if he had been *pure* Indian" while she imagines her mother as "an Indian princess" (91; emphasis added). When April identifies with settlers, she negates her differences (her American Indian ancestry), whereas when Cheryl identifies with American Indians she ignores her settler ancestry.[11] Cheryl's desire for racial purity is evident when she tells April that she wishes "we were whole Indians" (45). Cheryl's statement is ironic because she too is denying part of her ancestry.

When Cheryl and April visit the Native Friendship Center, Cheryl appropriates a romantic metaphoric language that she has learned from books. She tells Thunderbird Woman that April's "vision was clouded but that when your vision cleared, you would be a good person for the Métis people" (175). Occasionally, Cheryl is cognizant of her own stereotypes. She admits that while her words to Thunderbird Woman sound noble and poetic, "actually, most Indians don't talk like that at all" (175). She confesses that she learned this rhetoric from "reading so many Indian books" (175). When she refers to Mrs. Semple and those who believe in the "Native girl syndrome" as "them," Cheryl quickly catches herself; in accusing all settlers, she realizes that she is "going that syndrome route" (68).

For the most part, however, Cheryl's cognitive map has not changed; she still operates within colonial stereotypes (metaphoric images). When she later sees her father, she cannot make reality fit her exotic images, and her cognitive framework collapses. She questions all her work at the Native Friendship Center and, like April, believes that "native people have to be willing to help themselves" (136).

Her fabrication of a stereotypical image of her father explains why it collapses so easily when confronted with reality. In her search for her parents, Cheryl writes in her journal: "I feel like April does, I despise these people, these gutter creatures. They are losers" (215). Unwilling to modify her beliefs to accommodate reality, she attributes the discrepancy between her beliefs and reality to a deficiency in "native people"—a metonymic stereotypic image.

Cheryl perceives that April is "horrified that this [gutter existence] was her legacy" (215). Similarly, when she later sees her father, Cheryl realizes that she is "hiding the horror which is boiling inside of me. . . . All my dreams to rebuild the spirit of a once proud nation are destroyed in this instant" (217–18). Cheryl's slides into a depression and she loses all interest in her family and her work (224). In her suicide letter to her sister, she requests that April "dream my dreams for me" (227). Cheryl's tragic flaw—her inability to liberate herself from metaphoric colonial stereotypes of desire—is the basis for her tragic trajectory and exposes the weakness in all stereotypes, both glowing, noble metaphoric ones as well as mean, petty metonymic ones.

In charting these stereotypes, Culleton illustrates how April's and Cheryl's identities are socially constructed. Identity is an effect of the material production of a colonial discourse that circulates around socially configured boundaries of nationality, gender, race, and class. On one occasion, Cheryl chooses not to identify herself as either "Indian" or Métis. At the Radcliffs' New Year's Eve party, two men ask her how she would categorize herself. She counters the racism underlying their question by making crossed categorizations salient. She identifies herself on the basis of her gender and nationality:

> 'Oh, I've read about Indians. Beautiful people they are. But you're not exactly Indians are you? What is the proper word for people like you?' one asked. 'Women,' Cheryl replied instantly. 'No, no, I mean nationality?' 'Oh, I'm sorry. We're Canadians,' Cheryl smiled sweetly. (116)

Both of Cheryl's categorizations are true. Further, identification by nationality is often more inclusive than racial categorization, which tends to be exclusive. Being part white rules her out of the category of white, whereas being part Canadian generally rules her into being Canadian.[12] Throughout much of the novel, Cheryl defines herself as Métis and/or Native. At the Radcliffs' party, however, she defines herself as a woman and as a Canadian in order to point out the exclusionary politics underlying these men's comments.

For the Métis subject, identity and questions of identification and positioning are significant. Historically, the colonial relationship has created fundamental structural conflicts between settlers and American Indians. In embodying the *métissage* of these two cultures, Métis subjects cannot ignore this conflict but have to decide, when choosing affiliations, how to position themselves.

Initially, Culleton represents Métis identity in a "narrative of ambivalence [which] is split into two figures" (Emberley 162). She illustrates split allegiances through her characterization of April (who initially validates her Irish ancestry) and of Cheryl (who validates her American Indian ancestry), yet also demonstrates how they each continually shift their positions and affiliations. When Cheryl dies, the narrative is no longer split into two figures. April no longer validates her Irish ancestry over her American

Indian ancestry, but now affirms her Métis identity—an identity that consists of differences.

The phrase, "in search of," in the title of the novel not only suggests that April has lost her identity but also underscores how identity formation is an ongoing process. By showing the ways in which each sister undergoes shifting affiliations and positionings, Culleton demonstrates that any single fixed concept of identity as cohesive and stable is flawed. Colonizers attempt to construct a single fixed identity that disavows differences of those they have colonized; however, identity is fluid and unstable. It is subject to processes of disruption and suturing as well as of deformation and transformation. Identity is an ever shifting process in which individuals articulate and are also defined by their changing multiple affiliations.

Multiple Positionings

Culleton maps out possible Métis affiliations: with settlers, with American Indians, with both, with neither, or with a distinct Métis identity and consciousness[13]—"the hybrid moment of political change" that is neither the one nor the other (Bhabha *Location* 28). Through her relationship with Cheryl, April continually shifts her affiliations and undergoes a complex process of re-positionings.

She starts from a position of denial of her father's American Indian ancestry and affirmation of her mother's settler ancestry. As a result of her sister's comments and her own experiences of racism and exclusion by her in-laws, April realizes that she cannot pass for "white." Later, when the rapists not only perceive her as Native but also mistake her for Cheryl, April realizes that, despite her fair skin, she has still been "identified" (161) as Métis. She re-positions herself again, but this time chooses to negate both her American Indian and her "Caucasian" ancestry. She decides that being Métis rules her out of American Indian as well as of settler affiliations:

> It would be better to be a full-blooded Indian or full-blooded Caucasian. But being a half-breed, well, there's just nothing there. You can admire Indian people for what they once were. They had a distinct heritage or is it culture? Anyway, you can see how much was taken from them. And

white people, well, they've convinced each other they are the superior
race and you can see they are responsible for the progress we have
today. Cheryl once said, 'The meek shall inherit the Earth. Big deal,
because who's going to want it once the whites are through with it?'
(156)

It is not until long after her rape—itself a symbol of the violence
and violation that settler society has inflicted on American
Indians and Métis—that April renounces this position. After
Cheryl's suicide, April smashes a liquor bottle and says, "I hate
you for what you've done to my people!" (214). Looking at
Cheryl's son, April realizes that she had "used the words 'MY
PEOPLE, OUR PEOPLE' and meant them" (228). In using "our
people," April no longer sees herself as different from Cheryl.

Given her part Irish and part American Indian ancestry,
April's construction of a collective identity, "MY PEOPLE, OUR
PEOPLE" (228) appears problematic if we read it as an identity
that is defined by difference from settlers. If she defines her
identity in terms of difference from the oppressor, then she cannot
assert her identity without "asserting that of the oppressor as
well" (Laclau 101–2). Margery Fee rightly points out that "what
saves this resolution from simply imposing a different, but equally
fraudulent dichotomy on the reader is that April has been through
the process of internalizing both the oppressor role and that of the
oppressed ("Upsetting Fake Ideas" 176). Through April, Culleton
"reclaims 'identity' over difference" (Emberley 162). Culleton has
mapped out colonial stereotypes to re-present identity politics
and provide a model which includes differences.

April now affirms a distinct Métis identity in which she eludes
colonial binaries by inhabiting a hybrid, "third space" (Bhabha
Location 38). She resists the colonial binaries that oppose
sameness to difference. Including the American Indian legacy that
Cheryl formerly claimed and the settler ancestry that April earlier
validated, April's Métis identity is neither the one nor the other.
Instead, it is an ever-shifting hybrid identity that is no longer the
same difference.

Chapter Five

Re-place That Monument

> The struggle of man against power is the struggle of memory against forgetting.
>
> Milan Kundera *The Book of Laughter and Forgetting* 4

In addition to colonizing the territories of American Indians, colonizers also engage in a process of cultural imperialism[1] in which they impose their language(s), ideology, and rules of recognition on others. They encourage the colonized to assimilate into the dominant society and disavow cultural differences. Paula Gunn Allen describes the dangers of cultural imperialism for American Indians when she observes that "wars of imperial conquest have not been solely or even mostly waged over the land and its resources, but they have been fought within the bodies, minds, and hearts of the people" (*The Sacred Hoop* 214). One way for American Indians to resist cultural imperialism and ensure their survival is by remembering and practicing their diverse cultural traditions:

> To that end the wars of imperial conquest have not been solely or even mostly waged over the land and its resources, but they have been fought within the bodies, minds, and hearts of the people of the earth for dominion over them. I think this is the reason traditionals say we must remember our origins, our cultures, our histories, our mothers and grandmothers, for without that memory, which implies continuance rather than nostalgia, we are doomed to engulfment by a paradigm that is fundamentally inimical to the vitality, autonomy, and self-empowerment essential for satisfying, high-quality life. (*The Sacred Hoop* 214)

Cultural imperialism is often evident in education and in the curriculum that is offered in schools funded and run by the dominant society. While all histories are cultural constructions, settler versions of history often marginalize or trivialize the histories of those they have colonized. Colonial versions of history remind readers and writers of the imperative of, to borrow Toni Morrison's term, "rememoration."[2]

The history of the process which led to the writing of *Slash*, written by Okanagan writer Jeannette Armstrong and published by the Indian owned and operated Theytus press in 1985, illustrates how Armstrong and others in the Okanagan community resisted cultural imperialism by revising the educational curriculum. In 1972, the National Indian Brotherhood issued a position paper on Indian Control of Indian Education. Seven years later, the Okanagan Indian Curriculum Project was formed as part of a community effort to provide Indian control of education. A year after this Curriculum Project was created, there was a Union of BC Indian Chiefs discussion paper (15 October 1980) on policy to implement Indian education which stated:

> The policy which would serve us best in the long run, would be one which forces the government to simply give total recognition to local Indian control . . . It is this whole idea of our right to make our own policy that must finally be included in the Constitution of Canada. (qtd. in Webber 175)

In its efforts to provide an "Indian" curriculum that would be meaningful to American Indian students, the Okanagan Indian Curriculum Project sought out writers who "could look at contemporary history and write something that students could connect and relate to other than just a dry history of dates" (Armstrong qtd. in Williamson 16).

While working as a researcher in 1981–82 for the Okanagan Indian Curriculum Project, Armstrong "developed the concept of filling a gap in the contemporary history of Native thought over the past twenty-five years" (Armstrong qtd. in Williamson 16). The experiences of the planning committee attest to the ways in which some settlers continue to colonize and exclude American Indian voices. When Armstrong proposed the names of American Indian unpublished authors who could write the material, one of the consultants took the position that "there was no use getting hold of these Native writers since none of them was well known" (Armstrong qtd. in Williamson 17). Armstrong objected and she and several other writers walked out of the meeting (Williamson 18). The result was that the consultant and the other non-Indian members of the committee left and the committee regrouped (Williamson 18). Through a collective effort and a process of consensus decision making, this committee played an integral role in what would later become *Slash*.

Initially, Armstrong did not have a novel in mind. She planned to "interview people and recreate the historical situation" (Armstrong qtd. in Williamson 18). Later, she conducted "massive interviews with people at all levels of the community" (Armstrong qtd. in Williamson 18). When she presented her outline of historical events to the Curriculum Department, the committee suggested "a novel or a story in which one character experiences some of these feelings first-hand and shows the effects on his family or friends or his people. In that way, when a person reads, they could experience the process as if they were going through it" (Armstrong qtd. in Williamson 18–19).

Armstrong wrote *Slash* as part of the process of revising the curriculum for grade eleven American Indian students. While she speaks Okanagan and English, Armstrong chose to write in English in order "to share these words . . . with anyone who speaks English, but especially with my people" (*Telling It* 27). *Slash* is "an important documentation for those people who colonized this country and continue to make mistakes in terms of the colonizing process in this country, attempting to assimilate people" (Armstrong qtd. in Lutz). *Slash* critiques the ways in which colonial education, specifically colonial accounts of history, fosters assimilation. By re-presenting aspects of these colonial histories within American Indian contexts, Armstrong raises the reader's consciousness of American Indians and their ongoing traditions of resistance; further, she enables settler readers to understand the effects that colonial histories have on American Indians. This awareness is an important part of the process of decolonizing minds.

Slash is the story of an Okanagan adolescent named Tommy Kelasket who is later re-named Slash.[3] Raised with the traditional values of his parents, Tommy later becomes alienated from these traditions.[4] He leaves his community and undergoes a journey in which he learns about diverse American Indians. In participating in political activities in the United States and in Canada, he learns the importance of collective resistance to colonization. At the same time, Slash's journey is also a process of spiritual renewal in which he later validates the traditions and values of his community. The narrative foregrounds the necessity for spiritual renewal along with political action and depicts political actions without spiritual renewal as ineffective.

On one level, Tommy's/Slash's story is his quest to define his difference from settlers and to re-member his "Indian" identity. His politicization can be briefly summarized. He initially validates the traditional ways of his parents. Later, he rejects these ways and rebels (it is at this stage that Mardi re-names him Slash). He becomes active in politics, but then becomes frustrated and impatient with the political route of accommodation. Disillusioned, he turns to alcohol and drugs. Next, he enters a more militant phase in which he advocates action and sanctions violence. He identifies himself as a "warrior," although he has not yet fully realized this role. In his explanation of what it means to be "a warrior from the Native perspective," Douglas Cardinal explains that "a warrior operates from commitment and a way of being":

> A commitment is to take a stand for what you believe in. . . . It is a willingness to sacrifice everything except your truth, your way of being, your commitment. The ultimate stand is your commitment to do something with your life that will make a difference. (Cardinal and Armstrong 32)

After his militant phase, Slash experiences a spiritual emptiness and once again turns to drugs and alcohol. Finally, he owns his spirituality, reaffirms the traditional values and ways of his parents, and accepts individual responsibility. In the end, Slash is committed to being a "a keeper of the ways" (205, 211).

On another level, Slash's journey is about the politicization and re-education of American Indians. His story is a metonym for, and a fictionalized history of, American Indian activism in the United States and Canada since the 1960s. Although the narrator acknowledges in the prologue that the events are "not meant to be portrayed as historically accurate," this fictionalized history is fairly faithful to actual events.[5] Like Slash's journey, the history of American Indian activism is a movement from disempowerment toward consciousness-raising awareness through debates, marches, meetings, occupations, and sit-ins to action—in some instances, militant action and in other instances, a spiritual and/or political path.

Slash re-inscribes American Indian histories to counter and re-place those of the dominant society. This re-inscription does not suggest that American Indians have lost their histories, but directs readers' attention to the ways in which most mainstream historical accounts often omit American Indian histories. Armstrong performs an "act of rememoration" that slashes colonial histories, an interruption that interrogates and disrupts settler attempts to author(ity). She not only displaces settler versions of the past but also draws on and contributes to American Indian social memories.

In addition to being a "source of knowledge" (26), social memory is "an expression of collective experience: social memory identifies a group, giving it a sense of its past and defining its aspirations for the future" (Fentress and Wickham 25).[6] Commemoration is "the *action* of speaking or writing about memories, as well as the formal re-enaction of the past" (Fentress and Wickham x) while rememoration is commemoration from a position of having been silenced. Rememoration is an act of resistance which, in turning "the present of narrative enunciation into the haunting memorial of what has been excluded, excised, evicted . . . becomes the *unheimlich* space for the negotiation of identity and history" (Bhabha *Location* 198). In *Slash*, commemoration leads to rememoration of American Indian social memories.

In rememorating historical events and the traditions which inform American Indians, Armstrong has created an innovative form of resistance writing. Barbara Harlow defines resistance writing as literature which draws attention to itself as political and becomes a site of struggle against the dominant discourse and ideological/cultural production. It is produced within a struggle for decolonization (Harlow 2). Writing from a position of "exile" or "occupation," authors of resistance literature often create new narrative forms in which they explore history and question the historical narratives of the colonizer (Harlow 2, 22).

Slash is a hybrid narrative that combines history, personal anecdotes, poetry, and fictional autobiography. In this respect, the narrative affirms and is informed by American Indian oral stories and traditions.[7] Armstrong re-places the language of the dominant discourse, of "correct" English, by deliberately using the vernacular and hybridized english. This use of hybridized language legitimizes variants of English and, as in oral stories, conveys rhythms and cadences of vernacular speech. Like many oral stories, *Slash* does not have a linear narrative. Instead, there are frequent digressions, embedded stories, accretion, and multiple perspectives. The author provides readers with "a staged representation, history as narrative, history as telling" (Godard 214).

Through a non-linear narrative, Armstrong contests the chronological time evident in many colonial histories and narratives. Gunn Allen has described how settler histories are usually linear and chronological, while those of American Indians are often achronological, mythic, and ceremonial (*The Sacred Hoop* 147, 149). Gunn Allen argues that chronological time structuring promotes and sustains settler industrialism. In addition, it reinforces the settler ideological validation of individualism and this, she says, "contrasts sharply with a ceremonial time sense that assumes the individual as a moving event shaped by and shaping human and nonhuman surroundings" (149). Similarly, Michael Harkin points out how "the chronotype of the white man is linear,"[8] whereas American Indian concepts of time are "circular chronotypes," "time-out-of-time" (119). Harkin writes that the settler chronotype is "driven by the notion of progress. As such, there can be no time-out-of-time, since time itself is seen to be one-dimensional" (119).

Although the titles of the four chapters in *Slash* might suggest a sequential narrative with a linear progression, it soon becomes apparent that Slash's experiences de-stabilize notions of linearity. He later comes to validate the traditions that his parents practiced and taught him. In this respect, his journey is a "circle," a "continuum" (Armstrong qtd. in Lutz 19). The four sections signify the "Four Directions" and the prologue and epilogue are the direction "above" and "below" us (Lutz 20). Within this circle, Slash's learning process is like a spiral. The emphasis is not on progress, but on the relationships that he builds. The spiral is an image of the "Native creative process":

The Native creative process places importance on the internal understanding of our individual selves as a process of building relationships, moving outward to all other things. This becomes a means of collective long term healthy continuance. This principle is expressed in the open ended kind of societal structures which contain a cooperative symmetry concerned with continuance and yet facilitating the individuals [sic] capacity to continuously change and be enhanced in a balanced way. The spiral rather than the circle is used as a fundamental symbol for this. (Cardinal and Armstrong 22)

In the prologue and epilogue that frame *Slash*, the narrator reveals his perception of history as a continuum between past-present-future. He has an individual as well as a social responsibility to understand and retell the past in order to understand the present and to make responsible decisions for future generations. He tells the reader in the Epilogue: "I have made my stand and chosen my path and I decide to tell my story for my son and those like him because I must." While the narrator may be Slash who, later in life, relates his story, the narrator might well be another member of the community who relates a story about Slash. By refraining from identifying the narrator, Armstrong suggests that this story is one which has resonance for all American Indians. At the same time, his view of history as a continuum affirms American Indian traditions and challenges settler notions of linear time and chronological histories.

In addition, *Slash* contests eurocentric ideologies of capitalism and liberalism and the accompanying validation of individualism. In emphasizing the individual, liberal ideology focuses on the right to freedom and the right to equality. This emphasis on individualism and on individual rights is aligned with the validation of egalitarianism—a notion that is problematic because of the underlying assumption that all individuals are the same. Liberal ideology which promotes equal access often disavows cultural differences and fails to acknowledge who is defining sameness.[9]

Armstrong debunks the American "myth" of an egalitarian "Great Society" (36). Tommy perceives the idea of such a society in which all people are treated equally as empty rhetoric at odds with the political and economic reality and covert policies of assimilation and extinction. He says:

I knew he [the American president] talked about the blacks or any people that upset the fake idea about a 'Great Society.' I thought about all the history books and stuff at school and in movies. How it was all like that, a fake, while really the white people wished we would all either be just like them or stay out of sight. (36)

When Tommy listens to a young man advocate equality and reform to the Indian Act, he perceives how the man's proposals for development projects only perpetuate colonization because he is operating within colonial rules of recognition. Tommy's perception of the man's colonial mimicry is evident in his observation that the man looked "like a white man" (42): "He kinda looked ridiculous, like a parrot does when it mimics a person" (43).

In challenging colonial versions of history and colonial discourse, Armstrong problematizes issues of representation. Whose history is being told and by whom is it told? How and why is it being told? Colonizers endeavor to destroy the histories and social memories of those they colonize. As Frantz Fanon remarked, "Colonialism is not satisfied merely with holding a people in its grip and emptying the native's brain of all form and content. By a kind of perverted logic, it turns to the past of the oppressed people, and distorts, disfigures, and destroys it" (*The Wretched of the Earth* 210).

Colonial historical narratives often displace and replace American Indian histories and stories. This often contributes to distortions in, or lack of, social memories and internal divisions within American Indian communities. The Okanagan elder Pra-cwa and Tommy's father describe how colonizers have created internal divisions in their community. Pra-cwa perceives how "our people are two now" and tells Tommy: "There is us and there is them that want to try all kinds of new stuff and be more like white people" (42). He believes that his community will "never again be as one" (48). Too many people have "lost their language, their ways" and believe that "things will be better if they do things the white way" (48).

Assimilation in language or culture involves not only learning new rules of recognition, but also unlearning old ones (Deutsch 125). The less communities remember, the more colonizers can impose their rules of recognition and assimilate American Indians. Karl Deutsch describes how group assimilation can be accelerated by reducing or destroying competing information that members of a community recall from an unassimilated past and by reducing or repressing unassimilated responses in the present (Deutsch 118). "No further self-determination is possible if . . . memory is lost" (Deutsch 168); hence, rememoration is necessary for cultural self-determination.

It is also essential for the incorporation of American Indian acts of resistance into their social memories, and for their survival. Without these social memories that challenge settler social memories and histories, cultural genocide results. In addition, the patrols during the 1960s and 1970s served to remember the genocide of American Indians. The Beothuck patrol in which Mardi participates commemorates and rememorates the Beothuck people who "were wiped out so the land could be open for settlement" (69).

In adopting the stance of moral superiority, the dominant society constructs the colonized as "inferior, uneducated, and uncivilized" to "justify imperial occupation and exploitation" (JanMohamed 62). Slash perceives how colonial histories reveal this assumption of moral superiority. In presenting selective accounts of historical events, settlers endeavor to justify the status quo and their exploitation of American Indians:

> I [Slash] wondered why they [colonizers] didn't show things that really happened. . . . I thought maybe the reason could have been that it was easier to go on stealing resources and land and oppressing people if you had an image of them from childhood that said 'those savages deserve it.' I guessed it was easier to say, 'Why don't them damn stupid Indians be like us, fit in, assimilate?', if they refused to look at how despicable their kind of people really were. (118–19)

Tommy/Slash identifies settler education as one of the primary causes for his initial confusion and alienation (80, 91). Settler education disavows his culture. Language is one of the main tools that the dominant culture uses to indoctrinate the colonized subject into the values and ideology of the dominant culture. In his description of the American Indian students who attend the town school, Tommy observes: "Most of the Indian kids talked English different too. That was hard on us. We got mostly E's in Grammar and everything else that we used English in, which was just about everything" (25).

Tommy's father tells him to resist oppression by being proud of who he is, by respecting and validating his different identity (87). Similarly, his Uncle Joe reminds him not to deny "the spirit" in him—the spirit "associated with our dance religion" (133). Mr. Kelasket's and Uncle Joe's positions reflect their traditional values. Armstrong contrasts these values with those in the "town school" Tommy attends. The town school erodes self-esteem by devaluing American Indian languages, practices, and values.

Tommy experiences confusion between two types of education; one based on a non-directive approach that validates experiential knowledge and one based on a directive approach that privileges rational discourse. In adhering to traditional ways, his family represents the former, whereas the town school represents the latter approach. The dominant society uses pedagogy to reinforce the status quo. As Slash observes, "schools are meant to teach the young of the middle class the best way to survive their society and to maintain its system. They are not meant to instruct those who do not have the values of that society" (212).

At the beginning of his journey, Tommy has little knowledge of American Indian histories or of their ongoing resistance. What little information he has he learned from his father, his Uncle Joe, and the Okanagan elder Pra-cwa. He re-educates himself in prison and throughout his journey by reading books, yet much of his re-education lies not in books but in listening to the stories and histories of other American Indians. When he later participates in the Trail of Broken Treaties Caravan, he says, "I hadn't even heard of it [the Trail of Tears], but then I guess that was the point of this whole trip: to educate" (95). Through listening to others (experiential, rather than textual, learning), Tommy/Slash perceives similarities as well as differences between diverse American Indians and undergoes a process of rememoration of his own community's cultural traditions.

Rememoration is essential because "memory conforms to interpretation" (Fentress and Wickham 35). When individuals encounter a discrepancy between a story—a history—that is inconsistent with their memories and interpretation, the memory of the parts of the story that do not conform to the interpretation of the subject often fade (Fentress and Wickham 35). In an attempt to ascribe meaning, individuals interpret stories in ways that will render them intelligible (Fentress and Wickham 35).

This is precisely what colonial versions of history attempt to achieve. By providing historical accounts in which American Indians are marginalized, or erased, settlers take events out of context. American Indian subjects are left with a historical account that is at odds with their experience and/or memories of past events. In the Sasquatch incident, Tommy describes the confusion that he experiences because of differing cultural rules of recognition. He perceives a double standard in which settlers dismiss Sasquatch as superstition yet "things like angels and the devil weren't superstitious to them" (34). Nevertheless, Tommy and his friends want "to forget" about Sasquatch because it does not make sense in light of what they have been taught in the town school:

> Most of us just wanted to forget it. It didn't make sense to most of us, I guess, because we knew it didn't fit in with what you learn in science books about animals and things that exist. So we didn't talk about it, even amongst ourselves. (35)

In an effort to find meaning, those, like Tommy's friend Jimmy, who assimilate choose to ignore the discrepancy and accept settler versions of history at the expense of self-annihilation.

A colonial mimic, Jimmy perceives cultural differences but does not understand the nature of racism. He erroneously equates the symbols of power, wealth, and status with the acquisition of real power (26). Unlike Mr. Kelasket and Slash, Jimmy fails to perceive that assimilation involves an "unlearning" (Deutsch 125), and, in some instances, a rejection of one's own language and cultural identity. Desperate for approval and acceptance, he cannot see how his ambition to assimilate and to "feel good" (44) temporarily is at the cost of self-effacement. He is unable, or unwilling, to perceive the systemic racism and power imbalance in the dominant society. Jimmy refuses to question the dominant discourse. Instead, he rejects "Indian ways" (44). He perceives traditional ways and those who choose this path as "backward" (84), as nostalgic for a past which cannot be recovered. What he fails to realize is that traditions are not static; they change and adapt over time as do traditional practices. Slash later perceives Jimmy and others who mimic colonizers as "Uncle Tomahawks"

(90).[10] The term evokes images of "Uncle Toms."

Like the young man who advocates development projects, Jimmy participates in his own oppression because he has internalized colonialism and adopted the colonizer's rules of recognition. Consequently, colonizers and colonized disavow him; neither American Indian nor settler organizations will hire him (220–21). In contrast to Jimmy, Slash and others who reject assimilation perceive settler versions of history as "discordant bits" that they tend to "forget" (Fentress and Wickham 35); instead, they choose to validate their interpretation and memories.

In describing Louis Mink's view of conflicting historical narratives, Srivastava writes: "One of the disturbing things about conflicting historical narratives . . . is that they displace each other in the reader's mind—they cannot co-exist as literary narratives can" (77). This perspective is an accurate description of the process of assimilation and colonial mimicry. In their desire to emulate settlers, colonial mimics accept settler versions of history at the expense of displacing their own. However, those who hold this view make a distinction between history and fiction instead of recognizing that both history and fiction are cultural constructions. Moreover, the argument that conflicting historical narratives displace each other in the reader's mind ignores the mind of the reader as a site of struggle.

AlterNative History

Armstrong subverts the colonialist discourse of the alter/Native history, constructing an alterNative history in which American Indians are not negated by positions of alterity; instead, they are positioned as subjects who have agency. Armstrong's use of the first person subverts the colonial discourse in which the American Indian is positioned as other. She re-presents "as a whole that which has always been seen as fragmented, the construction of a Native 'I' performs a shift from that which has always been constituted as Other to Self" (Fee 171–72). The first person point of view conveys immediacy, subjectivity, and intimacy and enables readers to identify with Slash and his journey (as the Okanagan Indian Curriculum Committee initially suggested). A limitation of the first person point of view is that the reader often only understands people and events insofar as the first person narrator does; the field of vision is singular.

Armstrong decenters the single narrative by providing multiple perspectives and points of view in the direct and reported speeches of other characters, as well as in the discrepancy between Slash's words and actions. The first-person narrative and the direct speech of the multiple characters, most of whom disagree with Slash, promote "the illusion that individuals speak for themselves, rather than out of a discursively constructed subject position—the illusion is compensatory" (Fee 172). The first person point of view can foreground the individual (and eurocentric concepts of individualism), but Armstrong subverts this by using multiple points of view to situate Slash in relation to his Okanagan community and to other American Indian communities. Slash's story and journey are not just his story, but the story of all those he meets and his relationships with them. He is part of a web in which everything and everyone is interconnected. As Armstrong explains, the "spiders [sic] web is a physical construct which many Native cultures draw on symbolically to imbed this principle in their storytelling as an expression of the creative process concerned with the connectedness of all things" (Cardinal and Armstrong 18). The diverse voices and positions that Slash hears and his own shifting position reflect a dialogic practice. There is no single voice or single perspective, but rather many voices engaged in an ongoing dialogue.

Slash's story also subverts patriarchal notions of history as (his)story. Armstrong illustrates the intersections between race and gender oppression. While she believes men were "at the forefront and engendered the thought of the American Indian movement," Armstrong also recognizes that there "were a lot of things wrong with this, including the male ego and a displaced philosophy regarding what role the Native woman played" (qtd. in Williamson 14). She argues that this "was wrong and false and that any movement forward for Native people, any healing, needed to reconcile this" (qtd. in Williamson 14). Armstrong chose to present a male protagonist to examine "the breakdown in our society in relation to the male role" and how American Indian men "affected the progress of the movement in the positive and negative sense" (qtd. in Williamson 14). Through her characterization of Slash, she endeavors "to understand and then present an alternative" (qtd. in Williamson 14).

Specifically, Armstrong examines those American Indian men who have been "torn between role and ego" (qtd. in Williamson 19). For Tommy/Slash, this conflict stems from his colonial education which alienates him from his cultural traditions. Colonized people who internalize the lens of the colonizer can, in an effort to alleviate feelings of inferiority, take on the role of the oppressor while still being oppressed. Tommy describes how the American Indian boys in the town school he attends have learned to devalue girls and women in order to fit in with the settler students: "none of the Indian girls ever got asked to dance at the sock-hop because us guys wouldn't dance with them because the white guys didn't" (35). That they "were too ashamed to even tell" (35) is an effect of internalizing colonialism. Tommy describes how he and his friends felt "like we just weren't good enough to mix with the white kids" (35).

Slash models an alternative for American Indian men "torn between role and ego" (Armstrong qtd. in Williamson 19). He moves beyond the psychic fragmentation of the split subject caught between conflicting cultures to achieve integration and balance. In the process, he undergoes a metamorphosis in which he "reconciled himself to his feminine qualities" (Armstrong qtd. in Williamson 19). Armstrong explains: "By 'feminine,' I mean the capacity for compassion, love, sensitivity, and understanding that's required by the soft non-aggressive approach" (qtd. in Williamson 19). In moving Slash toward the "reconciliation of both male and female and the wholeness and healthiness of who we are as human beings" (Armstrong qtd. in Williamson 19), Armstrong contextualizes his transformation within the Okanagan "order of life learning" that she outlines in *The Native Creative Process*:

> In the Okanagan, as in many Native tribes, the order of life learning is
> that you are born without sex and as a child, through learning, you move
> toward full capacity as either male or female. Only when appropriately
> prepared for the role do you become a man or woman. The natural
> progression into parenthood provides immense learning from each other,
> the love, compassion and cooperation necessary to maintain family and
> community. Finally as an elder you emerge as both male and female, a

complete human, with all skills and capacities complete. (102)

The strong women characters and their diverse voices further decenter the single dominant male voice and the alter/Native, patriarchal discourse. Slash later acknowledges that

> It's really the women who keep things going smooth. All Indian men know that. We learned early from our mothers and grandmothers that it is women who are the strength of the people. We all know it was the women, too, who shake up any system if they get riled. (153)

Maeg, Mardi, Elise, Slash's mother, and Mardi's mother challenge Slash and cause him to question and modify his perspective. In using these women's voices, Armstrong challenges the notion of history as *his* story, history that is the product of a patriarchal society that privileges the white male; instead, her alterNative history is composed of *his/her* stories.

Each of the women teaches Slash. His mother perceives and points out his self-deception and teaches him traditional values and ways. She makes the discrepancy between Slash's militant words and apathetic actions apparent to him when she asks: "How you gonna fight, as you say, for your people, if you do the very stuff that you are fighting against?" (166). Like Elise, Slash's mother alludes to the dangers of cultural imperialism and of the internalization of colonial rules of recognition when she tells him "this is a land claims fight," but it is also "more than that" (166). Elise teaches Slash to examine not only the symptoms and effects of colonization but also the underlying complex political issues and politics of power and domination (96). She reminds him that the diseases which killed American Indians were not the enemy; rather, colonizers are because they "continue to use the disadvantaged conditions as a means of control" (96).

Mardi re-names Slash and teaches him the importance of political participation and activism. She gives him a name which commemorates and rememorates his experience. Literally, slash refers to a knife wound that Tommy receives. On a metaphorical level, the name Slash signifies Tommy's new militant identity and perception of himself as a warrior. The name, like Red Power, subverts settler meanings by transforming the word into a term of empowerment.

Maeg teaches Slash the value of the "Indian way" of "resistance" which, she explains, is non-violent (225). She tells him that his "way doesn't guarantee anything but opposition and resistance"; instead, she advocates the need to secure Aboriginal rights "and maintain our land bases, free of taxation" (243). She provides yet another voice, and political position, to Slash's.

These diverse voices re-place colonial narratives with ones that re-tell history. Armstrong records events and relates American Indian exclusion from, and angry responses to, government policies of assimilation. Alluding to policies of enfranchisement (18), taxation (19), regulation of alcohol distribution (20), and the White Paper (28), Armstrong re-presents these policies from American Indian perspectives. In so doing, she calls them into question and contextualizes American Indian resistance. American Indian readers become aware that they are not alone, but part of a larger community while settler readers are given a different lens to re-view the events of the 1960s and 1970s.

Armstrong's narrative calls into question official and unofficial colonial histories. The dominant society negates and/or marginalizes the history of colonized people as a means of domination and control. While this is done through education, specifically an educational system that presents history from the vantage point of settlers, the media also play a role in "manufacturing consent."[11] Since newspaper and other media coverage of events is selective, American Indian events are marginalized, deemed non-essential, and/or trivial. Slash becomes aware of the selective reporting, the whitewashing of instances of police discrimination and brutality at Wounded Knee (114, 117) and elsewhere in the United States and in Canada (82, 89, 99, 100, 109). He perceives the racist double standard wherein the incident about an American Indian in California who was shot was white-washed (103), while the white man who stabbed an American Indian was not charged for murder (109). What is even more ominous is the absence of the histories of the colonized.[12]

Slash observes that the missing persons are, significantly, all American Indian activists. In describing the death of one woman activist, he notices how the government attempts to eliminate not only individuals but also organizations that threaten the status quo:

I had heard stuff about a woman who had been found earlier in the year,

supposedly dead of exposure, in the States somewhere. The woman was
from Canada and she had been a pretty well known activist. People said
that the F.B.I. were probably responsible for her death and that her
people had asked for a second autopsy. From what I heard there had been
a lot of really brutal things like that which were carried out to
neutralize AIM. (194)

Armstrong strategically refrains from identifying this activist as
Anna Mae Aquash. By referring to Aquash in general terms and
alluding to telling details, the author encourages readers to engage
in acts of rememoration; readers piece missing bits of the puzzle
together by sifting through their memories, and in so doing
commemorate not only Anna Mae Aquash and the activities for
which she died but also others like her. While Armstrong bases
many of her characters on real people, she explains that she
"wanted to be able to make and draw together characters who in
people's minds form real characters" (qtd. in Lutz 17). By
alluding to historical events in the 1960s and 1970s, Armstrong
also encourages those readers who do not know or remember these
events to educate themselves and raise their consciousness of
American Indian histories.

   Slash draws attention to the atrocities committed by settlers
while at the same time emphasizing contemporary resistance and
the necessity for remembering, not forgetting, the past. Chapter
three, "Mixing It Up," focuses on the "Trail of Broken Treaties
Caravan" in which American Indians retraced the historic Trail of
Tears of 1838 in the fall of 1972 and occupied the Bureau of
Indian Affairs headquarters in Washington, DC. As a
consciousness raising event, the caravan not only serves to
remember history but also to re-inscribe it—to set the record
straight:

We stopped [Slash explains] at one place where a monument had been
erected in Minnesota where thirty-eight Sioux were hanged for trying to
protect their people. The leader of the Caravan made a statement that the
Indians were going to replace that monument with a replica of the scaffold
that was used to hang those Sioux. He told the people Abraham Lincoln
had authorized that execution, only one day after the Emancipation
Proclamation for the blacks was made. (98; emphasis added)

As he learns about American Indian events in British Columbia
and the rest of Canada as well as those in the United States,
Slash begins to perceive the struggle against oppression as a

collective one. For instance, Armstrong juxtaposes the struggle over fishing rights at Puyallup in Washington state (71) and the "salmon fish-in" on the Fraser River in Chilliwack, British Columbia to protest the government's imposition of fishing rights (71). She also compares the American Indian Movement's protest in Nebraska to protest an autopsy that "was whitewashed" (87) and the inquest for an "Indian up north who had been killed" (88). Through these, and other, juxtapositions, the author disavows constructed political and social borders and illustrates the concerns and values that diverse Aboriginal peoples share. Slash realizes that, as the president of the National Indian Brotherhood explains, "Indians from Canada were no different and that there was really no border recognized by Indians. . . . we had the same objectives as US Indians" (92).

In describing Slash's political involvement, and that of other American Indian people, Armstrong illustrates how American Indian resistance has been an ongoing process for hundreds of years. The "Indian way" of resistance, as Maeg explains, is non-violent (225). This is not to suggest that violence never occurs, however. Armstrong does describe Slash's militant involvement and those more radical members of the American Indian Movement (AIM) and other organizations who become impatient with accommodation.

Through his rememoration of the actions and words of his father, Uncle Joe, and Pra-cwa, Slash later rejects violence. His cousin Chuck (140), Uncle Joe, and a medicine man whom Slash meets in Alberta (89) each mitigate Slash's advocacy of militant action and temporary endorsement of violence. Chuck sees politics as the means to achieve the desired ends, while the medicine man and Uncle Joe teach Slash to validate his identity, culture, and spirituality (140–41). Slash learns that AIM is primarily a "spiritual movement" that advocates "the Indian way" (120–21). He eventually takes a spiritual, rather than a militant path.

Armstrong articulates the integral role spirituality plays in American Indian world views. Whereas settler society often distinguishes between "ordinary" and "non-ordinary" or "extra-ordinary" realities, many American Indians perceive both existing simultaneously (J. Dumont 79). Settler attempts to differentiate between fact and myth, ordinary and extraordinary in settler versions of histories about American Indians serve to inscribe settler ideologies upon American Indians—to colonize them. Many American Indians perceive stories, myths, rituals, and ceremonies to be the world as it is; moreover, they are history, and the commemoration of these constitutes historical practice. This historical practice, in turn, is essential for cultural survival.

Throughout the text Armstrong alludes to war dances, sun dances, winter dances, potlatches, traditional feastings and giveaways, sweat and pipe ceremonies, prayer gatherings, pow-wows, legends, myths, stories, drumming, and Indian songs. These are all acts of commemoration—re-enactments of the past. Whenever Slash participates in these acts of commemoration, he experiences a feeling of health and well-being.[13] They are what "was missing" and necessary for Slash's survival, and that of subsequent American Indian generations (180).

In writing about the importance of remembering and practicing traditions in a book, Armstrong is careful not to tell too much about American Indian communities. That she only alludes to traditions foregrounds the "impossibility of re-presenting the oral in a written form" and suggests that this written partial re-presentation is "supplementary to the oral" (Emberley 143). The silences (or lack of details about aspects of American Indian traditions) also give American Indian communities the "sense of being on the inside" (King qtd. in Rooke 74). By alluding to American Indian traditions, the author encourages American Indian readers to engage in acts of commemoration and rememoration of traditions in their own communities. In this way, *Slash* supports, rather than supplants, American Indian traditions.

In foregrounding American Indians and their traditions, Armstrong presents a syncretic perspective in which she illustrates how it is possible neither to turn back the clock and return to a pre-contact culture nor to forget the history of colonization. Slash's process of commemorating and rememorating his traditions enables him to decolonize his mind; he liberates himself from colonial rules of recognition when he later ceases to define himself according to the colonizers' rules or terms.

Rememoration affirms identity by articulating differences— between diverse American Indian and settler values —while also celebrating continuity of American Indian traditions. While imprisoned, Slash undergoes an inner liberation that enables him to survive when he visualizes himself at home at the winter dance and begins to sing Uncle Joe's dance song (67–68). Here, and elsewhere, acts of commemoration become acts of rememoration. His imagination triggers familial and social memories that sustain him because they remind him not only of his "Indian" identity but also of the social community that shapes and informs his identity. Slash realizes that he is not alone, but part of a continuum, or as he once observed about his father, he was "apart from everything and also a part of everything at the same time" (70). This affiliation with his social community counters the destructive, paternalistic filiation that he experiences in prison and in settler society.

When he eventually tries to articulate what being "Indian" means, Slash describes his identity in terms of feelings, "a really old part of me that I couldn't explain away as teachings from my Elders" (182). He acknowledges the need to cultivate cultural awareness, "to develop a certain kind of awareness and self-confidence" (183). While he wants to be "proud to be Indian," and to believe that "being Indian was special, not something to be forever ashamed of" (184–85), he still searches for what "was missing" (185). It is not until later, when he ceases to think in colonial terms, that he shifts his attitude and takes pride in "being Indian."

Community Identity Formation

As I discussed earlier, Armstrong delineates how American Indian world views, traditions, and cultural practices differ from those of settlers.[14] *Slash* resists eurocentric concepts of individualism, progress, and linear time and foregrounds American Indian cultural traditions. Armstrong articulates these, and other, cultural differences not only to interrogate the colonial discourse but also to signal shared values across diverse American Indians. These shared values become the basis for the construction of a collective identity. In examining the novel within the context of the colonial relationship, I have two main concerns: first, to explicate the relationship between community identity formation and historical consciousness and practice; second, to examine how Armstrong constitutes the larger collective identity of American Indians.

There needs to be an interaction between historical narrative and a social group to create a meaningful social memory:

> ... the highest and most meaningful level at which narrated events and historical reality are mutually validating—that is, on which a historical narrative is 'real'—is precisely that on which the historical narrative and a bounded social group merge to create a collective historical consciousness and practice .... (Harkin 101)[15]

Commemoration and rememoration are aspects of historical practice. Historical consciousness lends meaning to and structures historical practice, which amplifies and nourishes historical consciousness. While no one is devoid of historical consciousness, there are individuals, like Jimmy, who adopt colonial historical consciousness and are unaware of and/or unwilling to acknowledge their American Indian historical consciousness. Although Jimmy is exposed to the historical practice of his community, he does not grow up practicing the "Indian way"; instead, he follows the non-traditional, assimilated practices of his parents. An individual can choose to practice the "Indian way," even though his/her personal history did not include this historical practice. Individuals construct their historical practice in an effort to render their experiences meaningful, and this historical practice can transcend personal history. Historical practice can change social memories by articulating differences. On a community level, shared historical consciousness is the backbone of social memories. Commemoration and rememoration are profound tools with which to sustain and create social memories.

Armstrong's text marks why and how American Indian social memories change. The social memories of colonization that American Indians share are those of dispossession and oppression. The dominant social memory within Canada in which official histories are constructed glosses over these with other historical constructs like exploration, discovery, and assimilation disguised as equality. This dominant social memory is in conflict with American Indian memories of their colonial oppression and with their social memories that pre-dated colonization. Even though American Indian rituals, ceremonies, and other acts of commemoration have changed over time they are still part of the lineage of the rituals and ceremonies of their ancestors.

Community identity is built from social memories which, in turn, contain and construct historical practice. The community shapes the subject, but individual subjects, in exercising historical practice through acts of commemoration and rememoration, form and contribute to the development of the community. These acts of commemoration and rememoration articulate differences, yet also establish continuity. For example, many American Indians share the experience of winter dances; however, the particular rituals, ceremonies, and dances may differ, and these differences articulate the social memories of that community. The community is also the container for the historical practice that individuals can access.

According to Benedict Anderson, communities are imagined; they are cultural constructions. Anderson writes that "communities are to be distinguished not by their falsity/genuineness, but by the style in which they are imagined" (6). In imagining a collective identity of American Indians, Armstrong forges a hybrid "Indian" identity that is multinational to better resist colonialism. She adopts this colonial term and subverts it (much like Red Power redeploys a pejorative term as one of empowerment).[16] As stated earlier, Armstrong recognizes the diversity of American Indians; hence, her construction of this collective identity is strategic essentialism to contest colonizers and their efforts to divide American Indians.[17] In articulating an "Indian" social memory, Armstrong illustrates how diverse American Indians share an understanding of colonization and oppression as well as values which differentiate them from colonizers. Historically, this validation of an "Indian way" has been a political strategy to facilitate the construction of an "Indian community" much larger and stronger than individual American Indians.

On one level, the configuration of "the Indian way" exists within the colonial context of a settler/American Indian opposition. In this context, it is a counter discourse and construct which, by operating within the binary field, is in danger of perpetuating and repeating the very binarism it seeks to undo. It is this trap that Mardi addresses when she tells Slash: "You see they only give us two choices. Assimilate or get lost. A lot of us are lost. We need to make a third choice" (70). Mardi alludes here to the necessity for political action. The third choice is akin to Homi Bhabha's "third space" (*Location* 38) and "hybrid moment of political change" that is *"neither the One . . . nor the Other . . . but something else besides,* which contests the terms and territories of both" (*Location* 28).

One of the limitations of resistance literature is that it is reactive; it is a response to an existing relationship. Although there is a counter-discourse embedded in *Slash* in which Armstrong articulates cultural differences and contests settler histories, she also moves beyond resistance literature. She presents a proactive third position wherein American Indians are no longer represented in relation to those who have colonized them, but rather in relation to their traditions—traditions which include ongoing resistance to colonization.

Tommy's father perceives the need for American Indians not to define themselves in relation to the colonial relationship and its rules of recognition. Slash later understands this as is evident when he suggests that Jimmy re-examine his colonial thinking:

> One of the effects of it is the way people see themselves in relation to those who are doing the colonizing. Everything that the colonizers do, tells the Indians that they are inferior, ... So it gets transferred in subtle ways by our own people. . . . They attempt to become the same as the colonizers in as many ways as they can, to escape being inferior, or being tainted by it. They don't want to hurt inside, you see. (221)

In rememorating and practicing the traditions of his community, Slash refuses to define himself in relation to settlers.

Identity lies in culture and the knowledge and practice of culture is essential for continuance, for survival. In "Racism: Racial Exclusivity and Cultural Supremacy," Armstrong writes:

> The thought or the world view, however, is the shaper of cultural process. . . . Culture centricity becomes entrenched as tradition, through underlying structures which reinforce the world view, because they reinforce stability and continuance. Continuance is assured in the methods used to teach cultural process to ensuing generations. (*Give Back* 78)

The title of chapter four, "We Are a People," attests to the importance of developing a sense of commonalty. It is not until this chapter that Slash discovers what he has thought was missing. As Old Man tells Slash, "It is not the culture that is lost. It is you. The culture that belongs to us is handed down in the sacred medicine ways of our people. . . . We will soon be as extinct as the buffalo if we don't go back to them things" (191). Self-preservation and American Indian survival require not only knowledge but also praxis of the "Indian" way (211). Slash must practice his culture, which includes speaking his language, to fulfill his role as "a keeper of the ways" (205, 211).

Slash realizes that cultural adaptation, without assimilation, is necessary to ensure the survival of his community (210). While this rebuilding involves both internal and external changes, Slash believes that the former is more important than the latter because without internal change—pride in being "Indian," in difference—external changes cannot be meaningful (218). He commits himself to fostering internal change by "rebuilding a worldview that had to work in this century, keeping the values of the old Indian ways" (232).

Re-membering Social Memory

Armstrong not only illustrates how social memory can be changed, she contributes to this change through her narrative of rememoration. She critiques settler society and its constructed social memories. Criticism is essential, but it is only the beginning. The rememoration of American Indian "historical (f)acts" (Godard 206–7) sustains existing American Indian social memories but can also create new ones. It is necessary to disseminate American Indian histories and traditions in order to create new historical practices within their communities. A change in social memories is a change in attitude in which American Indians throw off the mantle of colonization, but do not forget the history/memories of colonial oppression.

Slash outlines a position based on mutual respect in which American Indians can take different perspectives yet still support one another (235). *Slash* offers a paradigm for decolonization, a third position of "dis-identification where one may signify otherness yet refuse the trope of subordination" (Godard 217). Through her rememorative telling/writing of the events of the past twenty-five years from American Indian perspectives, Armstrong speaks the unspoken and commemorates American Indian traditions and histories. In so doing, she fosters social memories of colonial oppression and resistance which reinforce the resolve of American Indians to forge a collective identity to resist colonization.

Chapter Six

Raven's Song

> Epidemic after epidemic had not birthed the shame Raven had hoped for among the people of white town, so the villagers remained staunch in their silence. It was not until this last 'flu epidemic that finally the seeds of shame were sewn. Raven grew excited.
>
> Lee Maracle *Ravensong* 191

In *Ravensong* Lee Maracle subverts the shame that often occurs when people engage in colonial mimicry or internalize the lens of the colonizer. The author illustrates how shame can be both a means of social control as well as social reform. The narrative describes how Stacey is caught between cultures. Celia, her sister, connects to the traditions and values of their ancestors through her visions while the trickster Raven attempts to wake Stacey and others in her village to transform the future.

> Far away the earth bled, her [Raven's] bleeding becoming an ulcer. Century by century, the ulcer intensified. It grew more serious millennium by millennium, until neither earth nor Raven had any choice. 'Bring them here to Raven's shore. Transform their ways. Deliver Raven to the whole earth.' (191)

As transformer and healer, the trickster's project is to liberate American Indians from their paralysis, their "drought of thought," to awaken the consciousness of American Indians so that she can "bring them across the bridge" (43–44). Equally important is Raven's plan to shame-teach settlers and "bring them to Raven's shore" (191). The trickster mediates between the town and Stacey's village, between the members of each community, and between the past, present, and future. As a catalyst for change, Raven articulates cultural differences and also signals the importance of cultural survival, which involves cultural adaptability and transformation. Raven and her song voice the social memories of this American Indian community and its experience of colonization.[1] The trickster's hybrid, syncretic vision offers an alternative paradigm of decolonization wherein American Indians can live with settlers without living as settlers.[2]

In many settler cultures, shame is perceived as a destructive emotion. The etymology of shame is to cover. Specifically, it is the need to cover that which is exposed, to conceal that which is vulnerable to a perceived threat (Schneider 30). As a process of validation and/or devaluation by others and oneself shame differs from guilt, although the two can be intertwined (Jacoby 2). When people experience guilt, they feel badly about their actions. When people experience shame, they feel badly about themselves—they internalize negative affect. Guilt often is linked to ethical or moral principles, whereas shame is not always a reaction to unethical behavior (Jacoby 1).

Some anthropologists distinguish between shame and guilt cultures, often attributing shame based cultures to non-western, "traditional" cultures and guilt based cultures to western (read "civilized," "superior") cultures.[3] According to this binary analysis, traditional cultures rely "on shame for social control; and modern societies, [rely on] guilt" (Scheff 79).

Shame is a social emotion which can be destructive and/or constructive. For instance, some degree of shame is required to establish and maintain respect for boundaries, which are often necessary to formulate and cultivate identity. Shame can protect the individual, and often communities, from unwelcome intrusions, invasions. It can be constructive when it encourages individuals to respect boundaries, which, in turn, protect individuality and identity (Jacoby 46). A person who is shameless often does not respect boundaries, however.

In *Ravensong* settlers use shame as a means of social control to erect and police cultural boundaries.[4] The American Indian villagers resist the shame which settlers try to ingrain. Through Raven's song, they raise their consciousness and articulate and validate their cultural differences. Stacey and some of the other villagers later learn to use shame as a means for social reform; they shame settlers into respecting the cultural differences of

American Indians.

Settler efforts to transform American Indians into colonial mimics involve a complex process of shaming the colonized. Shame involves "a perception of negative evaluation of the self by self or others" (Scheff 86). As used by settlers for social control, shame is destructive. It facilitates assimilation, and the conformity and concurrent destruction of American Indian cultures that assimilation entails. Shame is a means of social and cultural adaptation precisely because it works on compliant individuals. Those with low self-esteem are more likely to conform than those who have a strong identity and self-esteem. Individual and community identity play crucial roles in the formation and development of self-esteem. Individual identity may be, as is the case with Stacey in *Ravensong*, strengthened through community affiliations. By validating her culture and community relations, Stacey later rejects colonial constructs and assimilation.

Domination by one group over another can lead to a loss of self-control, which, in turn, shames and erodes self-esteem (Erikson 254). Colonizers often erode American Indian identities, both on individual and community levels. They try to shame American Indians by constructing a Manichean opposition in which individual subjects are transformed into collective objects, others. In dehumanizing them, settlers may shame those who think within this colonial binary construct. American Indians may experience interpersonal shame (between oneself and others) if they accept settler negative evaluations of them and/or intrapersonal shame (the way the self sees itself) if they internalize this negative evaluation.

The more individuals assimilate, the more likely it is that they will internalize settler values and come to perceive themselves as inferior. This form of intrapersonal shame is invidious because one contributes to one's own annihilation. Shame is intertwined with a process of recognition in which the subject comes to view him/herself through the lens of another. "Shame is by nature *recognition*. I recognize that I *am* as the Other sees me. . . . Thus shame is shame of *oneself before the Other*" (Sartre 222). When colonizers attempt to fix the identity of colonized people by constructing them as objects, colonized people experience disempowerment. Shame is often an expression of one's consciousness of inferiority (Schneider 24). Assimilated individuals, for instance, who perceive themselves as inferior not only experience shame but also become ashamed. Being ashamed is also a consequence of loss of freedom. Jean-Paul Sartre writes: "I can be ashamed only as my freedom escapes me in order to become a given object" (261). Shame does not always mean being ashamed, however. The word ashamed has a destructive connotation, whereas shame can also be constructive.

American Indians who assimilate may come to identify, or desire to identify, with settler society. This identification often involves a disidentification with their own culture. Internalized colonization occurs when American Indians view themselves, and/or their community, through the lens of settler society. This "process may underlie assimilationist strivings and be the factor that leads the individual to lose himself totally in the dominant group" (Allport 151). In some cases, the colonized may identify with the aggressor/colonizer, at the expense of self-annihilation. In their efforts to thwart settler devaluation, such individuals may devalue themselves (Jacoby 27).

Colonial Mimicry

In *Ravensong* Benny exemplifies the colonial mimic who has identified with the aggressor at the expense of alienation from his own community and culture. His participation in the colonizer's war overseas shames his mother and other members of the community because he is unwilling to combat injustice at home, yet is able to do so on behalf of his oppressors: "Her mother burned with shame. Benny had gone halfway 'round the world to kill young boys in a fight against something that he had not been willing to fight at home" (53).

Colonial mimics evaluate themselves in relation not only to those in their American Indian community but also to those settlers who perceive them as inferior. Shame serves as a form of recognition, which for colonial mimics can never be complete.[5] Instead, the colonial mimic always experiences a *partial recognition*, a split wherein the settler colonizer refuses to recognize the colonial mimic as equal.

A strong identity and high self-esteem play crucial roles in an individual's ability to resist shame. Individuals who have intact social bonds often experience pride in themselves and in their American Indian community/ies. Whereas pride often indicates an intact social bond, shame signals a threatened one (Scheff 71). In their assimilation projects, settlers attempt to sever social bonds within and between American Indian communities so that patterns of affiliation are replaced by ones of servile filiation.

Historically, many American Indians have been subject to settler practices that deny them the right to practice their lifestyle, to speak their languages, to practice their spirituality, and customs. In *Ravensong*, for instance, Maracle describes settlers and some of the effects of colonization:

> They [settlers] gobbled up the land, stole women, spread sickness everywhere, then horded the precious medicine which could heal the sickness. With each sickness the silence of the villagers grew. The silence grew fat, obese. (191)

Residential schools have also played a key role in fracturing the social bonds within American Indian communities as children have been separated from their families and taught to deny their culture.[6] In fragmenting American Indian communities, settlers deprive American Indians of their cultural context(s). This loss of context displaces American Indians.

Shame occurs when the individual is put into a context that is at odds with that within which he/she wishes to be interpreted, and the individual becomes conscious of "felt experiences of incongruity" (Schneider 35). At the beginning of *Ravensong* Stacey experiences the paralysis of the assimilated colonial mimic. She cannot hear Raven and is alienated from her culture. She lacks the cultural context to comprehend either Raven or the significance of her grandmother's funeral (16). As Raven observes, Stacey "judged the world through a pair of glasses whose colours did not match reality. Stacey behaved as though she did not share the context of her clanswomen" (22). At this point in the novel, she has yet to *feel* the incongruity. She needs to become aware of it to resist the spiral of shame.

Shame can be either "an emotional response to the violation of social norms" and/or "the violation of an inner value system associated with the ego ideal" (Jacoby 21–22) and can create conflicts for the person experiencing shame. The individual may experience fear of rejection by others and/or fear of self-betrayal. Snake, the abusive villager who is later ostracized by the village, experiences the first kind of shame because he has violated social norms in abusing his wife and children. Stacey comes to experience both forms of shame when she violates taboo by going unchaperoned on a walk with Rena and Judy (121). When faced with her mother's anger and threat of ostracism (124), Stacey experiences a conflict in her shame experience because she realizes that she not only has violated social norms but also has betrayed her self.

Conflicts may also arise when the individual experiences a contradiction between the shame of individualization and the shame of social adaptation (Jacoby 21). In the above incident when Stacey violates taboo, she initially experiences a conflict within her shame experience. Her attempt to individuate herself and ignore her mother conflicts with social adaptation within her community. She experiences shame when she recognizes that she has been "unmindful of the way" (127), and this recognition begins to dispel her inner conflict. Stacey's shame, here, serves to "safeguard certain agreed-upon boundaries that one violates only at the risk of social sanctions and personal exposure" (Jacoby 21). By giving her daughter a cultural context, Stacey's mother enables Stacey to realize that she has violated not only the cultural Law but also her cultural values. Stacey's conformity to societal norms leads to self-betrayal. She experiences a discrepancy between her values and those of settler society.

The colonial relationship between American Indians and settler society renders this situation even more problematic. American Indians not only have to negotiate between their own values and those of their community but also between their values, the values of their American Indian community, and those of settler society. Conformity to settler society is often at odds with conformity to American Indian societies. If American Indian individuals experience a discrepancy between their values and their American Indian society as well as between their values and settler society, then the level of alienation increases significantly.

The process of colonial mimicry involves a disavowal of one's American Indian culture. This leads to a conflict between one's values and those of one's American Indian community. To wit, the colonial mimic desires to become like settlers, which often necessitates becoming unlike American Indians. The consequence of settler disavowal for assimilated colonial mimics is that they encounter a double bind; they become alienated not only from their American Indian culture and themselves but also from settler society. Allport accurately depicts this double bind when he writes: "But more mysterious are the cases where the individual is hopelessly barred from assimilation and yet mentally identifies himself with the practices, outlook, and prejudices of the dominant group. He accepts his state" (151).

According to Raven Stacey's community has contributed to its own alienation, and the chasm between its village and settler society, because the villagers have come to accept their state. In internalizing shame, they have confined themselves. Raven believes that this "drought of thought" stems from "the parochial refusal of her own people to shape the future of their homeland. . . . her people had given up, . . . withdrawn into their imagined confinement" (43). That Raven emphasizes their "imagined confinement" is itself a resistance strategy. Raven suggests that the villagers shift their attitude. They can resist settler attempts to disavow them by refusing to accept or engage in colonial terms. The villagers must first become aware of the ways in which they have been paralyzed by settler shaming tactics.

Raven is a catalyst for change, but she cannot change those who are either unwilling or unable to hear her song: "It had taken Raven almost a century to drive the people from the village, still the villagers would not communicate with the others" (191). People have to become agents of their own change; Raven merely points the way. She directs people's attention in her efforts to wake them up. Raven is also a catalyst for raising the consciousness of American Indians and, directly or indirectly, of settlers. When Stacey rationalizes the consequences of the epidemic, Raven squawks (28) in an attempt to direct Stacey's attention to Polly's (a settler's) suicide. She encourages Stacey to pay attention to this event and to what it teaches about those who are rootless, and thus lose the will to survive (39).

Stacey's journey toward cultural affirmation begins when she attempts to engage with the settler town. In observing it, she compares it to her village and begins a process of individual and cultural differentiation. Initially, this differentiation process emerges as a bipolarization, albeit a reversal of the bipolarization inherent in settler assumptions of their superiority. Stacey focuses not on what settlers have, but rather on what they lack.

As she becomes more aware, Stacey becomes more critical of settler society and further articulates and validates the ways of her people. In defining cultural differences, however, she reverses the Manichean binarism. Stacey believes: her community values interconnectedness, whereas settler society lacks this connectedness (17); her community is not capitalistic, not wasteful, not consumer-oriented, whereas settler society is capitalistic, wasteful, and consumer-oriented; her people are respectful of the land and of one another, whereas settlers are disrespectful; her people are passionate and discreet, whereas settler society is "dispassionate" (34) and indiscreet. Stacey attributes this dispassion, and many other settler ills, to their lack of connectedness (17, 61)—their discreteness.

She also perceives patriarchy as part of the problem in settler society, although she also acknowledges that it has become part of the problem in her village. Colonization has required "a new moral sensibility and the old culture died just a little after that" in which "never again would wolf women serve men in quite the same way" (10). When Stacey visits Mr. and Mrs. S. she notices that, "Mrs. S. had no more rank in her own house than the children" (35). In contrast to her village, here there are no support systems for white women (81). Stacey juxtaposes settler society with its rigid moral code to her community and to the ways of Dominic, the village medicine man:

> In Dominic's mind morality was irrelevant. What lived inside was a set of laws which were to be obeyed at all times regardless of the circumstances. His belief in their ways kept him on a trail of gentle social affection. He would not believe that anyone could consider that committing an indiscretion was worse than committing a crime. Lawlessness, over-indulgence and deception were just other words for thievery—only what you stole was the sacred right of others to choose based on clear knowledge. Deception robbed the hearts of others. Now Polly's life lay stilled in some graveyard because she had dared to be indiscrete [sic]. They weren't very likable people, Stacey decided. (64)[7]

Ravensong points to the indiscretion of settler society and illustrates how settler forms of "disgrace-shame" (Schneider 22) lead to disintegration of one's world, whereas forms of "discretion-shame" (Schneider 22) sustain the individual and the community.

Schneider differentiates between "discretion-shame" and "disgrace-shame" (21–22). "Discretion-shame" is shame which occurs before a harmful act and serves as a warning (18). "Disgrace-shame" is shame which a person feels after a harmful experience. For example, Polly feels "disgrace-shame" when her classmates taunt her. Shame before a harmful act precipitates a sense of discretion. "Discretion-shame" is constructive because it acts as a social restraint for valued relations (as opposed to social repression). Polly's classmates, for instance, lack the necessary "discretion-shame" and publicly humiliate her. If they had experienced "discretion-shame," then they would have been more sensitive and might well have refrained from humiliating her.

Re-visioning

In raising Stacey's and others' consciousness, Raven encourages the people to articulate and validate their cultural differences. Gradually, Stacey's initial desire to be like settlers becomes more ambivalent as she observes her increasing dislike for them: "I am obsessed with living like these people but I can't stand them anymore" (37).

As I discussed in chapter five, one way to ensure cultural survival and to cast off the shaming effect of the colonizer is to not forget the past—to remember the experience of colonization. This holotropic remembering also makes it increasingly difficult to share the belief system of settlers.

Through visioning, Stacey and her sister, Celia, re-affirm their cultural context. Celia, undergoes a series of visionings in which she re-members the advent of settlers in a ship, and the deleterious effects that resulted: the dwindling numbers of American Indians (resulting from epidemics, diseases, and deaths) and the destruction of a clan system (10). As Celia realizes, the advent of settlers/colonizers meant that, "A new moral sensibility was required and the old culture died just a little after that" (10).

Through her visionings with the past, Celia resists .the alienation and disconnectedness that has resulted from colonization because she re-establishes linkages with her ancestors and rememorates traditional ways. Similarly, Raven images up memories for Stacey, and it is through these memories, these voices from the seemingly absent dead, that Stacey regains a sense of connection, of rootedness, of kinship. That these voices are often the voices of those who have died reinforces the idea that the dead remain present if the living are willing to listen.

Stacey's grandmother's voice, for instance, reassures her that she will understand the significance of her grandmother's funeral when she is ready and when she "need[s] to know" (16). The voice of Nora, an elder in Stacey's community who has recently died, often reminds Stacey that there is "no use thinking about it" (25). While these voices from the past comfort Stacey, other voices from the past remind her of the dangers of assimilation.

She remembers how her cousin, Shelly, married a white man, and consequently, lost her Indian status (70). Shelly's ghost comes to Stacey when she is with Steve, a white boy. This act of rememoration guides her thinking about Steve, and the potential consequences of any relationship that she might have with him.

Later, when Stacey feels betrayed by her settler friend, Carol, she remembers her father's words, " Remember, if they [settlers] ever have to choose between each other and you, they will always choose themselves" (89). His words enable her to put Carol's betrayal in perspective; she sees it in the context of settler-American Indian relations and firms her resolve to seek support and validation from herself and her community.

Raven is emblematic of change, of adaptation that is essential for cultural survival. She perceives American Indian people "heading for the kind of disaster they may not survive" (14). In an attempt to prevent cultural annihilation, she creates a catastrophe to "wake the people up, drive them to white town to fix the mess over there" (14). Although Raven deems change necessary, she does not perceive it as destructive, but rather as a form of "birth":

> Change is serious business—gut-wrenching, really. With humans it is important to approach it with great intensity. Great storms alter earth, mature life, rid the world of the old, ushering in the new. Humans call it catastrophe. Just birth, Raven crowed. (14)

In viewing a catastrophic epidemic as "birth," Raven resists settler binary thinking and re-places it with an American Indian perspective that emphasizes the natural cyclical process of birth-death-birth. This perspective enables the villagers to retain hope and determination to survive by encouraging them to take a longer range perspective; they participate in the present while at the same time articulating the future. By reminding them of their connection to the land and by her plan to create an epidemic, Raven endeavors to bring the villagers, and ultimately settler society, together so that death can become a transformative birth in which the people re-affirm their culture and spirit.

Raven and her song articulate the risks which are often necessary for cultural survival and for liberation and transformation. As trickster, Raven exemplifies both folly and wisdom. At times, members of Stacey's community tell her that she has "too much Raven" while, at other times, she does not have enough Raven. Too much Raven can lead to folly or to freedom. It can symbolize the courage, awareness, and determination that underlie necessary risks and acts of liberation. Not enough Raven can also lead to folly or, in some instances, be a wise course of self restraint. Whether one has too much or too little Raven is dependent on the context.

Hearing Raven's song, Stacey learns that articulation and validation of cultural differences are part of an ongoing process of liberation. American Indians, according to Raven, must bridge cultural differences by teaching settlers. They need to identify on some level with settlers so that they can re-place settler patterns of filiation with ones of affiliation. While it is not possible to erase colonization or colonizers— "Raven could never again be understood outside the context of the others" (191)— Maracle subverts colonial constructs of superiority by positioning settlers as others. Before the villagers can learn how to shame-teach settlers, they must undergo a process of affiliation. In some instances, Raven suggests, they may internalize colonialism before they will finally be roused from their drought of thought: "Until the villagers began to feel as ugly inside as the others, none could come forward to undo the sickness which rooted the others to their own ugliness" (191). Raven recognizes the need for the villagers to "learn how it is we are to live with these people" (192).

In chastising Stacey's mother for her hardheartedness toward settlers who visited her house during the Depression, Raven argues that "the law must always be obeyed, particularly when it is difficult" and "upholding the law is personal,—a thing of the spirit" (54). From Raven's perspective, Stacey's mother missed an opportunity to "teach these men" (54). As in the incident where Raven chastises Stacey's mother's heartlessness toward her settler visitors, Stacey's resistance and heartlessness toward Steve is, from Raven's perspective, another missed opportunity to teach settler society.

Initially, Stacey is unable to identify with Polly or to decipher the significance of Polly's suicide because she is trapped in a binary mode of thinking. Her cultural differentiation has come to necessitate a disaffiliation with settler society; she refuses to allow herself to see or *feel* Polly's shame and loss of will to survive. She has become *heartless*, lacking in Raven spirit.[8]

Raven endeavors to teach Stacey to feel Polly's shame:

> 'Polly . . . suicide . . . feel the life of Polly draining from her perfect body. Wander around Polly's insides, feel your way through decades, generations of lostness. Capture the moment, the precise minute in which the will to survive melts down to disappear in the millennia of futility her lineage has been. Discover her spirit, bent, then broken. Re-invent Polly, re-imagine her, hang onto the picture of perfect being letting go, spiralling down into shame. Picture the rootlessness she must feel.' (38–39)

Stacey does not "feel" for Polly at this point, but she later empathizes with Polly. Polly's rootlessness is brought home to her when Stacey reviews her relationship with her own mother. Initially, she is ashamed of her mother because she thinks her mother lacks discretion and has disgraced the family; however, Stacey later realizes that her judgments of her mother are not very different from those made by Polly's peers.

Stacey recognizes the similarities and differences between Polly and her own mother; Stacey's mother lives in a culture that accepts and allows her to be passionate, whereas Polly's judgmental peers disavow her passion. Stacey eventually abandons her heartlessness toward her mother and realizes: "Polly and Momma were the same woman—good-hearted and passionate. In the white world her momma would have perished. In her own world of choice and acceptance, Momma was safe"

(106). Stacey has moved beyond reversing the negative binary categorizations of colonizer/colonized to articulate and affirm her American Indian culture. She has carved out a space in which she can feel some empathy, some common ground with settlers while still validating her culture and cultural differences. Stacey now chooses points of affiliation with settlers on her terms.

Her ability to empathize with them is crucial to this process; otherwise, her unresolved anger and bitterness sever potential channels for communication. As Stacey has learned from Old Dominic, it is necessary to move beyond anger and revenge:

> 'We have a right to the anger of any given moment. What we are not entitled to do is hold onto it until it becomes bitter bile spilling out indiscriminately, so that the other person receiving the anger ends up paying for the misdeeds of others.' (130)

This process of empathy and choosing affiliations should not be confused with universalism that obliterates cultural differences and ignores power relations and the differences that they create. As is evident in Stacey's realization of the similarities between Polly and her mother, this form of empathy is a teaching tool. Through Polly and her experience, Stacey acquires a greater appreciation for cultural differences. Understanding is possible because Stacey has undergone a process of self and cultural individualization. She no longer desires to be like settlers. She has also moved beyond a reverse racism wherein she earlier transformed settlers into inhuman objects. Her empathy succeeds as a teaching tool precisely because it does not ignore existing power imbalances in the colonial relationship, but addresses them. To wit, Stacey perceives similarities between Polly and her mother, but she does not identify with the aggressor; instead, her empathy for Polly and settlers enables her to articulate and affirm her culture and community relations. This affirmation process enables her to resist colonial constructs and shame.

Stacey challenges the school principal, Mr. Johnson, and his authoritarian paternalism because of her reclaimed conviction in herself and her culture. She deconstructs the master-slave script he represents when she refuses to obey or to retract her position: "What was disturbing for Mr. Johnson was her quiet faith in herself, her absolute belief that she had the right to disobey a direct command from him" (69). When Stacey later decides not to pursue her relationship with Steve, she realizes that this action, like her resistance to Mr. Johnson, is evidence that the "slave had just given an order to the master, which made him an ex-master" (75).

Stacey is partially able to shame-teach Steve because, although she empathizes with him, she does not sympathize or pity him. She understands his alienation, but does not internalize or share his colonialism. He asks: "'Is it because I am white?'" "'No,'" she said softly, "'it's because you aren't Indian'" (185). Her reply reveals a distinct shift in her thinking; she now refuses to view the world on the colonizers' terms. Her reply suggests that it is time for Steve and other colonizers to shift their thinking. Until this occurs, he will never understand Stacey or her culture because he "had no context for seeing her as she really was" (185). "Without context, any relationship is doomed" (185). Stacey uses Steve's alienation to shame-teach him, and others, in settler society.

Raven is a catalyst to help settlers raise their awareness of the effects of colonization. As long as settlers do not allow themselves to empathize with American Indians, they can continue to perpetrate victimization and other forms of social injustice. Raven's plan is to use shame to facilitate their affiliation with colonized American Indians. This is a difficult task. The danger is that settlers will resist; if they further deny their feelings, then alienation will increase. This will burn the bridge that is necessary to eliminate victimization.

When Stacey confronts Steve and provides him with the context from which to formulate understanding by giving him graphic details of the horror of the epidemic, he fails to understand until he remembers that his father was one of the doctors who refused to treat American Indians. This memory is at odds with the ideal image that his father has given him: "He had so easily persuaded his son of the interests of his patients" (186). The discrepancy between Steve's ideal image of his father and the reality shames him. In light of this discrepancy, he can either reject his ideal image of his father and accept reality or he can reject reality. Steve is unable to adjust his inner values and ideal image of his father. He is not yet capable of learning from his shame. Instead, he leaves the village behind (186). Even though Steve has not yet modified his behavior, he has experienced the ambivalence of constructive shame. In departing, Steve experiences shame because he is alienated from Stacey, whom he still loves: "In shame, the object one is alienated from, one also loves still" (Schneider 28). Stacey has planted, as Raven observes, "this seed [of shame] in the heart of young Steve" (191).

In the epilogue, Stacey tells the story to her son Jacob in an attempt to answer his question: "Why did little Jimmy [Stacey's nephew] shoot himself?" (197). Stacey relates how "the village fell apart" (197) and "they would not let us build our school" (198). Her son (who symbolizes the next generation) asks: "Why did anyone pay attention to them?" (198). Stacey's reply is "Not enough Raven" (198). Jacob has yet to understand what this means, but the women do. They assure him: "You'll know the answer when you need to" (199). The story, like Raven's plan to shame teach settlers decolonization, is ongoing.

Chapter Seven

Tricking In/Subordination

. . . there is no recognition of master and slave, there is only the matter of
the enslaved master, the unmastered slave.

Homi Bhabha *The Location of Culture* 131

The slave had just given an order to the master, which made him an ex-
master.

Lee Maracle *Ravensong* 75

Tomson Highway in *The Rez Sisters* and *Dry Lips Oughta Move to
Kapuskasing* and Thomas King in "The One About Coyote Going
West" unsettle colonization through trickster strategies of
insubordination. Both authors adapt traditional trickster figures
(Nanabush and Coyote, respectively) to create post-colonial
ones.[1] Through their trickster discourses, these writers subvert the
colonial discourse and present literary paradigms of
decolonization. They articulate and affirm cultural differences
through tricksters that escape inside-outside dichotomies. Like
Maracle, Highway and King map terrains of insubordination to
resist being placed in positions of subordination.

Trickster Traits

It is paradoxical to analyze American Indian tricksters
because they defy and transcend categories, definitions, and
analysis. Tricksters embody the paradox of human existence and
the world as we know it. As First People, tricksters existed prior
to the origin of human beings. While they did not create the world,
they are *bricoleurs* (Lévi-Strauss qtd. in Bright 36) who attempt to
fix it up and who have "instituted human life and culture" (Bright

xi). Once human beings were created, these First People were transformed into animals. While they can have animal names (Raven, Bluejay, Spider, Hare, Coyote) and can change shapes, appearing at times as animals, tricksters are not animals (Bright xi).[2]

Trickster is a "transformer-culture hero" (Ricketts qtd. in Bright 21) and/or a mythic figure that transcends time and space. According to Gerald Vizenor, the "trickster is a comic sign, neither a real person nor a character with 'aesthetic presence'" (*Narrative Chance* 207). Taking issue with settler attempts to marginalize and appropriate American Indians and their stories, Vizenor explains that trickster is "a healer and comic liberator in narratives, not an artifact or a real victim in historical summaries" but "a communal sign in imagination, a comic holotrope and a discourse that endures in modern literature" (*Narrative Chance* 205).

For many American Indian people, trickster is not mythic in the sense of being unreal. Peter Blue Cloud expressed this well when he asked William Bright: "You sure Coyote is a myth?" (Bright xix). Settlers have often marginalized American Indian myths by hearing and reading them in the same vein as fairy tales, fables, and children's stories. In many settler cultures, myths frequently connote unreal or untrue stories, whereas in many American Indian contexts, tricksters and the term *myth* do not signify that which is not real.

Tricksters not only have remarkable powers but are also empowering. Like Raven, in Lee Maracle's *Ravensong*, tricksters are often catalysts for others' empowerment. They can mimic others as well as change their shape and assume different guises. Tricksters embody a timeless quality that transcends limits and limitations. For instance, Coyote is often referred to as Old Man Coyote, alluding to trickster's timelessness (Bright 177). Able to traverse boundaries and elude definitions, tricksters often mediate between humans and deities, humans and animals, men and women, young and old. They also remain unfettered by time and space and wander freely between the past, the present, and the future.

Tricksters remind listeners/readers of the importance of social intercourse and exchanges between cultures as well as cultural continuity. Often bawdy, lecherous, greedy, they have insatiable appetites and exhibit "an enormous libido without procreative outcome" (Babcock 162), although they often leave others impregnated. Indeed the fact that they are not defined by gender and referred to as he/she illustrates how tricksters transcend gender. Trickster also articulates the importance of cultivating and integrating both male and female aspects of human nature.[3] Their ability to appear as male and/or female also reflects linguistic differences. In many American Indian languages "there is no gender," and trickster is "neither exclusively male nor exclusively female, or is both simultaneously" (Highway *Dry Lips Oughta Move to Kapuskasing* 12).

Ever changing, trickster reminds listeners and readers of the mutability of life and the importance of adaptability for cultural and personal survival. While trickster invented death and occasionally dies, it is only momentarily, for trickster not only embodies survival but is a survivor. Trickster's invention of death reminds human beings to appreciate life (Bright 48) and, because of our common mortality, to show compassion for others (Bright 119). With their vibrant energy and inquiring minds, tricksters foreground the importance of taking risks and remaining inquisitive. While they trick others, tricksters are also often duped. Trickster stories and exploits remind us of the unpredictability of life and remind us to laugh at uncertainty and indeterminacy.

Perpetually curious, trickster is a restless wanderer and traveler who challenges socially constructed borders, boundaries, rules, and regulations. Trickster's traveling articulates the process of cultural transmission and translation.[4] Trickster's refusal to be pinned down and his/her role as mediator (and anti-mediator) is evident in the ways in which he/she often inhabits or make appearances in crossroads: intersections, market places, thresholds. In so doing, trickster signals the processes of becoming, of cultural adaptability. Never static or fixed, trickster transcends spatial, temporal, and cultural boundaries.

As liberators and healers, tricksters often model cultural transformations and the artistic/creative process. They create and destroy, do good as well as evil as they balance and unbalance the world. They are reminders that change, growth, survival often involve some unsettling, some necessary risks. Death and destruction are not opposed in trickster discourses, but intertwined and part of life and creation. In many respects, tricksters embody imagination and enable listeners and readers to imagine alternative paradigms, a liberated world. As Griever, Gerald Vizenor's trickster figure, explains: "Listen, imagination is the real world, all the rest is bad television" (*Griever* 28).[5]

Tricksters transform others without providing overt direction; rather, they enable American Indians to see not only themselves and their cultures but also possibilities. In many instances, tricksters are associated with mirrors. Mirrors suggest how tricksters can reflect and exemplify human behavior. Trickster mirrors call into question issues of representation and identity. Through their behavior, tricksters "express a concomitant breakdown of the distinction between reality and reflection" (Babcock 163). As mentioned previously, tricksters can both reflect and refract the colonial discourse and rules of recognition. They partially mirror the double-voiced colonial discourse. However, subversive tricksters also give us refracted images in which the colonial discourse is re-contextualized within trickster discourse. By re-presenting settlers and their rules in a refracted image, they enable listeners and readers to recognize not only ourselves as we are but also ourselves as we might be.

Often attired in motley (reminiscent of Coyote's motley coat), tricksters may evoke images in the minds of settler readers of the fool, clown, or buffoon. Tricksters often are wise fools who teach through comic examples and/or counter examples. Paul Radin has described how trickster is both "creator and destroyer" who "knows neither good nor evil yet is responsible for both" (xxiii), but tricksters often do not take responsibility for their actions. In many instances, they are quite irresponsible as well as irrepressible as they flout conventions, customs, and rules. As Coyote and the four Indians in *Green Grass, Running Water* illustrate, tricksters often "add disorder to order and so make a whole, to render possible, within the fixed bounds of what is permitted, an experience of what is not permitted" (Karl Kerényi qtd. in Radin 185). Defiant of authority, they often achieve this by transgressing cultural boundaries, rules, and taboos.[6] At times, their challenge of cultural customs remind listeners and readers to heed them. At other times, trickster's transgressions of taboos serve as a counter example, a route not to take or perhaps one to travel with more awareness of possible consequences. At times, trickster's transgressions signify the importance of the process of cultural adaptation—the need to question boundaries and limits and to adapt customs and conventions to the changing times. In these instances, trickster's transgressions are liberating because they articulate new directions.

In order to understand the cultural resonances of trickster stories and the ways in which trickster inverts or transgresses social customs and practices, listeners and readers require some familiarity with the American Indian culture and cultural contexts in which the trickster is situated. Those unfamiliar with the specific cultural codes and allusions will miss the mark. At the same time, adaptations of oral trickster discourses into written form can be useful modes of resistance that are not forbidden by settler society precisely because the dominant society does not fully understand the discourse and its underlying cultural codes. By articulating cultural differences through trickster discourses written in the language of colonizers, Highway and King subvert colonial discourse from within. Their trickster discourses signify "the historical movement of hybridity as camouflage . . . a space in-between the rules of engagement" (Bhabha *Location* 193). Camouflage and humor may well prevent settlers from perceiving the discourse as a threat. Settlers may also undergo a translation/transformation process whereby they collaborate in the decolonization process, helping to undo the very colonial and imperial structures of which they are a part.

In Highway's plays and King's short story, Nanabush and Coyote respectively contest colonial rules of recognition and re-present alternative paradigms of decolonization and cultural survival. In King's short story, Coyote is a *bricoleur* who attempts to fix the world. His/her efforts to balance it also involves unsettling colonial rules of recognition. King's trickster, like Maracle's Raven and Highway's Nanabush, foregrounds the agency of American Indians and subverts colonial efforts to disempower them. Coyote comically re-presents the effects of colonization and, in trickster fashion, often becomes both the trickster as well as the one who is tricked. In Highway's plays, Nanabush often engages in subversive mimicry and represents the effects of colonialism and of internalized colonialism to re-present alternatives; readers imagine a liberated world free from colonial oppression. Like Maracle and King, Highway offers readers a paradigm for decolonization in which he alters the colonial cultural landscape.

Cultures under Construction

The United States' and Canada's cultural landscapes are not homogeneous. Their borders are impossible to define with any degree of precision and there are significant regional variations. The entire panorama is in a state of dynamic change. Yet, there are recognizable landmarks (football and hockey fights, congressional and constitutional fights). As we gaze on this panorama much remains invisible to settler eyes. What we perceive to be the landmarks and sign posts of settler cultural landscapes are the constructions of settlers whose ancestors arrived here within the past five hundred years. Reconstructing colonial cultural landscapes in North America is a matter of survival for American Indians. Through their processes of cultural self-determination, they create new spaces in which to speak.

For many American Indians, cultural survival involves continuity with the past. American Indian writers can create spaces—discourses of difference(s)—in which settler society is disavowed and no longer "sublates otherness" (Bhabha *Location* 173). Affirming continuity with the past often consists of American Indian engagement with shared social memories of colonization and its deleterious effects. It also involves active rememoration—an affirmation and re-inscription—of their unique social memories that settler society has marginalized and/or erased. Like Maracle, Highway and King subvert settler society precisely by playing in the cultural cracks in-between settler and American Indian societies.

In *The Rez Sisters* (1988) the trickster Nanabush embodies the survival of American Indian cultures despite colonization.[7] As Highway explains:

> Some say that Nanabush left this continent when the white man came. We believe he is still here among us—albeit a little worse for wear and tear—having assumed other guises. Without him—and without the spiritual health of this figure—the core of Indian culture would be gone forever. (xii)

Marie-Adele's observation that "he [Nanabush] won't fly away" but "just sits there. And watches me" refers to Nanabush's persistence in this particular scene, but also alludes to one of his roles in American Indian culture—namely, to watch the people and to remain with them (19).[8] At the same time, Nanabush exemplifies the ability of American Indians to liberate and heal themselves through affirmation of their cultures. Trickster exists in-between American Indian realms. He/she also "straddles the consciousness of man and that of God, the Great Spirit" and "teaches us about the nature and the meaning of existence on the planet Earth" (*Rez* xii). This liberation process indicates the ability that people and their cultures have to adopt survival strategies.

Trickster exemplifies adaptability. American Indians can subvert settler society from within by inhabiting spaces in-between law and taboo, English and American Indian languages, God and the Great Spirit. Able to transmute her/himself, the post-colonial Trickster refutes colonial binary oppositions and definitions.[9] Embracing fluidity, he/she can move between realms while belonging to neither. Trickster's refusal to be pinned down and trapped in stereotypes is liberating: "In trickster narratives the listeners and readers imagine their liberation; the trickster is a sign and the world is 'deconstructed' in a discourse" (Vizenor *Narrative Chance* 194).

American Indian tricksters embody indeterminacy. Barbara Babcock's view of trickster as a "liminal figure" that inhabits in-between spaces and lives "interstitially" is useful when considering the post-colonial trickster (154). The apparent duality that Radin uses to describe traditional tricksters as male/female, human/non-human, good/evil, creator/destroyer, and trickster/duped not only misses the mark when audiences and readers encounter the post-colonial trickster but becomes the mark; the post-colonial trickster exposes and challenges this cultural binarism underlying much of settler thinking and language.

Nanabush's ambivalent position in *The Rez Sisters* is evident in his ability to articulate presence in what some perceive as absence.[10] Only Marie-Adele and Zhaboonigan perceive trickster's presence. Even then, there are times when they are unaware of him. Marie-Adele gives no indication of her awareness of Nanabush when he plays havoc with her laundry (70). Similarly,

Zhaboonigan appears to be unaware of trickster when he knocks her off her stool (70). Nevertheless, Marie-Adele and Zhaboonigan are often aware of him, whereas the other women on the reservation are unaware of Nanabush's presence, and believe he is now absent from their culture. They hope that if they take action to improve conditions on the reservation, then trickster may return. Here, Highway reinforces the idea that "*some* say that 'Nanabush' left this continent when the whiteman came" (xii; emphasis added). Trickster is in-between not only spiritual and natural realms but also seen and unseen realities. Nanabush's straddling of presence-absence suggests that realities exist that some see; others do not see. For instance, settler audiences visually observe Nanabush on stage; however, they may or may not see (or validate) American Indians and their diverse cultures. To recognize trickster, even if only to perceive his visual presence, is an acknowledgment of trickster's and American Indians' cultural survival.

In *Dry Lips Oughta Move to Kapuskasing* (1989), Highway presents, what he calls, the "'flip-side' to *The Rez Sisters*— Nanabush is female" (12). Unlike his first play, here Highway provides stage directions for a lower as well as an upper realm. The set was "designed on two levels, the lower of which was the domain of the 'real' Wasaychigan Hill," whereas "the upper level of the set was almost exclusively the realm of Nanabush" (*Dry Lips* 9). The "soundscape," specifically Zachary's "idealized" form of harmonica playing, evokes the blues and mimics human voices.[11] The musician's absence-presence symbolizes "a dynamic intertextuality by forces outside the text upon the actual play" (Imboden 114) while simultaneously reinforcing the dream world and the interplay between the two levels/realms. By having both realms visible, Highway again suggests that there is more than one reality, or if there is one reality, aspects of it are visible to some, but not to others. The apparent dichotomy between the two levels: the dream world of Nanabush and the "reality" of the reserve—is not clear cut. What we first perceive to be "reality" later appears to be Zachary's dream. Through apparent dream/visions and through Nanabush, the problem manifests itself, namely the men fear domination, loss of identity, and cultural extinction.

Just as Marie-Adele and Zhaboonigan Peterson are the only

women who occasionally sight Nanabush, so Simon Starblanket and Dickie Bird Halked are the only ones who see the trickster. Like Marie-Adele, Simon Starblanket believes that the people must speak their language and validate their culture. As he tells Zachary, "I'm gonna go out there and I'm gonna bring that drum back if it kills me" (*Dry Lips* 52). When he is later fatally wounded, Simon speaks Cree and intersperses references to apple pie. The Cree words displace these English words so that they "develop an unrecognizability, an inaudibility that makes them strangely alien, as if the meaning they usually convey is absent" (Imboden 122). Here, and throughout the play, Highway's use of Cree also articulates colonizers' efforts to dispossess American Indians of their languages.

Displaced, Zhaboonigan and Dickie Bird symbolize the dispossession and fragmentation of the people on the reservation. Whereas Zhaboonigan lost her parents in a car accident, Dickie Bird, the illegitimate son of Big Joey, is in search of the true identity of his father. Zhaboonigan re-members being raped by white boys, while Dickie Bird Halked perpetuates the victimization that he has experienced when he rapes Nanabush/Patsy (*Dry Lips* 99). His rape of her with a crucifix symbolizes the way that settler society violated American Indians in the name of Christianity.

In *The Rez Sisters* men are absent, but figured through Nanabush in the guise of a male dancer. In *Dry Lips Oughta Move to Kapuskasing* women are absent, but figured through Nanabush in her various appearances as the "spirit" of Gazelle Nataways, Patsy Pegahmagahbow, and Black Lady Halked. Nanabush embodies what the men both fear and desire (*Dry Lips* 14).

The inversion of stereotyped gender roles in what Pierre St. Pierre defines as a "world topsy-turkey" is depicted by the "Wasy Wailerettes," (the all women hockey team), Spooky Lacroix's knitting, and Zachary's baking (*Dry Lips* 109). Threatened by the "Wasy Wailerettes," the men feel disempowered by the newly liberated women on the reserve. The men's sexism is reflected in the way each envisions, or has visions of, Nanabush. In her various guises of different women on the reserve, Nanabush has oversized sexual characteristics: as Patsy, she has a big bottom; as Black Lady Halked, she has a big belly;

as Gazelle Nataways, she has big breasts. Having internalized colonialism, these men exhibit the patriarchal values and sexism of settler society. Big Joey's misogyny, as he explains, stems from his fear of loss of power and is analogous to the domination of American Indians by settler society, "I hate them fuckin' bitches. Because they—our own women—took the fuckin' power away from us faster than the FBI ever did" (*Dry Lips* 120).

Zachary's/Nanabush's dream is not only a neat device but also a trickster mirror which exposes and re-presents the poison of colonization. The play enacts the imbalance of power relations, and the human costs of cultural genocide. It illustrates how patriarchal colonial structures underlie settler society's racism and sexism. Nanabush critiques the patriarchal structures in settler society and the sexism that results from these structures. She provides a comic commentary on Marilyn Monroe, a sex symbol in settler society, when a flag drops from the Monroe poster and Nanabush "farts" (107). Norma Jean's cinematic persona also embodies the cinematic commodity. The poster of Marilyn is also "an image of illusion that led to drug abuse and suicide" which, by the end of the play, "is exorcised" (Imboden 119). By framing the play as an apparent dream/vision—a dream of a colonized American Indian man—Highway critiques the psychology of those American Indian men who have adopted patriarchal colonial values. The seven men on the reservation are not just distinct individuals, but symbolic of different facets of the colonized American Indian male and manifestations of his dreams and fears.

In-between American Indian and settler societies, trickster is the means by which Highway exposes the savagery of Christianity and its civilizing mission. Highway satirically alludes to biblical figures in his choice of names: Spooky LaCroix, Pierre St. Pierre, Simon, and Big Joey. Zhaboonigan appears at the bingo table "banging a crucifix." "The scene is lit so that it looks like 'The Last Supper'" (*Rez* 102). As the Bingo Master, Nanabush's garish dress parodies settler society and its emphasis on consumerism, media (talk shows), and materialism. Highway satirizes settler society's emphasis on quantity, as well as Toronto's assumed hegemonic importance and centrality in Canada. The stage directions read:

> Instantly, the house lights come on full blast. The Bingo Master—the most
> beautiful man in the world—comes running up center aisle, cordless mike
> in hand, dressed to kill: tails, rhinestones, and all. The entire theater is
> now the bingo palace. We are in: Toronto!!!! (*Rez* 100)

Nanabush has found some cracks, too, in the temporal
landscape. He does not follow the linear time of settler culture,
but moves between past and present, articulating future
possibilities. He often triggers memories of the past. In the guise of
a gull Nanabush attempts to grab Zhaboonigan, which triggers her
recollection of being raped. That her rapists were two "white
boys" (*Rez* 47) reminds the audience of settler violations of
American Indians. Nanabush's "agonizing contortions"
throughout this scene enact Zhaboonigan's pain, as well as that of
colonized American Indians. Trickster's ambivalence enables him
to elude restrictive categories and boundaries; here, for instance,
he re-presents victimization without being victimized.

In the epigram of *Dry Lips Oughta Move to Kapuskasing*,
Highway cites the words of American Indian leader, Lyle
Longclaws, to articulate the problem: ". . . before the healing can
take place, the poison must first be exposed . . . ." Nanabush not
only enunciates American Indian cultures but also critiques settler
society and the cultural baggage it has left with American Indians.
Specifically, she exposes the poison of colonization so that the
healing can take place.

Nanabush occupies an ambivalent hybrid space in which she
travels freely between diverse American Indian and settler
cultures. In parodying settler society, and its concept of a
patriarchal Christian God, she re-forms it. Highway re-places
settler concepts of an omniscient, omnipotent, paternalistic God
with the ambivalent, comic trickster. Nanabush is neither good nor
bad, but playfully nonchalant. Zachary appeals to "God of the
Indian! God of the Whiteman" and asks: "Why are you doing this
to us?" (*Dry Lips* 116). By way of reply, the audience is given a
vision of Nanabush "sitting on a toilet having a good shit":

> He/she is dressed in an old man's white beard and wig, but also wearing
> sexy, elegant women's high-heeled pumps. Surrounded by white, puffy
> clouds, she/he sits with her legs crossed, nonchalantly filing his/her
> fingernails. (117)

Simon, and later Patsy, tells Dickie Bird Halked that the cross is not "right for us" (*Dry Lips* 96); instead, both Simon and Patsy advocate following traditional medicine ways. They tell him that this medicine is good, unlike the ways of settlers which are destructive—poisonous.

In the opening conversation between Philomena and Pelajia in which they discuss problems on the reservation, Pelajia attributes the problems to the erosion of American Indian cultures, to the loss of "the old stories, the old language" which are "almost all gone" (*Rez* 5). She recalls a time when "Nanabush and Windigo and everyone here could rattle away in Indian fast as Bingo Betty could lay her bingo chips down on a hot night" (*Rez* 5). She describes how times have changed: "Everyone here's crazy. No jobs. Nothing to do but drink and screw each other's wives and husbands and forget about our Nanabush" (*Rez* 6). Marie-Adele and Zhaboonigan Peterson are the only two, out of the seven, women who can partially perceive Nanabush. Pelajia, on the other hand, believes that Nanabush will only "come back" once the roads are repaired and trickster can have "paved roads to dance on" (*Rez* 59).

When Marie-Adele perceives Nanabush (in the guise of a white gull), she speaks to the trickster in Cree. Highway gives an example of hybrid space. By interspersing Cree and Ojibway in a predominantly English text, he unsettles readers; they confront cultural difference because there is a linguistic sign post in their cultural landscape(s) that they do not comprehend. Highway's use of Cree serves to alienate and displace settler audiences; they must struggle with language and the problems of translation. They have a small sampling of the alienation and dispossession that many American Indians have experienced when they have not been allowed to speak their languages, but have been required to speak English. While audiences can deduce much of the meaning from the linguistic and situational contexts, their alienation and displacement may enable some to interrogate settler attempts to erode or eliminate American Indian languages. Marie-Adele's use of Cree when talking to trickster suggests that American Indian languages—and cultures—still survive, but just barely. That Marie-Adele speaks Cree and is one of the few who can perceive trickster reinforces the idea that languages are a central part of American Indian cultures and essential for their survival.

Nanabush illustrates how the imposition of English has alienated American Indians. When a language is imposed on another culture, many experiences are untranslatable; others are translated/transformed when expressed in the language of the colonizer. In a comic scene between Nanabush/Patsy and Simon, for instance, Simon insists that Nanabush is male while Nanabush persists in defining herself as female. The debate is resolved when Simon realizes that the problem lies in English, and the gender distinctions that exist in the language. Instead, Simon embraces his language. Speaking in Cree, he reminds himself and the audience that in his language Nanabush is "weetha ('him/her'—i.e., no gender)" (*Dry Lips* 110). The subsequent debate in which Simon says "and thisaway" only to have Nanabush comically respond with "and thataway" (*Dry Lips* 111) parodies the binary thinking underlying much of colonial language and discourse. Nanabush patterns resistance in which the colonial game of Simon says falls apart.

Settlers often encourage American Indians to fit their cultural landscape—to become colonial mimics and assimilate. In this reconstruction of the colonial landscape, performance is the trick which transforms colonial mimicry into subversive mimicry. Consider stories of American Indian speakers who converse with settlers all the while performing gestures of Raven, or Coyote. In her explanation of "the silent language of physical metaphor," Lee Maracle writes:

> Each facial expression, change in tone of voice, cadence or diction has meaning for us. I have watched such orators as Philip Paul, George Manuel and Ellen White pull the legs of government officials by posturing raven while complimenting the official. For us this is hilarious, because not only does the posture go over the heads of the official listening, but also because the joke does not go by the Native audience watching the interplay. (*Sojourner's Truth* 12–13)

In Highway's plays, gestures undermine the spoken words and communicate to American Indian audiences a different message, one that subverts colonial mimicry. These trickster performances enable American Indian audiences to realize: "In these instances of social and discursive alienation there is no recognition of master and slave, there is only the matter of the enslaved master, the unmastered slave" (Bhabha *Location* 131). The knowing wink, gesture, destroys the existing cultural landscape and substitutes American Indian spaces.

Trickster is a mimic without succumbing to colonial mimicry. His/her subversive mimicry is analogous to that of impersonators, who mimic others through exaggeration, caricature, mockery, and satire without being disavowed. In adopting the persona of the target subject, the impersonator creates the illusion that he/she is the target in order to critique the actual target audience, and to translate it through laughter. The impersonator's ability to shift positionalities succeeds in large part because both the audience and impersonator are aware, on some level, that the repetition that the impersonator performs is a performance.

Performance becomes a dialogic game in which there are multiple voices interacting, at times competing at times cooperating. The impersonator is the agent of his/her actions, as well as the catalyst for the audience's potential transformation. On another level, the impersonator is not the sole agent. The success of the impersonation relies on the impersonator's understanding of and ability to caricature the target subject as well as on the interaction between the impersonator and the audience. The audience's acceptance of the impersonation—of the performance—largely determines the success of the illusion. The audience, in this respect, also becomes the agent of the impersonator's transformation performance.

Performance can allow the writer to shift the target subtly, to take aim at settlers in such a way that they may or may not realize that, in laughing at the performance, they are laughing at themselves. Whether or not they perceive themselves to be the target depends on the extent to which they have made an identification between the apparent and the actual target. This kind of doubling of impersonations is a repetition in which affiliation can become a subversive splitting, a splintering of identifications.

In *The Rez Sisters*, Nanabush's role as a mimic/impersonator is evident when the seven women "march" to the store (35). Still in the guise of the white gull, Nanabush (played here by a male dancer) follows the women, playing tricks and mimicking their movements. Nanabush's role is ironic because, although most of the women do not see Nanabush, the audience does. The effect is comical as Nanabush follows the women in their determined trek to the "band office" to appeal for funds to attend the biggest bingo event ever in Toronto. The seven women, and later seven drumbeats accompanying the women as they round up funds for their trip to the biggest bingo ever in Toronto, symbolize the seventh generation in which American Indians are liberated. As Highway explains:

> Legend has it that the shamans, who predicted the arrival of the white man and the near-destruction of the Indian people, also foretold the resurgence of the native people seven lifetimes after Columbus. We are that seventh generation. (qtd. in Wigston 9)[12]

In dancing along with them, Nanabush is a comic sign of American Indian cultures and of liberation.

That Marie-Adele and Zhaboonigan are, throughout this scene, playing "games" with each other reinforces the overall metaphor of the game of bingo as chance in life. Marie Adele's and Zhaboonigan's games highlight Nanabush's significance as a "comic holotrope," in which "the signifier in a Trickster narrative, is signified in *chance*" (Vizenor *Narrative Chance* 189). Highway depicts a dialogic game wherein "the Trickster sign is communal" and the "author, narrator, characters and audience are the signifiers and comic holotropes in the Trickster narrative" (Vizenor *Narrative Chance* 188).[13]

The dialogic interaction between sign and signifiers, between Trickster and author, characters and audiences articulates American Indian cultural differences because it is a "communal sign" which is informed by, and informs, American Indian social memories. This dialogic interaction enunciates the present as well as the past and future; it enacts a fluid process of becoming.

As a "sign," trickster is not solely agent; rather, it is in the dialogic interaction between sign and signifiers that American Indian cultures are enunciated. This point is crucial because it reminds us not to read Nanabush as agent, as director, of the women and their transformations. Instead, it is in their interactions with each other and with Nanabush, either directly or indirectly, that the women realize their own liberation.

When Marie-Adele dances in the arms of the Bingo Master, later transformed into the black night hawk, it is clear that she has now accepted her approaching death and is willing to leave with

Nanabush (104). After returning to the reserve where they bury Marie-Adele, the other women, who have also undergone transformations, now accept their lives. In his guise of gull, Nanabush closes the play by perching on Pelajia's rooftop (unseen by her) and dancing to the beat of her hammer, reminding us once again that Nanabush has survived.

In *Dry Lips Oughta Move to Kapuskasing*, Nanabush appears to direct Simon (in the scenes with the dancing bustles) and the others, but she is not the agent of change. These men, not settlers, are the agents of their actions and transformations. They achieve what they do because each comes to terms with the past in his own way and in his own time. Nanabush is a catalyst perhaps, but only to those who seek direction.

Nanabush expresses and re-enacts the past in the men's minds and in the communal memory. She perches on an old jukebox which has a "mystical" effect and which hangs, as Highway explains in the production notes, "in the night air, like a haunting and persistent memory" (*Dry Lips* 10). The circumstances and origins of Dickie Bird's birth still haunt the community. When Nanabush appears on the upper level as Black Lady Halked, Dickie Bird is the only one able to perceive her. He prays to this "vision of 'the Madonna' (i.e., his own mother), which he actually sees inside his own mind," while Spooky Lacroix remains oblivious to Nanabush's presence (*Dry Lips* 52). Dickie Bird Halked's visionary experience with the Madonna/his mother is shattered when Pierre St. Pierre recounts the origin of Dickie Bird's name and tells him who his father really is (*Dry Lips* 57).

Nanabush articulates the social memory of this particular community by re-enacting the downfall of Black Lady Halked and the tragic birth of Dickie Bird Halked. Significantly, the background music for this scene is Kitty Wells' "It Wasn't God Who Made Honky Tonk Angels" (93). Nanabush provides visions of the past which enable the members of the community to acknowledge and come to terms with the dark memories of that fated night seventeen years ago, and all that resulted from it, to heal themselves.

The most telling scene of holotropic time in which past and present fuse is when Nanabush is on the upper level re-enacting Gazelle Nataway's striptease on the night of Dickie Bird's birth seventeen years ago.[14] On the lower level, Zachary, Spooky, and Pierre do not appear to recognize Nanabush, but slip into the past and participate in the striptease until they are interrupted and literally caught with their pants down by the entrance of Simon Starblanket.

Nanabush embodies a survival strategy for American Indians; they can exist in a hybrid realm where, even though they live with settlers, they do not live *as* settlers. They can co-exist with settler cultural landscapes, while practicing/validating their different cultures. Further, they can stake out cultural spaces which neither exclude nor assimilate, but embrace differences. Trickster is the articulator of differences. In *The Rez Sisters* the women are dominant and Nanabush appears as a male dancer, whereas in *Dry Lips Oughta Move to Kapuskasing* the men dominate the lower stage and Nanabush appears in various female guises. Trickster signifies that what is perceived to be absent is in fact present—the absent women in *The Rez Sisters* and the absent men in *Dry Lips Oughta Move to Kapuskasing* still have a presence. The spiritual realm is present. Their culture is present.

American Indians can articulate those differences that threaten the dominant culture in a way that settler society does not recognize or in a way that no longer threatens it; they can develop strategies that play on settler blind spots and alter the colonial rules of recognition. Highway alters these rules not only by comedy and parody but also by framing the play as an apparent dream and by Nanabush's visionary appearances. While the most convenient way to make *Dry Lips Oughta Move to Kapuskasing* fit Western settler cosmology is to interpret the play as a dream (and Highway certainly makes this interpretation available), another way to interpret it is to accept that these are Zachary's experiences. Dreams and visions are real, past-present-future exist simultaneously in a holotropic time, and Nanabush has never left.

In the stage directions near the end of the play, Highway writes:

> Zachary 'sleep walks' through the whole lower level of the set, almost as though he were retracing his steps back through the whole play. Slowly, he takes off his clothes item by item, until, by the end, he is back lying naked on the couch where he began the play, except that, this time, it will

be his own couch he is lying on. (*Dry Lips* 124)

Hera bends over and kisses Zachary on his bottom at the end of the play. She speaks Cree and has a silvery Nanabush laugh which is echoed by the absence-presence of a "magical arpeggio" on the harmonica off-stage (130). These details circle back to the beginning when Gazelle Nataways kisses Zachary on his bottom, and later gives a throaty laugh that echoes Big Joey's. On one level, the circle is complete: Zachary and Hera are reconciled, Dickie Bird has found his father and the events of his birth have been worked through, and the poison of colonization has been exposed. On another level, the circle is ongoing. When Zachary lifts his infant daughter, who symbolizes the next generation, into the air he reminds the audience that this is just one reconstruction project among many to come. Zachary is not the same person that he was at the beginning of the play and neither are we, thanks to Nanabush.

Decolonizing Minds and Inventing Souls

In his short story, "The One About Coyote Going West," Thomas King also provides settlers with a literary paradigm of decolonization. He reconfigures a traditional trickster tale to weave a work of post-colonial criticism, a hybrid text. He deconstructs the *grand récit* of North American history to reveal how colonizers sought to eradicate American Indians and their histories. Specifically, King challenges colonial views of history in which historians described North America as a *tabula rasa*, an empty continent that needed to be discovered and mapped by the "imperial eyes"[15] of European settlers determined to "civilize" the "savages."

By drawing parallels between Coyote and settlers, King wields a scalpel that surgically cuts into colonial discourse, and its rules of recognition, to heal American Indians.[16] In mimicking aspects of settler discourse and values, Coyote functions as a comic trickster mirror through which readers can view internalized colonization as a mistake. Settlers initially claimed legitimacy and superiority in the name of civilization and Christianity, using the Bible—an "old book"—to justify their exploitation of American Indians in the name of conversion. Similarly, Coyote uses books to try to gain authenticity (68). She erroneously equates books—the printed word with legitimacy and authority, whereas the grandmother audience interprets "those books" as a constructed narrative, "a good story." When Coyote chimes in, "I been reading about that history . . . about who found us Indians" (68), the grandmother audience[17] again redefines Coyote's history as "those old ones" and encourages Coyote to "tell me your story" (68). From the grandmother audience's perspective, history is just another narrative; it is another story that conveys a relative, rather than an absolute, truth. What grandmother is telling Coyote is that your story may be different from mine.

King creates an identification between the Bible—the settler tool in the civilizing mission—and a store catalogue, which signifies Western materialism and consumerism. The dialogue between the personified Mistake and Coyote emphasizes the "mistake" that the settlers made by imposing a consumer culture and filling "up this world" with "stuff" (76). When Coyote goes west, grandmother tells us, "there is a pile of snow tires," as well as televisions, vacuum cleaners, pastel sheets, an air humidifier, a portable gas barbecue, a hydraulic jack, toaster ovens, a computer with a color monitor, a golf cart, and golf balls (75–76). It is ironic that Coyote asks the Mistake to stop and "give me that book (a store catalogue), before the world gets lopsided," because she is bending the world. Once again, Coyote makes the mistake of identifying a book with power.

King re-presents settler history in which Europeans discover Indians, and out of this settler agency comes American Indian subjugation. Here, the ducks are not discovered; instead, they transform themselves into Indians, and are agents of their own subjectivity (79). Through the play of multiple voices, King replaces the concept of a single, authoritative narrative/history with an alternative paradigm of dynamic multiplicity that positions itself neither in relation to nor in opposition to a colonial hegemonic center.[18]

In places, the narratives are self-referential; they alert readers to the ways stories and histories are cultural constructions. At one point, the narrator steps outside the story to comment on Coyote to the audience: "Well, that Coyote don't know what to do. So she tells them ducks to go ahead because this story is pretty long and it's getting late and everyone wants to go home" (77). Earlier, the narrator tells Coyote: "This story is going to be okay. This story is doing just fine. This story knows where it is going. Sit down. Keep your skin on" (72). In this way, King contrasts the grandmother's narrative with the settlers' and implies that this story has a life of its own; the story has its own knowledge. However, the context in which King presents this statement points to the indeterminacy of knowledge. He encourages us to question whether this, or any, story can know, or ever claim to know.

The participatory interaction between tellers, both in the frame tale between Coyote and grandmother and in the inner tales about Coyote, destabilizes the centrality and closure in many eurocentric narratives. Similarly, the first ending (the ending to the inner tales) refuses closure because it circles back to the beginning. Once again, Coyote "starts to think about a healing song" (79). King interrogates and critiques the notion of a central, authoritative (his)tory/story with a "sense of an ending."[19]

In an oral story the interactive relationship between the speaker (teller), the subject (tale), and the audience is based not only on content but also on context—the reason, and the occasion, for telling the tale. The speaker must consider not only how and what s/he presents but also the audience to whom s/he is speaking. The audience often participates in the story, helping to shape and determine it.

There is a colonial assumption that narratives that draw heavily on American Indian traditions of storytelling are relics or reproductions of dead or dying cultures—museum artifacts of limited impact and import. King's work contradicts this assumption because he demonstrates that such narratives are capable of great power, sophistication, and contemporary relevance to American Indian and settler readers.

As Walter J. Ong points out, "narrative originality lodges not in making up new stories but in managing a particular interaction with this audience at this time—at every telling the story has to be introduced uniquely into a unique situation, for in oral cultures an audience must be brought to respond, often vigorously" (42). By choosing to write in English, King is "managing a particular interaction with this audience at this time"; this is a criticism for those who have read the book—the Bible and the *grand récit* of settler history.

He encourages settlers to engage in a deconstructive reading practice. A deconstructive reading examines the text's critical difference from itself; the text says something other than what it appears to say. Such a reading practice is particularly relevant to hybrid texts like King's which subvert and deconstruct colonial narratives while also demonstrating the conflicting discourses and forces of signification within the text. In so doing, King unsettles any and all claims of domination or privileging of one discourse or mode of expression over another.

In King's story the conflicting forces of signification are settler and American Indian discourses and oral and written literatures. King is not teasing out the subtleties of signification, but foregrounding them to critique settler society and its oppression of American Indians. The "denied knowledges" that estrange settler society's rules of recognition (Bhabha *Location* 114) are the narratives that unsettle Coyote's, and settlers', tales and actions.

Right from the beginning of King's text, the grandmother narrator illustrates how Coyote exemplifies these battling forces of signification. She warns us to be on guard for the discrepancy between what Coyote says as opposed to what she does (67–68). When Coyote tells the grandmother audience she is going to fix the world, grandmother expresses concern and hints by the addition of the word "again" that Coyote often does more damage than good: "Oh boy, pretty scary that, Coyote fix the world, again" (67).

The traditional Coyote trickster figure is emblematic of hybridity: creator and destroyer, good and evil, trickster and tricked, male and female.[20] Coyote provides a trickster mirror not only of what we are but also of what we fear and desire. Through Coyote, King enacts what Bhabha terms, "a dialectical play of 'recognition.'" The effect of this hybrid strategy is that:

> The displacement from symbol to sign creates a crisis for any concept of authority based on a system of recognition: colonial specularity, doubly inscribed, does not produce a mirror where the self apprehends itself; it is always the split screen of the self and its doubling, the hybrid. (*Location* 114)

The trickster's role, Tomson Highway explains, is "to teach us about the nature and the meaning of existence" (12). The question here is what does King's Coyote teach and whom does she teach?

King uses the trickster figure, and humor, as a "subversive weapon" in which he ambushes the reader (Atwood 244). He plays with the context to create a con/text in which Coyote is contextualized both as American Indian trickster as well as settler reader. In Coyote's latter role, she is caught in her own text of confidence tricks. Coyote's role as trickster is established in the comic description of her ability to leave her skin, "sneak around," and "make you jump"(68).

In performing the part of settlers, Coyote suggests that settlers are the ones in need of instruction, but are reluctant to learn. King transforms Coyote into a disempowered trickster figure; like the settler, "her mouth is in other places" and her "ears don't hear anything" (71). As she loses her mouth, she tries to sing out of her nose, ears, and finally her "butt hole" (71). When she endeavors to sing her healing song "out her butt hole," "things don't smell so good in that hole" and her "butt hole" now appropriates her song and pursues her. King has transformed the initial hole that Coyote fell into when she made her mistake into Coyote's butt hole (70–71). By linking the two holes, King parodies Coyote's and settlers' mistakes. King comically reduces Coyote to the level of the absurd and emphasizes her loss of power—both as a character within the story and as audience who has lost her role as narrator. The image of Coyote being chased by her own bodily part—her butt hole—serves to ridicule her and is further evidence of her humiliation. She is eager to be the center of attention, but not the butt of the joke.

Like settlers, Coyote wants agency, to be the originator/creator of everything in the world. Whenever she tries to attribute agency to herself and co-opt those around her, she is usually undermined and disavowed:

> Maybe she makes that beautiful rainbow, says Coyote. No, I says. She don't make that thing. Mink makes that. Maybe she makes that beautiful moon, says Coyote. No, I says. She don't do that either. Otter finds that moon in a pond later on. Maybe she make the oceans with that blue water, says Coyote. No, I says. Oceans are already here. She don't do any of that. (69–70)

Like Maracle and Highway, King illustrates how American Indians can deploy trickster strategies of insubordination to reject and subvert colonial tropes of subordination.[21] Rather than reverse colonial binarisms and oppression, King offers a relational trickster discourse that unsettles oppositional concepts of identity.

Whenever Coyote attempts to relate an origin type tale "about who found us Indians" (68), her tale is dislocated and repeatedly written over and reinscribed by the multiple narrators: the grandmother, the personified Mistake, Coyote's butt hole, and the ducks. Initially, the grandmother audience takes over the narrative; Coyote now becomes the audience, not the storyteller, and the grandmother audience shifts back to her initial role of narrator as she challenges and reinscribes Coyote's version of history. As narrator, the grandmother relates the story about Coyote—the one who really discovered "Indians"—heading *west* (67). According to the grandmother, Coyote, like the settler, is only an agent of mistakes: "The first thing Coyote makes, I tell Coyote, is a mistake" (70). Once she has fallen into the hole and made the mistake, Mistake "jumps up and down on Coyote until she is flat" and now takes over Coyote's role as it "wanders around looking for things to do" (71).

By having Coyote transpose and combine the names of settlers, King presents us with iconic explorers. Coyote tells the grandmother audience: "Maybe I tell you the one about Eric the Lucky and the Vikings play hockey for the Old-timers, find us Indians in Newfoundland" or "Maybe I tell you the one about Christopher Cartier looking for something good to eat. Find us Indians in a restaurant in Montreal" or "Maybe I tell you the one about Jacques Columbus come along that river, Indians waiting for him" (68). In each instance, Coyote describes the settlers as finding the Indians, and specifically of finding them in a state of civilization determined by the settlers. Indians are found playing hockey and eating in a restaurant. Moreover, Coyote portrays the Indians as anxious to be found.

In contrast to Coyote, the grandmother dismisses this version of history as "Whiteman stories" (68) and re-places this "white" (his)tory. As the grandmother points out, American Indian people had to find the "lost" settlers, not the other way around (69).

Grandmother is constantly interrupting and disrupting Coyote's narrative. She ironically undercuts Coyote, and her narrative, by means of dramatic asides. On one level the grandmother audience's asides serve to cast suspicion on Coyote and the credibility of her narrative; Coyote, the grandmother audience tells us, is sneaky; she is not to be trusted. Like the settlers with their civilizing mission and treaties which they did not honor, Coyote can slip out of her skin and "bite them toes" (68).

In the grandmother's version of the origin of Indians, she initially claims that Coyote found the Indians, but as her "origin tale" progresses it becomes evident that Indians came into being without, and despite, Coyote and the settlers. By critiquing the imperialist project that seeks to inscribe, to discover, and map, King uncovers and challenges these settler presuppositions. In the dialogue between Coyote and the ducks, King satirizes the myth of discovery and colonial assumptions that settlers mark the point of origin, the center. He parodies Coyote's pose of being a critical know-it-all audience and the way in which she, like settlers, perceives herself to be the origin/creator. It is significant that Coyote does not, for instance, make the ducks (that later transform themselves into Indians) just as settler did not find Indians:

> Where did you ducks come from? I didn't make you yet. Yes, says them ducks. We were waiting around, but you didn't come. So we got tired of waiting. So we did it ourselves. (72)

Like the narrator, the ducks take over Coyote's place within the story. They deflate her by suggesting: "Maybe you're looking for Indians" and "Coyote is real surprised because she hasn't created Indians, either" (73).

In one version of the story of trickster's encounter with ducks which Paul Radin relates, Coyote deceives the ducks by telling them that they must not open their eyes or they will become red. By means of this ploy, Coyote is able to devour most of the ducks until one finally opens its eyes and warns its fellow ducks (Radin 14–16). In King's story, however, Coyote is unable to devour the ducks because the personified Mistake catches Coyote in the act and warns them (77–78). Coyote's request that the ducks close their eyes reminds us of the grandmother narrator's earlier request that Coyote "close your eyes, too" because the "first mistake in the world" is "pretty scary" (70). The grandmother's request serves as a clue that she also plays the role of trickster. Coyote now becomes the one being duped, rather than the one deceiving the ducks. Like settlers, Coyote's attempt to deceive the ducks (later, Indians) is undone, and revealed for the trickery and deception that it is.

Later, when the Coyote audience interrupts yet again and suggests that she knows the end of the story, postulating that Indians come out of the eggs, the narrator delegitimizes and negates Coyote's claim to author and authority. The narrator deflates Coyote by giving her a literal answer: "No, I says. You are one crazy Coyote. What comes out of those duck eggs are baby ducks" (78).

Throughout the story, King sets up what appears to be an opposition between two terms: "flat" and "bent" to play on the various significations of both words and transform this binary thinking into a decentered, fluid form of multiple narratives. He satirizes iconic settler characters and demonstrates how colonial icons and stereotypes are destructive.

King appears to create a flat Coyote, and a flat story. However, through the subtle identification that he weaves between the settler audience and Coyote, King subverts the reader's expectations. He ironically undercuts this seemingly flat character and story. Flat can mean a type character that fulfills our expectations, and bent can signify not flat, as well as crooked. Settlers and Coyote attempt to bend the world, to mold and re-create it to suit their expectations and fulfill their desires. Like Coyote, settlers were looking for Indians and intent on "bending the world" to suit their preconceptions. Coyote's remark that "this world is getting bent" is a tangential allusion to the narrator's former references to Coyote's flatness (73, 71). What follows are descriptions of how Coyote, in "fixing the world," literally bends it; she makes the straight river crooked, the round mountain craggy just as settlers tried to bend American Indians to fit their colonial world view. The result is that, like Coyote, settlers fell into a big hole and made a big "mistake" (70).

Coyote and the settler remain flat in the sense that they are unable to bend the world, yet they are themselves bent by King's manipulation of them. In transforming the meanings of these terms, King illustrates how when Coyote or settlers attempt to bend the world, they, and their stories, are flattened. There is a discrepancy between what Coyote (and by association, the settler) attempts to do and what she achieves; she attempts to re-create (bend) the world, but she destroys it. As the grandmother narrator suggests, Coyote may "fall on top of this story and make it flat" (78). Flat also refers to print and to unimaginative stories. Here, King adapts oral story telling techniques to bend the limitations of printed words. The multiple dialogues engage readers and, as in oral stories, encourage them to participate in this dialogue—to move beyond the flat print on the page and visualize these scenes in their imagination.

The ducks later transform into Indians who, dissatisfied with their human form, need to unbend Coyote. So they "stomp all over Coyote until she is flat like before" (79). The grandmother narrator announces the story is over, but the dissatisfied Coyote audience refuses to accept the ending: "But what happens to Coyote, says Coyote. That wonderful one is still flat" (79). Grandmother replies, "Some of these stories are flat, I says. That's what happens when you try to fix this world. This world is pretty good all by itself. Best to leave it alone" (80).

Like settlers, Coyote is unable or unwilling to accept the story or world the way it is. A *bricoleur*, Coyote sets out to fix the world (again). We laugh when grandmother warns: "When that Coyote's wandering around looking to fix things, nobody in this world is safe" (80), but ultimately we are really laughing at ourselves. The effect is unsettling.

New Relations, New Directions

> Moving from silence into speech is for the oppressed, the colonized, the exploited, and those who stand and struggle side by side, a gesture of defiance that heals, that makes new life, and new growth possible.
>
> bell hooks "*Talking Back*" 340

bell hooks describes the importance of "talking back" and explains that it is "no mere gesture of empty words"; rather, it is "the expression of moving from object to subject, that is the liberated voice" ("Talking Back" 340). Recontextualizing stereotypical terms and colonial rules of recognition within American Indian contexts, Jeannette Armstrong, Thomas King, Lee Maracle, Tomson Highway, Ruby Slipperjack, and Beatrice Culleton "talk back" to settlers and unsettle their colonial discourse, their "terminal creeds" (Vizenor *Bearheart* 192–93). Through their different trickster-like narratives which elude settler definitions, these writers move toward alternative positions of political change that contest the colonial relationship but do not replicate its terms or discourse.

In describing "a new cultural politics which engages rather than suppresses difference and which depends, in part, on the cultural constructions of new ethnic identities," Stuart Hall visualizes a "more diverse conception of ethnicity" that "does not represent itself as an ethnicity at all" ("New Ethnicities" 257). He sees the need to split ethnicity between "the dominant notion which connects it to nation and 'race'" and "a positive conception of the ethnicity of the margins, of the periphery" ("New Ethnicities" 258). Hall's paradigm of "new ethnicities" is appealing because it acknowledges that we are all "ethnically located" and "speak from a particular place, out of a particular history, out of a particular experience, a particular culture, *without being contained by that position*" ("New Ethnicities" 58; emphasis added).

In the colonial relationship, settlers in North America have repeatedly sought to contain the identities of American Indians, to sublate cultural differences and to position diverse communities and peoples into settler images. Settlers have disavowed cultural differences while at the same time invoking them to justify the civilizing mission and ongoing processes of assimilation. Colonial mimicry plays an integral role in settler efforts to assimilate American Indians; hence, it is crucial to be aware of how settlers have encouraged those they colonized to mimic them and the ways colonial mimicry has undermined diverse American Indians and their processes of cultural self-determination.

For the colonized to escape the vortex of colonial mimicry and cultural imperialism is a considerable challenge. If the colonial regime is long-standing, pre-colonial traditions may simply be out of reach in time and memory. If the colonial regime has accomplished a geographical displacement of the colonized peoples, their ancestral heritage is likely irretrievable. If the colonized have been dispossessed of their traditional economies and political infrastructures their grasp of their own rules of recognition may be weakened. If they have also suffered the loss of their own language(s), then the colonial power has succeeded in fracturing a fundamental bond between the people and their culture. What culture then survives is inevitably hybridized.

Many American Indian communities are endeavoring to re-construct their cultures from the impacts of colonization. In using the term re-construct, here, I am not suggesting that American Indians can return to a pre-contact culture nor am I suggesting that efforts to re-construct aspects of their cultures which have been eroded or lost implies that the impacts of colonization were not great. Instead, I am using the term to describe American Indian practices of self-determination in which they continue to define and determine their diverse cultures. This process is challenging because of the amount of misinformation that exists.

In mimicking and appropriating aspects of American Indian cultures, settlers erode American Indian cultures and communities.

Stereotypical images in television, literature, and other media have led American Indians in some communities to adopt customs and traditions from other American Indian cultures. For instance, I have heard about Northwest coast children who want to wear a headdress or buckskin outfit in a ceremony because they saw it on television, even though their community never wore war bonnets or buckskin outfits. In re-constructing their cultural traditions, each American Indian community has to sort through conflicting information within as well as outside their community. This process of defining what their respective cultures are is compounded because individuals may have different ideas about what constitutes their community's traditions.

Like cultures, traditions are not static. They change with the times and involve "an unceasing activity of selection, revision and outright invention" (Mulhern 253). At times, traditions can function "to defend identity against the threat of heterogeneity, discontinuity and contradiction" and "to bind (and necessarily, therefore, to exclude)" (Mulhern 253). Traditions often unite people in any given community as they commemorate shared values, beliefs, and stories. As trickster stories illustrate, traditions can also be challenged, subverted, and transformed in efforts to forge transcultural relationships. Ultimately, the issue is not what is authentic, but rather who has the right to determine authenticity. All community self-definition involves a certain amount of invention, but for American Indians the process is compounded by the need to "re-invent the invention" of "Indianness" (Blaeser 39) which settlers have constructed.

American Indians have already undergone a process of colonial hybridization. At present, there is a need for settlers to undergo a process of decolonizing *métissage*. While hybridity is a problematic term which often evokes images of colonial efforts to assimilate others and sublate cultural differences into a homogeneous construct of the settlers' making, it can also connote a creative process in which writers draw on diverse cultural traditions in their writing to re-configure them. Through hybrid narratives that draw on diverse American Indian and settler traditions and works, the authors I have examined infiltrate and alter settler perspectives and offer transcultural bridges in which readers can imagine alternative relationships and possibilities.

Their writing charts possible directions for, what Homi Bhabha terms, a "third space" (*Location* 38) of political change. These diverse relational discourses foreground American Indian relations, as well as the necessity for forging new relationships. Subversive mimicry plays with the "contradiction at the heart of mimesis wherein to mime means a chameleon-like capacity to copy any and everything in a riot of mergers and copies posing as originals" (Taussig 42). Often, the trickster-like narrative resembles a complex dance wherein it is difficult to ascertain who is copying whom. In his discussion of mimesis as "a space permeated by the colonial tension of mimesis and alterity," Taussig observes that "it is far from easy to say who is the imitator and who is the imitated, which is copy and which is original" (78). By providing multiple voices and perspectives, these narratives subvert hierarchies and dance along the colonial precipice. In choreographing shifting positions and affiliations, these writers illustrate how identity and power relationships are ever-shifting.

Through their relational, dialogic narratives, the works discussed in this book engage readers in alternative reading practices. The narratives foreground the ideological, social, political, historical, and material conditions that inform the text, its production, and its subject matter as well as the reader's own reading practice. Through subversive mimicry, these writers deploy rules of recognition which are familiar to the colonizer and re-present them in new contexts so that American Indian rules and forms of knowledge infiltrate the dominant discourse and "estrange the basis of its authority" (Bhabha *Location* 114). These innovative narratives challenge mimetic readings and engage readers in other reading practices.[1] Readers who think that they are reading a familiar literary form and interpret American Indian narratives according to settler literary principles and values find themselves tricked. They often experience a shock of recognition which may well lead them to interrogate the colonial relationship and discourse.

Like the oral storytelling traditions that inform them, these fluid, open-ended narratives approximate oral storytelling performances in which there is an ongoing interaction between the teller, the tale, and the audience. As in oral stories, these authors and their narratives do not presume to explain or offer new rules but open dialogues in which readers create and re-create meaning each time they read and re-visit these stories. Dialogic narrative strategies enable these writers to present exchanges in which cultural differences remain heterogeneous while at the same time mapping out terrains in which writers and readers can bridge (not eliminate) cultural differences. The interplay of intertextual references from diverse cultures transforms the settler narratives to which they allude so that readers no longer read them without also remembering these new contexts.

These narratives also offer new paradigms for teaching American Indian literature, and literature generally. In his critique of contemporary education, Paulo Freire uses the metaphor of a banking system in which educators, wielding power and authority as so-called experts, deposit their knowledge into the minds of their students. According to this model, the students are passive; their minds are like empty receptacles. This banking model of education is not unlike the colonial view of the New World as a *tabula rasa* and the civilizing mission wherein missionaries and educators imposed their language, values, and beliefs on American Indians.

In contrast to this colonial image of education, the narratives discussed in this volume encourage a dialogic model in which teachers and students learn from one another and from the narrative and their interactions with it. Those readers and instructors who lack the American Indian cultural codes and frames of reference implicit in these texts may become othered, and this experience can heighten their awareness of the disempowering effects of colonial constructs of alterity. Their unfamiliarity with American Indian cultural contexts unsettles colonial assumptions of authority. At the same time, these new contexts articulate cultural differences and encourage readers to recognize the different signifying practices at play in these works and to acknowledge their own positions.

Throughout this book, I have analyzed how these narratives unsettle readers and facilitate the process of decolonization. Academics engaged in post-colonial studies have complicity in the colonizing process because of their institutional affiliation and position of privilege. Marcia Crosby observes: "The academics get the M.A.s and the Ph.D.s—they are the ones whose prestige increased with their degrees in their own communities. Their research and publications, however, often only produce another Imaginary Indian" (108). Crosby's comments underscore the power imbalance that continues to exist in North America and foregrounds issues of access and voice. Elaborating, she writes: "Western interest in Aboriginal peoples has really been self-interest" (85); their interest does not represent American Indians. Joy Asham Fedorick argues that in scrutinizing American Indians, the settler frequently "procrastinates from looking at 'self'" (55). While I agree with Crosby that settler readings of American Indian literature reveal the reader's interests and assumptions, I do not think this means that only American Indians can write about American Indian material.[2] To take such a position is, as Margery Fee points out, another form of oppression, of silencing (178–79). Moreover, settlers who refrain from reading or studying American Indian literature contribute to the disavowal and marginalization of American Indian writers and their works.

The subversive strategies used by the writers addressed in the preceding pages have relevance to all writers and readers engaged in the ongoing process of decolonization. These writers, and their works, are also an inspiration to literary critics who seek alternative theoretical approaches to contest colonial binary oppositions (First World-Third World, Subject-Object, Us-Them, Civilized-Savage). Their inclusion of the double-voiced colonial discourse critically acknowledges the historical reality of colonialism and power relations. By partially representing while also re-presenting this discourse in multi-voiced relational narratives, writers can disavow the colonial discourse and offer alternative literary paradigms. Through trickster strategies, they can cast off colonial definitions, offering readers a world in which colonialism no longer exists. Writers can refuse to be confined by settler definitions of nationalism and ethnicity. Like tricksters, their multi-voiced narratives elude easy definitions and stereotypes. Subversive mimicry unsettles colonial discourse and encourages readers to imagine other possibilities.

Notes

Preface

1. Throughout the book, I primarily use the term *American Indians*, although I also use *Natives, First Nations, Aboriginals,* and *Indians* to refer to the nations and peoples that inhabited North America prior to the arrival of settlers. I primarily use the term *American Indians* to refer to diverse peoples that live in Canada and in the United States. Many American Indians do not recognize the validity of the border between Canada and the United States and have traditional territorities that pre-date settler boundaries. I also refer to Okanagan, Cree, Ojibway, and Cherokee peoples. In using these different terms, I have respected what each individual chooses to call him/herself.

2. Gayatri Spivak discusses the importance of strategic essentialism in *The Post-Colonial Critic* 11–12, 45.

3. The term "civilizing mission" refers to the process wherein settlers attempted to "civilize" those they colonized.

4. I use Homi Bhabha's phrase "rules of recognition" (*Location* 114) throughout the book. Henceforth, I do not put these terms in quotation marks.

5. Throughout, I use the term *settler* as a descriptive term that points to the historical process of colonization which continues to this day.

6. Brydon does not use the concept "literary contamination" in a pejorative sense. Nevertheless, I prefer to use the term *literary infiltration* to highlight the agency of American Indian writers.

7.   For a useful discussion of hybridity, see Robert Young's *Colonial Desire: Hybridity in Theory, Culture and Race*. The first chapter of his book provides a good overview of the history of racist theories and discourse and of the ways in which literary critics have considered literary and linguistic hybridity.

8.   There are several good introductions to American Indian literature. *Looking at the Words of Our People: First Nations Analysis of Literature* provides essays written by American Indians while Penny Petrone's *Native Literature in Canada: From Oral Tradition to the Present* (1990) provides an introduction to the study of the literature from a non-Native perspective. A. LaVonne Brown Ruoff's *American Indian Literatures* provides an introduction to, and excellent bibliographic review of, American Indian literatures while *Studies in American Indian Literatures* is a good teaching tool for scholars in the field and provides both essays and suggestions for course designs.

Chapter One. Dancing along the Precipice

1.   Graham Huggan discusses mimesis as it pertains to cartography. Michael Taussig provides an extensive analysis of mimesis in *Mimesis and Alterity*.

2.   As I will later illustrate, writers may use mimicry subversively to estrange readers from colonial rules of recognition so that readers may "become Other" (Taussig xiii).

3.   The following chapters illustrate how writers can assert agency and subvert this power imbalance through modes of subversive mimicry in which their re-presentation claims, or takes away, power from the original.

4.   For a more detailed discussion of residential schools, see Celia Haig-Brown's *Resistance and Renewal: Surviving the Indian Residential School*.

5.   Joe Hovaugh's name is a satirical allusion to Jehovah. The

name Red Matthews alludes to the apostle Matthew and recontextualizes this biblical figure within an American Indian framework. King is also alluding to Robin Matthews, a leftist (Red) Canadian nationalist.

6. Rose explains that Cherokee critic Geary Hobson coined the expression "whiteshaman movement." The term "whiteshaman" refers to those settlers "who in their poems assume the persona of the shaman" (Rose 403).

7. For a historical analysis of the "Indian problem" see Noel Dyck's "Negotiating the Indian 'Problem.'"

8. James Baldwin used the expression, "bear the burden," in a piece in the London *Observer* (Williams and Chrisman 434). Achebe discusses the English language and the challenges that African writers face (*Morning Yet on Creation Day* 91–103).

9. Thiong'o writes in his native Gikuyu, a language spoken in Kenya. He is willing to translate his texts into English, however. For his discussion about the effects of speaking, writing, and reading in English see "The Language of African Literature" in *Decolonising the Mind: The Politics of Language in African Literature*.

10. For an extended discussion of "epistemic violence" see Gayatri Spivak's "Can the Subaltern Speak?"

11. I use the lower case, here, to indicate english variants that writers use to articulate cultural differences which may include, for instance, dialects, colloquial, and idiomatic expressions. These english variants often serve to challenge Standard English.

12. Michael Taussig describes how "the copy takes power from the original" (59).

13. I do not intend to suggest that these works do not operate on multiple levels and speak to diverse voices. They do. In drawing on Bakhtin's terminology, I am well aware that I am opening myself up to the charge of perpetuating the very

colonial binary oppositions I am investigating. However, my intent is not to perpetuate this opposition but to examine how these writers re-deploy it to create multi-accented texts.

14.   The story of the witchery exemplifies the refusal to assign blame to any single individual, gender or group (134). No one knows what tribe the witch who tells the story is from, and no one knows whether the witch is a man or a woman.

15.   In *The Pedagogy of the Oppressed*, Paulo Freire discusses how the oppressed can only liberate themselves, they cannot liberate/change the oppressor.

16.   Throughout I use subversive mirror and trickster mirror to describe how they both reflect and refract the colonial discourse and rules of recognition.

17.   I am drawing on Homi Bhabha's discussion of hybridity in which he argues that "other 'denied' knowledges enter upon the dominant discourse and estrange the basis of its authority—its rules of recognition" (*Location* 114).

Chapter Two. To Know the Difference

1.   The experiences of colonization differ substantially between and within diverse American Indian and West Indian communities. Like Thomas King's work, Derek Walcott's poem speaks about particular colonial contexts yet has resonance for many colonized people around the world.

2.   I am indebted to Pat Stone for her on-line posting to the Native Literature discussion. *"The Durbin Feeling's Cherokee-English Dictionary* translates the epigrams in King's novel: 1. East Red 2. South White 3. West Black 4. North Blue" (Pat Stone, NativeLit serve @cornell, 1 May 1996). As I later discuss, by using Cherokee scripts at the beginning of each section King defamiliarizes readers.

3.   According to Paula Gunn Allen, First Mother "enjoined cooperation and sharing on all her children" and is "deeply connected to water" (*The Sacred Hoop* 3, 25). Changing

Woman is the "major goddess figure among the Diné,
particularly connected to puberty ceremonies and healing
(Gunn Allen *Grandmothers of the Light* 235). "Grandmother
Spider, Thought Woman, thought the earth, the sky, the
galaxy, and all that is into being, and as she thinks, so we
are" (*Grandmothers of the Light* 28). Thought Woman
embodies survival and weaves human beings "in a fabric of
interconnection" (*The Sacred Hoop* 11).

4   Although King cites Harry Robinson's *Write It on Your Heart*
      as the only "complete example we have of interfusional
      literature," *Green Grass, Running Water* provides yet another
      example of this hybrid form of writing ("Godzilla" 13). King
      writes that Robinson has been "a source of inspiration and
      influence" for him ("Godzilla" 14).

5.   There are many variations on this phrase. For instance, see
      the discussion of treaty negotiations in "As Long as the Sun
      Shines and Water Flows: An Historical Comment" (Getty
      and Lussier 1–26).

6.   When one holds the paperback edition of *Green Grass,
      Running Water* (Toronto: HarperPerennial, 1994) up to the
      light, the image of Coyote is superimposed on the
      photograph of Thomas King.

7.   Coyote can be either male or female and referred to as either
      he or she.

8.   As tricksters, the four Indians are capable of constructive as
      well as destructive acts. Hawkeye tells Babo that they
      "fixed up part of the world," although Ishmael also
      acknowledges that "part of it got messed up, too" (357).
      Overall, however, the four Indians have attempted to redress
      the mistakes and imbalances of settler society. They
      appropriate Babo's, Dr. Hovaugh's, Charlie's, and Alberta's
      cars and use them to sabotage the dam, although it is also
      Coyote's singing and dancing that causes the earthquake
      that leads to the breakup of the dam. They also help Lionel
      reunite with his community, and they revise the ending of the
      Hollywood western so that the Indians are victorious. John

Wayne, who typifies a settler icon of the "rugged individual" that tames the "savage" frontier, dies.

9. Henceforth, when I refer to mimics in this chapter I am talking about colonial mimics.

10. This scene has resonance for those readers who are familiar with King's satiric short story, "A Seat in the Garden," where Joe Hovaugh (Jehovah) yells at the Indian standing in his garden, "This is private property. You people ever hear of private property?" (*One Good Story, That One* 84).

11. The reference to the "blackwhalesbian" (163) also foreshadows the friendship between Changing Woman and Moby-Jane.

12. King critiques miscegenation by describing how the western that Eli reads, like most of the westerns he has read, always concludes with the Indian chief who sends the white woman away and returns to "his people." As Eli points out, "Western writers seldom let Indians sleep with whites" (166).

13. As I discuss further on, King critiques the ways settler institutions imprison Indians. There are frequent retellings of how American Indians have been imprisoned in Fort Marion. Lionel is incarcerated. Dr. Hovaugh's treatment of the four Indians at his hospital, the doctors' treatment of Lionel at the Hospital for Sick Children in Toronto, and the medical professionals' treatment of Alberta often result in mistakes and reveal settler prejudices.

14. For a historical account of the controversy over the Great Whale River and the James Bay and Northern Quebec Agreement of 1975, see Dickason's *Canada's First Nations: A History of Founding Peoples from Earliest Times* (405).

15. Congress later passed the pueblo lands act which was supposed to guarantee the Pueblos titles to their lands.

16. King makes the allusion to Christopher Columbus more obvious when Portland explains that C. B. Cologne stands

for Crystal Ball Cologne, a fragrance C. B.'s mother liked
(152).

17. For a historical analysis of the White Paper (1969) and its
consequences, see Dickason's *Canada's First Nations: A
History of Founding Peoples from Earliest Times* (385–89).

18. I am alluding to V. S. Naipaul's term, which he uses in his
novel entitled *The Mimic Men*. The term refers to colonial
mimics.

19. I have not included the four Indian tricksters because at
times they are four men and at other times they are First
Woman, Changing Woman, Thought Woman, and Old
Woman.

20. Significantly, the gynecologist whom she consults for
information about artificial insemination is called Dr. Mary.

21. King alludes to figures in settler literature and history in his
choice of names for Alberta's students: Henry Dawes, John
Collier, Mary Rowlandson, Elaine Goodale, Hannah Duston,
Helen Mooney. All the names with the exception of Helen
Mooney refer to the authors of captivity narratives.

22. Like Harlan in *Medicine River*, Norma exhibits trickster-like
characteristics. She meddles in Lionel's relations with
Alberta and encourages him to attend the sun dance.

23. Elijah Harper, a member of the provincial Manitoba
legislature, delayed ratification in the Manitoba legislation
thus allowing the Meech Lake Accord to expire before a
sufficient number of provinces had ratified it. For a historical
account of Harper's role, see Dickason's *Canada's First
Nations: A History of Founding Peoples from Earliest Times*
(409).

Chapter Three. Listening to Silences

1. Gregory Bateson first used the term *frame* in 1955 "to explain
how individuals exchange signals that allow them to agree
upon the level of abstraction at which any message is

intended" (Tannen "What's in a frame?" 141).

2. The phrase "all my relations" alludes to the importance of relatives and of relationships. In Thomas King's introduction to *All My Relations*, an anthology he edited, he explains that the phrase is "a reminder of who we are and of our relationship with both our family and our relatives" (ix). However, it also refers to the relationship people have with "all human beings" and with "all the animate and inanimate forms that can be seen or imagined" (ix). Thus, the phrase conveys the "web of kinship" (ix). King adds that the phrase is "an encouragement for us to accept the responsibilities we have within this universal family by living our lives in a harmonious and moral manner (a common admonishment is to say of someone that they act as if they have no relations)" (ix).

3. Throughout, I use "a language of silences" to refer to the unspoken silent words of Ojibway traditions and the characters' thoughts, feelings, and memories. I use language to remind readers that these silences are part of the continuum of language.

4. For numerous examples of the ways in which silence and speech complement each other, see Adam Jaworski's *The Power of Silence: Social and Pragmatic Perspectives*.

5. Gregory Bateson coined the term *double bind*.

6. Jensen and Tannen discuss the ambiguity of silence. They analyze silence within binary constructs, whereas Slipperjack refutes binarism because she depicts the multiple meanings inherent in the ambiguity of silence.

7. I am referring to the cover, which Slipperjack illustrated, on the paperback edition of *Silent Words* (Saskatoon: Fifth House, 1992).

8. Visual stimuli can interfere: "When interaction is structured through silence, for example, in a dance or a football game, dependence on the visual channel is so great that any talk that *accompanies* the interaction (but does not turn away

from it) is secondary to the co-occurring visual stimuli and physical activities (Philips qtd. in Jaworski 50). Similarly, Lord discovered, and Ong reiterates, "Learning to read and write disables the oral poet," because it "introduces into his mind the concept of a text as controlling the narrative and thereby interferes with the oral composing processes, which have nothing to do with texts but are 'the remembrance of songs sung'" (Ong 59).

9. Here, I am arguing that rememoration is commemoration from a position of having been silenced. Toni Morrison coined the term *rememoration* ("Unspeakable Things Unspoken" 1–34). In *The Location of Culture*, Homi Bhabha elaborates on Morrison's term (198).

10. I am using *holotropic* to refer, as the word suggests, to holistic.

11. Thomas King discusses how *Honour the Sun* is an example of "associational literature" ("Godzilla" 15). The characteristics of "associational literature" that he outlines here are also evident in *Silent Words*.

12. I use english with a lower case e here to differentiate it from Standard English. Throughout her novel, Slipperjack validates Ojibway variants of the english language by using dialect and colloquial language.

Chapter Four. Stereotypography

1. When Culleton's first novel was reissued in 1984, the title changed to *April Raintree*. The reissued version deletes the emphasis on the search for an identity and only provides the name of the protagonist.

2. Homi Bhabha discusses this simultaneous process of sameness and difference in the colonial discourse and the civilizing mission. He describes how "stereotypical racial discourse is a four-term strategy" (*Location* 77) and writes: "In any specific colonial discourse the metaphoric/narcissistic and the metonymic/aggressive positions will

function simultaneously, strategically poised in relation to each other" (*Location* 77).

3.   I am extending George Lakoff's view of stereotypes as "cases of metonym" here. Lakoff writes: "social stereotypes are cases of metonymy—where a subcategory has a socially recognized status as standing for the category as a whole, usually for the purpose of making quick judgements about people" (79).

4.   Bhabha's conception of the construction of otherness and his four-term strategy of the colonial stereotype are consistent with his analysis of the colonial relationship as one in which colonizers encourage the colonized to mimic them, but the colonized are disavowed.

5.   Some cognitive theorists confirm Bhabha's conception of stereotypes in their suggestion that, "stereotypes may reflect a justification or rationalization for emotions felt when around the outgroup" (Vanman and Miller 228).

6.   An illusory correlation is a false equation in which a person makes a judgment based on two or more variables that were not linked in the information that the person originally received (Hamilton, Stroessner, and Mackie 44).

7.   The term *apple* is a derogatory reference that suggests that an American Indian is red on the outside and white on the inside. While Cheryl's nickname is a term of endearment rather than a derogatory term here, the reference foreshadows Cheryl's later perception that her sister is denying her identity.

8.   While skin color may be used as a basis for racial discrimination, it is not the underlying cause.

9.   This is the American ideal of the "Great Society" which President Johnson voiced in the 1960s. Like Slash, Cheryl sees this as a myth, a "fake idea" (*Slash* 36).

10. Examples of Cheryl's validation of an alterNative discourse abound (57, 75, 77–78, 84–85, 95, 168–70).

11. While April identifies with her mother's fair skin and Cheryl identifies with her father's American Indian ancestry, their parents are métis. Their mother is Irish and Ojibway and their father is "of mixed blood" (9).

12. These statements are particular to these cases and not generalizable to all races and nationalities.

13. Duke Redbird describes the importance of raising Métis consciousness and discusses a distinct Métis identity (Redbird in Moses and Goldie 121–28).

Chapter Five. Re-place That Monument

1. The term *cultural imperialism* was coined in the 1960s. Edward Said describes how Jacques Lang made this term fashionable (*Culture and Imperialism* 291). I agree with John Tomlinson that "the concept of cultural imperialism must be assembled out of its discourse" and often involves "a variety of different articulations which may have certain features in common, but may also be in tension with each other, or even mutually contradictory" (9).

2. See Toni Morrison's "Unspeakable Things Unspoken."

3. I refer to the protagonist as Tommy for all incidents that occur prior to the scene when Mardi renames him Slash.

4. Armstrong describes how she decided to make Slash "a traditional person who goes through a metamorphosis" because the traditional "was what I was most comfortable with myself" (qtd. in Williamson 19).

5. For further details about Armstrong's research and creative processes see her interview with Janice Williamson (*Sounding Differences* 14–18).

6. I agree with Fentress and Wickham's observation that social memory can be selective and inaccurate, but this is not always the case (xi). As they point out, the question of accuracy is not particularly relevant to the meaning of social memory which "is little affected by its truth; all that matters

is that it be believed, at least on some level" (xi).

7. In an interview with Karin Beeler, Armstrong explains that she "wanted to see how the narrative [*Slash*] would work with the transfer of orality into a written form" (qtd. in Beeler 146).

8. Michael Harkin adapts Mikhail Bakhtin's idea of chronotypes here.

9. To wit, the Constitution of the United States claims that "all men are created equal"; women are absent and other groups are marginalized and/or excluded by settler constructions that deem them inhuman, not men.

10. Clyde Warrior used the term "Tomahawks" to describe "young people coming home who are somewhat verbal, who have some knowledge of how the mechanics of government and American institutions work" (Robert Warrior 28–29).

11. In examining propaganda, Walter Lippmann used the term "manufacture of consent" (Herman and Chomsky xi). Edward Herman and Noam Chomsky analyze how media are often shaped by an elite consensus in *Manufacturing Consent: The Political Economy of the Mass Media*.

12. When I have taught this text, many of the students commented that they learned a lot about American Indian histories and had not been aware of most of these events, or of the extent of American Indian activism in Canada.

13. In an interview with Karin Beeler, Armstrong discusses the scene where Slash sings Uncle Joe's dance song: "Songs in the Okanagan are very healing." She points out that "for a person like Slash, the ability to rebalance and the ability to heal and to put things back together on an emotional and a spiritual level are not possible without the songs" (qtd. in Beeler 147).

14. See Julia Emberley's diagram of the cultural differences in chapter one in *Slash* (*Thresholds of Difference* 133).

15. Michael Harkin is drawing on the work of Paul Ricoeur (*Temps et recit*, vol. 1, 127–28) and Martin Heidegger (*The Basic Problems of Phenomenology* 261–74).

16. In an interview with Janice Williamson, Armstrong says:
    But because there are categories of people in North America, there needs to be some word which describes us in a generic sense, and so I prefer *Indian*, mainly because it is a word that was used in some of Columbus's writings to describe who we were, *Indian* coming from *in deo*, meaning 'in with God' (qtd. in Williamson 11).

17. In outlining how the different people Slash meets have diverse positions, Armstrong depicts the diversity of political perspectives during this period of history. For a historical overview of this period, see Robert Allen Warrior's *Tribal Secrets: Recovering American Indian Intellectual Traditions* (26–44 and 87–98). Alvin M. Josephy's *Red Power: The American Indians' Fight for Freedom* includes documents about resistance activities during this period while Kenneth S. Stern's *Loud Hawk* provides an interesting discussion of Anna Mae Aquash and of others in the American Indian movement.

Chapter Six. Raven's Song

1. Maracle illustrates how songs facilitate memories in the scene where Grampa Thomas sings "searching for memory; singing helped him unleash the memory of his ancestors" (97).

2. Maracle refers to Raven as "she" throughout the novel. In so doing, she reinforces the transformative and creative power of women in Stacey's village. In keeping with *Ravensong*, all references to this trickster will use the feminine form.

3. For further information on this topic, see Millie R. Creighton's "Revisiting Shame and Guilt Cultures: A Forty-Year Pilgrimage." Orthodox psychoanalytic theory also sets up a dichotomy between shame and guilt, viewing guilt as

"the adult emotion of self-control, with shame thought of as 'regressive'" (Scheff 79).

4. Stacey's village also uses shame as a means of social control as is evident when Snake is banished. However, this chapter focuses on the shame that often arises when colonized people internalize the lens of the colonizer.

5. Schneider also discusses shame as recognition (25).

6. For a more detailed discussion of residential schools, see Celia Haig Brown's *Resistance and Renewal: Surviving the Indian Residential School.*

7. I have used *sic* because Dominic's comment about indiscretion suggests that Maracle meant indiscreet, not indiscrete, here.

8. Maracle explains how Raven is the heart of the people (qtd. in Lutz 174).

Chapter Seven. Tricking In/Subordination

1. I use the term *traditional* here to refer to the oral traditions of trickster stories. I do not intend to suggest that there is a single tradition.

2. William Bright discusses how trickster appears as Raven and, in some instances, as Bluejay in the Pacific Northwest. In the Northern Plains, trickster appears as Spider while in the Southeast, he/she is called Hare (4). Tomson Highway discusses how trickster is called "'Weesageechak' in Cree, 'Nanabush' in Ojibway, 'Raven' in others, 'Coyote' in still others" (*Dry Lips Oughta Move to Kapuskasing* 12). Louis Owens describes how in many parts of Canada and the United States, there are references to Nanabush, "wenebojo (or manibozho, nanibozhu, and so on)" (239).

3. As mentioned in chapter five, Jeannette Armstrong describes the Okanagan order of life learning in which individuals are encouraged to "move toward full capacity as either male or female" (Cardinal and Armstrong 102). As elders, they

"emerge as both male and female, a complete human, with all skills and capacities complete" (Cardinal and Armstrong 102).

4. Henry Louis Gates also makes this observation in his analysis of African trickster figures (19).

5. Griever's use of the word *listen* reminds readers of the importance of listening to oral stories.

6. In describing the Winnebago trickster cycle, Babara Babcock gives an example of this cultural transgression and satiric inversion (173).

7. Henceforth, I abbreviate *The Rez Sisters* as *Rez* and *Dry Lips Oughta Move to Kapuskasing* as *Dry Lips*.

8. Marie-Adele's comment also foreshadows her liberation and subsequent death.

9. In this chapter, all subsequent references to trickster refer to post-colonial trickster figures, unless stated otherwise. Gerald Vizenor also describes how trickster, as a communal sign in a language game does not participate in binary categories (*Narrative Chance* 202).

10. I refer to trickster as he when discussing *The Rez Sisters* and as she when discussing *Dry Lips Oughta Move to Kapuskasing* because Highway does. The reader, however, should bear in mind that trickster is "weetha" (him/her).

11. For an interesting discussion of how Tomson Highway draws on the blues tradition, see Roberta Imboden, "On the Road with Tomson Highway's Blues Harmonica in 'Dry Lips Oughta Move to Kapuskasing.'" Imboden also discusses how the harmonica can "mimic the human voice" (114).

12. Highway plans on writing a "cycle of 'rez' plays, seven in all" (Denis Johnston 263).

13. I am using Mikhail Bakhtin's definition of this term:
    Dialogism is the characteristic epistemological mode of a world dominated by heteroglossia. Everything means, is understood, as a part of a greater

whole—there is a constant interaction between meanings, all of which have the potential of conditioning others. Which will affect the other, how it will do so and in what degree is what is actually settled at the moment of utterance. This dialogic imperative, mandated by the pre-existence of the language world relative to any of its current inhabitants, insures that there can be no actual monologue. (426)

14. I am using *holotropic* to mean whole, three-dimensional.

15. I am borrowing the phrase, "imperial eyes," from Mary Louise Pratt.

16. In reference to another of his stories, Atwood describes King's technique as: "a double-bladed knife" (244).

17. S/he is the narrator of the frame story in which she is also at times Coyote's audience. King only uses the term grandfather once. The rest of the time she is called grandmother. For the purpose of concision, I will refer to her as grandmother, although the reader should bear in mind that, like a trickster, she can be either male or female. Likewise, Coyote can be male or female but I will refer, as King does, to Coyote as she. The grandmother/grandfather figure is an Elder. King also uses dialogues between Coyote and an Elder in *Green Grass, Running Water*.

18. I refer to this as a paradigm because the role of the teller(s) is ironic; King creates what appears to be a series of dialogues—interactions between teller and listener (Narrator-Coyote, Coyote-Narrator, Narrator-Coyote). The apparent freedom of multiple levels of discourse and of interpretations is illusory.

19. I am borrowing Frank Kermode's phrase here. See *The Sense of an Ending: Studies in the Theory of Fiction*.

20. In reiterating some of trickster's hybrid characteristics here, I use "and" to avoid binary oppositions.

21. In a similar vein, David Moore states that, although "the ontology within Euroamerican colonialism has been concerned with agency within subjectivity," American Indians "have become concerned since contact more directly

with agency within subjection" (373). Here, however, I am arguing that trickster strategies of insubordination foreground the agency of American Indians and contest subjection without perceiving themselves in colonial constructs or terms.

Epilogue. New Relations, New Directions

1. In his discussion of post-colonial texts, Homi Bhabha also warns against mimetic readings and argues that readers need to undergo a shift in reading strategies ("Representation" 95, 98).

2. All readings, interpretations, of literature reveal the reader's interests to some extent.

Bibliography

Achebe, Chinua. *Morning Yet on Creation Day*. New York: Anchor, 1975.

——. "The African Writer and the English Language." *Colonial Discourse and Post-Colonial Theory: A Reader*. Eds. Patrick Williams and Laura Chrisman. New York: Columbia UP, 1994. 428–35.

Acoose, Janice. *Iskwewak-Kah' Ki Yaw Ni Wahkomakanak: Neither Indian Princesses Nor Easy Squaws*. Toronto: Women's Press, 1995.

Adam, Ian, and Helen Tiffin, eds. *Past the Last Post: Theorizing Post-Colonialism and Post-Modernism*. Calgary: U of Calgary P, 1990.

Adorno, T. W., E. Frenkel-Brunswik, D. J. Levinson, and R. N. Sanford. *The Authoritarian Personality: Studies in Prejudice*. New York: Norton, 1950.

Allen, Paula Gunn. *Grandmothers of the Light*. Boston: Beacon, 1991.

——. *The Sacred Hoop: Recovering the Feminine in American Indian Traditions*. Boston: Beacon, 1986.

——. "Teaching American Indian Oral Literatures." *Studies in American Indian Literature Critical Essays and Course Designs*. Ed. Paula Gunn Allen. New York: MLA, 1983. 33–51.

Allport, Gordon, W. *The Nature of Prejudice*. Unabridged. 1954. Reading: Addison-Wesley, 1979.

Anderson, Benedict. *Imagined Communities: Reflections on the Origin and Spread of Nationalism*. 1983. Rev. ed. London: Verso, 1991.

Anzaldúa, Gloria, ed. *Making Face, Making Soul: Creative and Critical Perspectives by Feminists of Color*. San Francisco: Aunt Lute, 1990.

Armstrong, Jeannette. *Breath Tracks*. Vancouver: Williams-Wallace/ Theytus, 1991.

——, ed. *Looking at the Words of Our People: First Nations Analysis of Literature*. Penticton: Theytus, 1993.

——. *Slash*. Penticton: Theytus, 1985.

Ashcroft, Bill, Gareth Griffiths, and Helen Tiffin. *The Empire Writes Back: Theory and Practice in Post-Colonial Literatures*. London: Routledge, 1989.

Ashcroft, W. D. "Constitutive Graphonomy: A Post-Colonial Theory of Literary Writing." *After Europe: Critical Theory and Post-Colonial Writing*. Eds. Stephen Slemon and Helen Tiffin. Sydney: Dangaroo, 1989. 58–73.

Atwood, Margaret. "A Double-Bladed Knife: Subversive Laughter in Two Stories by Thomas King." *Native Writers and Canadian Writing. Canadian Literature: Special Issue*. Ed. W. H. New. Vancouver: U of British Columbia P, 1990. 243–54.

Auerbach, Erich. *Mimesis: The Representation of Reality in Western Literature*. Trans. Willard. R. Trask. Princeton: Princeton UP, 1953.

Babcock, Barbara. "A Tolerated Margin of Mess: The Trickster and His Tales Reconsidered." *Critical Essays on Native American Literature*. Ed. Andrew Wiget. Boston: Hall, 1985. 3–185.

Bakhtin, M. M. *The Dialogic Imagination*. Ed. Michael Holquist. Trans. Caryl Emerson and Michael Holquist. Austin: U of Texas P, 1981.

Baldwin, James. *The Fire Next Time*. 1962. New York: Vintage, 1993.

Becker, Alton, L. *Beyond Translation: Essays Towards a Modern Philology*. Ann Arbor: U of Michigan P, 1995.

Beeler, Karin. "Image, Music, Text: An Interview with Jeannette Armstrong." *Studies in Canadian Literature* 21.2 (1996): 143–54.

Benjamin, Walter. *Illuminations: Essays and Reflections*. Trans. Harry Zohn. Ed. Hannah Arendt. New York: Schocken, 1968.

——. *Reflections: Essays, Aphorisms, Autobiographical Writings*. Trans. Edmund Jephcott. Ed. Peter Demetz. New York: Schocken, 1978.

Bentley, D. M. R. "Savage, Degenerate, and Dispossessed: Some Sociological, Anthropological, and Legal Backgrounds to the Depiction of Native Peoples in Early Long Poems on Canada." *Native Writers and Canadian Writing. Canadian Literature: Special Issue.* Ed. W. H. New. Vancouver: U of British Columbia P, 1990. 76–92.

Berger, John. *Ways of Seeing.* London: BBC, 1972.

Berkhofer, Robert F. Jr. *The White Man's Indian.* New York: Random, 1979.

Bhabha, Homi K. "Cultural Diversity and Cultural Differences." *The Post-Colonial Studies Reader.* Eds. Bill Ashcroft, Gareth Griffiths, and Helen Tiffin. London: Routledge, 1995.

——. "Difference, Discrimination and the Discourse of Colonialism." *The Politics of Theory.* Ed. Francis Barker et al. Colchester: U of Essex P, 1983. 194–211.

——. "DissemiNation: Time, Narrative, and the Margins of the Modern Nation." *Nation and Narration.* Ed. Homi K. Bhabha. London: Routledge, 1990. 291–322.

——. *The Location of Culture.* London: Routledge, 1994.

——. "Of Mimicry and Man: The Ambivalence of Colonial Discourse." *October* 28 (84): 125–33.

——, ed. *Nation and Narration.* London: Routledge, 1990.

——. "The Other Question: Homi K. Bhabha Reconsiders the Stereotype and Colonial Discourse." *Screen* 24.6 (1983): 18–36.

——. "Representation and the Colonial Text: A Critical Exploration of Some Forms of Mimeticism." *The Theory of Reading.* Ed. Frank Gloversmith. Brighton: Harvester, 1984. 93–122.

——. "Signs Taken for Wonders: Questions of Ambivalence and Authority under a Tree Outside Delhi, May 1817." *Critical Inquiry* 12 (1985): 144–65. Rpt. in *"Race," Writing, and Difference.* Ed. Henry Louis Gates, Jr. Chicago: Chicago UP, 1986. 163–84.

Blaeser, Kimberly M. *Gerald Vizenor: Writing in the Oral Tradition.* Norman: U of Oklahoma P, 1996.

Bloom, Harold. *The Anxiety of Influence: A Theory of Poetry.*

180 Bibliography

Oxford: Oxford UP, 1973.

Boire, Gary. "Sucking Kumaras." Rev. of *Fear and Temptation*, by Terry Goldie. *Native Writers and Canadian Writing. Canadian Literature: Special Issue*. Ed. W. H. New. Vancouver: U of British Columbia P, 1990. 301–6.

Boldt, Menno, and J. Anthony Long in association with Leroy Little Bear, eds. *The Quest for Justice: Aboriginal Peoples and Aboriginal Rights*. Toronto: U of Toronto P, 1985.

Bouson, J. Brooks. *The Empathetic Reader: A Study of the Narcissistic Character and the Drama of the Self*. Amherst: U of Massachusetts P, 1989.

Bright, William. *A Coyote Reader*. Berkeley: U of California P, 1993.

Brody, Hugh. *Maps and Dreams: Indians and the British Columbia Frontier*. 1981. Vancouver: Douglas & McIntyre, 1988.

Bruchac, Joseph. *Survival This Way: Interviews with American Indian Poets*. Tuscon: U of Arizona P, 1987.

Bruneau, T. J. "Communicative Silences: Forms and Functions." *The Journal of Communication* 23 (1973): 17–46.

Brydon, Diana, and Helen Tiffin. *Decolonising Fictions*. Sydney: Dangaroo, 1993.

——. "The White Inuit Speaks: Contamination as Literary Strategy." *Past the Last Post: Theorizing Post-Colonialism and Post-Modernism*. Eds. Ian Adam and Helen Tiffin. Calgary: U of Calgary P, 1990. 191–203.

Bynum, David E. *The Daemon in the Wood: A Study of Oral Narrative Patterns*. Cambridge: Harvard UP, 1978.

Campbell, Maria. *Halfbreed*. Toronto: Goodread Biographies 1983. Originally published by McClelland and Stewart, 1973. Published in a Seal Books edition in 1979.

——, and Doreen Jensen, Joy Asham Fedorick et al., eds. *Give Back: First Nations Perspectives on Cultural Practice*. Vancouver: Gallerie Women Artists' Monographs, 1992.

Cardinal, Douglas, and Jeannette Armstrong. *The Native Creative Process*. Penticton: Theytus, 1991.

Cassidy, Frank, and Robert L. Bish. *Indian Government: Its Meaning in Practice*. Lantzville: Oolichan, 1989.

Césaire, Aimé. *Discourse on Colonialism*. Trans. Joan Pinkham. New York: Monthly Review 1972. Originally published as *Discours sur le colonialisme* by Présence Africaine, 1955.

Chambers, Iain, and Lidia Curti, eds. *The Post-Colonial Question: Common Skies, Divided Horizons*. London: Routledge, 1996.

Chatterjee, Partha. *Nationalist Thought and the Colonial World: A Derivative Discourse?* Delhi: Oxford UP, 1986.

Clark, Ella Elizabeth. *Indian Legends of Canada*. 1960. Toronto: McClelland & Stewart, 1992.

Coltelli, Laura. *Winged Words: American Indian Writers Speak*. Lincoln: U of Nebraska P, 1990. 135–53.

Commager, Henry Steele, and Milton Cantor, eds. *Documents of American History Since 1898*. Vol. II. Englewood Cliffs: Prentice Hall, 1988. 852–55.

Cornell, George L. "The Imposition of Western Definitions of Literature on Indian Oral Traditions." *The Native in Literature: Canadian and Comparative Perspectives*. Eds. Thomas King, Cheryl Calver, and Helen Hoy. Oakville: ECW, 1987. 174–87.

Cove, John J., and George F. MacDonald, eds. *Tricksters, Shamans and Heroes: Tsimshian Narratives I*. Collected by Marius Barbeau and William Beynon. Ottawa: Canadian Museum of Civilization, 1987.

Creighton, Millie R. "Revisiting Shame and Guilt Cultures: A Forty-Year Pilgrimage." *Ethos: Journal of the Society for Psychological Anthropology* 18.3 (1990): 279–308.

Crosby, Marcia. "Construction of the Imaginary Indian." *By, For & About: Feminist Cultural Politics*. Ed. Wendy Waring. Toronto: Women's Press, 1994. 85–113.

Cruikshank, Julie. In collaboration with Angela Sidney, Kitty Smith, and Annie Ned. *Life Lived Like A Story: Life Stories of Three Yukon Native Elders*. Lincoln: U of Nebraska P 1990. Vancouver: U of British Columbia P, 1990.

Cuddon, J. A. *The Penguin Dictionary of Literary Terms and Literary Theory*. 3rd ed. London: Penguin, 1976.

Culleton, Beatrice. *April Raintree*. Winnipeg: Pemmican, 1983.

———. *In Search of April Raintree*. 1983. Winnipeg: Peguis, 1992.

Currie, Noel Elizabeth. "Jeannette Armstrong & the Colonial Legacy." *Native Writers and Canadian Writing. Canadian Literature: Special Issue.* Ed. W. H. New. Vancouver: U of British Columbia P, 1990. 138–56.

Damm, Kateri. "Dispelling and Telling: Speaking Native Realities in Maria Campbell's 'Halfbreed' and Beatrice Culleton's 'In Search of April Raintree.'" *Looking at the Words of Our People: First Nations Analysis of Literature.* Ed. Jeannette Armstrong. Penticton: Theytus, 1993. 93–113.

Davey, Frank. *Post-National Arguments: The Politics of the Anglophone-Canadian Novel Since 1967.* Toronto: U of Toronto P, 1993.

Davidson, Arnold E. *Coyote Country: Fictions of the Canadian West.* Durham: Duke UP, 1994.

Derrida, Jacques. *Writing and Difference.* Trans. Alan Bass. Chicago: U of Chicago P, 1978.

——. *Dissemination.* Trans. Barbara Johnson. Chicago: Chicago UP, 1981.

Deutsch, Karl W. *Nationalism and Social Communication: An Inquiry into the Foundations of Nationality.* Cambridge: MIT, 1953.

Devine, Patricia G., and Margo J. Monteith. "The Role of Discrepancy-Associated Affect in Prejudice Reduction." *Affect, Cognition, and Stereotyping: Interactive Processes in Group Perception.* Eds. Diane M. Mackie and David L. Hamilton. San Diego: Academic, 1993. 317–45.

Dickason, Olive Patricia. *Canada's First Nations: A History of Founding Peoples from Earliest Times.* Toronto: McClelland & Stewart, 1992.

Donald, James, and Ali Rattansi. *'Race,' Culture & Difference.* London: Sage, 1992.

Donaldson, Laura E. "Noah Meets Old Coyote, or Singing in the Rain: Intertextuality in Thomas King's *Green Grass, Running Water.*" *Studies in American Indian Literature* 7.2 (1995): 27–43.

Dovidio, John F., and Samuel L. Gaertner. "Stereotypes and Evaluative Intergroup Bias." *Affect, Cognition, and Stereotyping: Interactive Processes in Group Perception.* Eds. Diane M. Mackie and David L. Hamilton. San Diego: Academic, 1993. 167–95.

Dumont, James. "Journey to Daylight-Land: Through Ojibwa Eyes." *The First Ones: Readings in Indian/Native Studies.* Eds. David R. Miller, Carl Beal, James Dempsey, and R. Wesley Heber. Piapot Reserve #75: Saskatchewan Indian Federated College, 1992. 75–80.

Dumont, Marilyn. *A Really Good Brown Girl.* London: Brick, 1996.

Dyck, Noel. "Negotiating the Indian Problem." *Out of the Background: Readings on Canadian Native History.* Eds. Robin Fisher and Kenneth Coates. Toronto: Copp Clark Pitman, 1988. 267–84.

Eisenberg, Nancy, ed. *Empathy and Related Emotional Responses.* San Francisco: Jossey-Bass, 1989.

Emberley, Julia V. *Thresholds of Difference: Feminist Critique, Native Women's Writings, Postcolonial Theory.* Toronto: U of Toronto P, 1993.

Engelstad, Diane, and John Bird, eds. *Nation to Nation: Aboriginal Sovereignty and the Future of Canada.* Concord: House of Anansi, 1992.

Erikson, E. H. *Childhood and Society.* New York: Norton, 1950.

Esses, Victoria, M., Geoffrey Haddock, and Mark P. Zanna. "Values, Stereotypes, and Emotions as Determinants of Intergroup Attitudes." *Affect, Cognition, and Stereotyping: Interactive Processes in Group Perception.* Eds. Diane M. Mackie and David L. Hamilton. San Diego: Academic, 1993. 137–67.

Fanon, Frantz. *Black Skin, White Masks.* Trans. Charles Lam Markmann. New York: Grove Weidenfeld, 1967. Originally published as *Peau Noire, Masques Blancs* by Editions du Seuil, Paris, France, 1952.

——. *The Wretched of the Earth.* Trans. Constance Farrington. New York: Grove Weidenfeld, 1963. Originally published as *Les damnés de la terre* by François Maspero éditeur, Paris, France, 1961.

Fedorick, Joy Asham. "Fencepost Sitting and How I Fell Off to One Side." *By, For & About: Feminist Cultural Politics.* Ed. Wendy Waring. Toronto: Women's Press, 1994. 53–68.

Fee, Margery. "Upsetting Fake Ideas: Jeannette Armstrong's 'Slash' and Beatrice Culleton's 'April Raintree'." *Native Writers and Canadian Writing. Canadian Literature: Special Issue.* Ed. W.

H. New. Vancouver: U of British Columbia P, 1990. 168–83.

Fentress, James, and Chris Wickham. *Social Memory*. Oxford and Cambridge: Blackwell, 1992.

Ferguson, Russell, Martha Gever, Trinh T. Minh-ha, and Cornel West, eds. *Out There: Marginalization and Contemporary Cultures*. New York: New Museum of Contemporary Art, 1990.

Findley, Timothy. *Not Wanted on the Voyage*. Toronto: Penguin, 1984.

Finnegan, Ruth. *Oral Traditions and the Verbal Arts: A Guide to Research Practices*. London: Routledge, 1992.

Fisher, Robin. *Contact and Conflict: Indian-European Relations in British Columbia, 1774–1890*. Vancouver: U British Columbia P, 1977.

——, and Kenneth Coates, eds. *Out of the Background: Readings on Canadian Native History*. Mississauga: Copp Clark Pitman, 1988.

Fiske, Susan T., and Janet B. Ruscher. "Negative Interdependence and Prejudice: Whence the Affect?" *Affect, Cognition, and Stereotyping: Interactive Processes in Group Perception*. Eds. Diane M. Mackie and David L. Hamilton. San Diego: Academic, 1993. 239–69.

Foucault, Michel. *The Order of Things*. New York: Random, 1970. Originally published as *Les Mots et les choses* by Editions Gallimard, France, 1966.

——. *Power/Knowledge: Selected Interviews and Other Writings 1972–1977*. Trans. Colin Gordon, Leo Marshall, John Mepham, and Kate Soper. Ed. Colon Gordon. New York: Pantheon, 1980.

Francis, Daniel. *The Imaginary Indian: The Image of the Indian in Canadian Culture*. Vancouver: Arsenal Pulp, 1992.

Freire, Paulo. *Pedagogy of the Oppressed*. Trans. Myra Bergman Ramos. 1970. New York: Continuum, 1993.

Frye, Northrop. *Anatomy of Criticism*. Princeton: Princeton UP, 1957.

Gates, Jr. Henry Louis, ed. *"Race," Writing, and Difference*. 1985. Chicago: U of Chicago P, 1986.

——. *The Signifying Monkey: A Theory of African-American Literacy*

Criticism. Oxford: Oxford UP, 1988.

Getty, Ian A. L., and Antoine S. Lussie, eds. *As Long as the Sun Shines and Water Flows: A Reader in Canadian Native Studies.* Vancouver: U British Columbia P, 1983.

Godard Barbara. "Listening for the Silence: Native Women's Traditional Narratives." *The Native in Literature.* Eds. Thomas King, Cheryl Calver, and Helen Hoy. Oakville: ECW, 1987. 133–58.

——. "The Politics of Representation: Some Native Canadian Women Writers." *Native Writers and Canadian Writing. Canadian Literature: Special Issue.* Ed. W. H. New. Vancouver: U of British Columbia P, 1990. 183–229.

——. "Voicing Difference: The Literary Production of Native Women." *A Mazing Space: Writing Canadian Women Writing.* Eds. Shirley Neuman and Smaro Kamboureli. Edmonton: Longspoon/ NeWest, 1986. 87–107.

Goffman, Erving. *Frame Analysis: An Essay on the Organization of Experience.* Cambridge: Harvard UP, 1974.

——. *Stigma: Notes on the Management of Spoiled Identity.* New York: Simon & Schuster, 1963.

Goldie, Terry. *Fear and Temptation: The Image of the Indigene in Canadian, Australian, and New Zealand Literatures.* Kingston: McGill-Queen's UP, 1989.

Goodchild, Peter, ed. *Raven Tales: Traditional Stories of Native Peoples.* Chicago: Chicago Review, 1991.

Grant, Agnes. "Contemporary Native Women's Voices in Literature." *Native Writers and Canadian Writing. Canadian Literature: Special Issue.* Ed. W. H. New. Vancouver: U of British Columbia P, 1990. 124–33.

Green, Rayna. "Native American Women." *Signs* 6.2 (1980): 248–67.

Guédon, Marie Francoise. "Dene Ways and the Ethnographer's Culture." *Being Changed by Cross-Cultural Encounters: The Anthropology of Extraordinary Experience.* Eds. David E. Young and Jean-Guy Goulet. Peterborough: Broadview, 1994. 39–70.

Haig-Brown, Celia. *Resistance and Renewal: Surviving the Indian Residential School.* Vancouver: Tillacum, 1988.

Hall, Stuart. "Introduction: Who Needs 'Identity.'" *Questions of Cultural Identity*. Eds. Stuart Hall and Paul du Gay. London: Sage, 1996. 1–17.

——. "New Ethnicities." *"Race," Culture & Difference*. Eds. James Donald and Ali Rattansi. London: Sage, 1992. 252–59.

Hamilton, David L., Steven J. Stroessner, and Diane M. Mackie. "The Influence of Affect on Stereotyping: The Case of Illusory Correlations." *Affect, Cognition, and Stereotyping: Interactive Processes in Group Perception*. Eds. Diane M. Mackie and David L. Hamilton. San Diego: Academic, 1993. 39–63.

Harkin, Michael. "History, Narrative, and Temporality: Examples from the Northwest Coast." *Ethnohistory* 35.2 (1988): 99–130.

Harlow, Barbara. *Resistance Literature*. New York: Methuen, 1987.

Henwood, Karen, Howard Giles, Justine Coupland, and Nikolas Coupland. "Stereotyping and Affect in Discourse: Interpreting the Meaning of Elderly, Painful Self-Disclosure." *Affect, Cognition, and Stereotyping: Interactive Processes in Group Perception*. Eds. Diane M. Mackie and David L. Hamilton. San Diego: Academic, 1993. 269–97.

Herman, Edward S., and Noam Chomsky. *Manufacturing Consent: The Political Economy of the Mass Media*. New York: Pantheon, 1988.

Hicks, Emily. *Border Writing: The Multidimensional Text*. Minneapolis: U of Minnesota P, 1991.

Highet, Gilbert. *The Anatomy of Satire*. Princeton: Princeton UP, 1962.

Highway, Tomson. *Dry Lips Oughta Move to Kapuskasing*. Saskatoon: Fifth House, 1989.

——. *The Rez Sisters*. Saskatoon: Fifth House, 1988.

Hoffman, Martin L. "Emotion, Attention, and Temperament." *Emotions, Cognition, and Behavior*. Eds. Carroll E. Izard, Jerome Kagan, and Robert B. Zajonc. Cambridge: Cambridge UP, 1984. 103–32.

——. "Empathy, Its Development and Prosocial Implications." *Nebraska Symposium on Motivation 1977: Social Cognitive Development*. Lincoln: U of Nebraska P, 1977. 169–219.

——. "Toward a Theory of Empathetic Arousal and Development." *The Development of Affect.* Eds. Michael Lewis and Leonard A. Rosenblum. New York: Plenum, 1978. 227–57.

hooks, bell. *Yearning: Race, Gender, and Cultural Politics.* Toronto: Between the Lines, 1990.

——. "Talking Back." *Out There: Marginalization and Contemporary Cultures.* Eds. Russell Ferguson, Martha Gever, Trinh T. Minh-ha, and Cornel West. New York: New Museum of Contemporary Art, 1990. 337–40.

Hoy, Helen. "'Nothing But the Truth': Discursive Transparency in Beatrice Culleton." *Ariel* 25.1 (1994): 155–85.

——. "'When You Admit You're a Thief, Then You Can Be Honourable': Native/Non-Native Collaboration in *The Book of Jessica.*" *Canadian Literature* 136 (Spring 1993): 24–39.

Huggan, Graham. "Decolonizing the Map: Post-Colonialism, Post-Structuralism and the Cartographic Connection." *Ariel* 20.4 (1989): 115–31.

Hughes, David R., and Evelyn Kallen. *The Anatomy of Racism: Canadian Dimensions.* Montreal: Harvest, 1974.

Hunt, Nigel. "Tracking the Trickster." Rev. of *The Rez Sisters and Dry Lips Oughta Move to Kapuskasing,* by Tomson Highway. *Brick* 37 (1989): 58–60.

Hutcheon, Linda. "'Circling the Downspout of Empire': Post-Colonialism and Postmodernism" *Ariel* 20.4 (1989): 149–75.

——. *Irony's Edge: The Theory and Politics of Irony.* London: Routledge, 1994.

——. "Modern Parody and Bakhtin." *Rethinking Bakhtin: Extensions and Challenges.* Eds. Gary Saul Morson and Caryl Emerson. Evanston: Northwestern UP, 1989. 87–103.

——. *Splitting Images: Contemporary Canadian Ironies.* Toronto: Oxford UP, 1991.

Hymes, Dell. "Bungling Host, Benevolent Host: Louis Simpson's 'Deer and Coyote.'" *American Indian Quarterly* 8.3 (1984): 171–98.

Imboden, Roberta. "On the Road with Tomson Highway's Blues Harmonica in 'Dry Lips Oughta Move to Kapuskasing.'" *Canadian Literature* 144 (1995): 113–24.

Izard, Carroll E., Jerome Kagan, and Robert B. Zajonc, eds. *Emotions, Cognition, & Behavior.* Cambridge: Cambridge UP, 1984.

Jacoby, Mario. *Shame and the Origins of Self-Esteem: A Jungian Approach.* Trans. Douglas Whitcher. London: Routledge, 1994.

Jaimes, M. Annette, and Theresa Halsey. "American Indian Women: At the Center of Indigenous Resistance in Contemporary North America." *The State of Native America: Genocide, Colonization, and Resistance.* Ed. M. Annette Jaimes. Boston: South End, 1992. 311–44.

Jameson, Fredric. *The Political Unconscious: Narrative as a Socially Symbolic Act.* Ithaca: Cornell UP, 1981.

JanMohamed, Abdul. "The Economy of Manichean Allegory: The Function of Racial Difference in Colonialist Literature." *Critical Inquiry* 12 (1985): 59–87.

Jaworski, Adam. *The Power of Silence: Social and Pragmatic Perspectives.* London: Sage, 1993.

Jensen, V. "Communicative Functions of Silence." *ETC* 30 (1973): 249–57.

Johnston, Basil H. *Indian School Days.* Toronto: Key Porter, 1988.

——. *Moose Meat and Wild Rice.* Toronto: McClelland and Stewart, 1978.

——. *Ojibway Ceremonies.* Toronto: McClelland and Stewart, 1978.

——. *Ojibway Heritage.* Toronto: McClelland and Stewart, 1976.

——. "One Generation from Extinction." *Native Writers and Canadian Writing. Canadian Literature: Special Issue.* Ed. W. H. New. Vancouver: U of British Columbia P, 1990. 10–19.

Johnston, Denis W. "Lines and Circles: The 'Rez' Plays of Tomson Highway." *Native Writers and Canadian Writing. Canadian Literature: Special Issue.* Ed. W. H. New. Vancouver: U of British Columbia P, 1990. 254–66.

Johnston, Gordon. "An Intolerable Burden of Meaning: Native Peoples in White Fiction." *The Native in Literature.* Eds. Thomas King et al. Oakville: ECW, 1987. 50–66.

Josephy, Alvin M. Jr. *Red Power: The American Indians' Fight for Freedom.* Lincoln: U of Nebraska P, 1971.

Kermode, Frank. *The Sense of an Ending: Studies in the Theory of Fiction*. London: Oxford UP, 1966.

King, Thomas, ed. *All My Relations: An Anthology of Contemporary Canadian Native Fiction*. Toronto: McClelland and Stewart, 1990.

——. *A Coyote Columbus Story*. Toronto: Douglas & McIntyre, 1992.

——. "Godzilla vs. Post-Colonial." *World Literature Written in English* 30.2 (1990): 10–16.

——. *Green Grass, Running Water*. Toronto: HarperCollins, 1993.

——. "Introduction: An Anthology of Canadian Native Fiction." *Canadian Fiction Magazine* 60 (1987): 4–10.

——. *Medicine River*. 1989. Toronto: Penguin, 1991.

——. *One Good Story, That One*. Toronto: Harper Collins, 1993.

——, Cheryl Calver, and Helen Hoy, eds. *The Native in Literature: Canadian and Comparative Perspectives*. Oakville: ECW, 1987.

——, and Greg Staats. "Native Writers of Canada: A Photographic Portrait of 12 Contemporary Authors." *Books in Canada* 23.5 (1994): 12–18.

Krupat, Arnold. "The Dialogic of Silko's Storyteller." *Narrative Chance: Postmodern Discourse on Native American Indian Literature*. Ed. Gerald Vizenor. Albuquerque: University of New Mexico, 1989. 56–68.

——, ed. *New Voices in Native American Literary Criticism*. Washington, DC: Smithsonian Institution, 1993.

——. "Post-Structuralism and Oral Literature." *Recovering the Word: Essays on Native American Literature*. Eds. Arnold Krupat and Brian Swann. Berkeley: U of California P, 1987. 113–28.

——. *The Turn to the Native: Studies in Criticism and Culture*. Lincoln: U of Nebraska P, 1996.

——. *The Voice in the Margin: Native American Literature and the Canon*. Berkeley: U of California P, 1989.

——, and Brian Swann, eds. *Recovering the Word: Essays on Native American Literature*. Berkeley: U of California P, 1987.

Kundera, Milan. *The Book of Laughter and Forgetting*. Trans. Aaron Asher. 1978. New York: Harper Perennial, 1996.

Lacan, Jacques. *The Four Fundamental Concepts of Psychoanalysis.* Trans. A. Sheridan. Ed. J. A. Miller. New York: Norton, 1978.

Laclau, Ernesto. "Universalism, Particularism and the Question of Identity." *The Identity in Question.* Ed. John Rajchman. London: Routledge, 1995. 93–108.

Lakoff, George. *Women, Fire, and Dangerous Things.* Chicago: The U of Chicago P, 1987.

——, and Mark Johnson. *Metaphors We Live By.* Chicago: The U of Chicago P, 1980.

——, and Mark Turner. *More Than Cool Reason: A Field Guide to Poetic Metaphor.* Chicago: U of Chicago P, 1989.

Lanser, Susan S. "Toward a Feminist Narratology." *Feminisms: An Anthology of Literary Theory and Criticism.* Ed. Robyn R. Warhol and Diane Price Herndl. New Brunswick: Rutgers UP, 1991. 610–29.

Lewis, Michael, and Leonard A. Rosenblum, eds. *The Development of Affect.* New York: Plenum, 1978.

Loomba, Ania. *Colonialism/Postcolonialism.* London and New York: Routledge, 1998.

Lundgren, Jodi. "'Being a Half-breed': Discourses of Race and Cultural Syncreticity in the Works of Three Métis Women Writers." *Canadian Literature* 144 (1995): 62–77.

Lutz, Hartmut. *Contemporary Challenges: Conversations with Canadian Native Authors.* Saskatoon: Fifth House, 1991.

Mackie, Diane M., and David L. Hamilton, eds. *Affect, Cognition, and Stereotyping: Interactive Processes in Group Perception.* San Diego: Academic, 1993.

Maracle, Lee. *Bobbi Lee: Indian.* Foreword by Jeannette Armstrong. Ed. Viola Thomas. Toronto: Women's Press, 1990. Originally published as *Bobbi Lee, Indian Sterling,* Liberation Support Movement, 1975.

——. *I Am Woman.* North Vancouver: Write-On, 1988.

——. *Ravensong.* Vancouver: Press Gang, 1993.

——. *Sojourner's Truth and Other Stories.* Vancouver: Press Gang, 1990.

——. *Sundogs.* Penticton: Theytus, 1992.

MacDonald, Mary Lu. "Red & White Men; Black, White & Grey Hats: Literary Attitudes to the Interaction between European and Native Canadians in the First Half of the Nineteenth Century." *Native Writers and Canadian Writing. Canadian Literature: Special Issue.* Ed. W. H. New. Vancouver: U of British Columbia P, 1990. 92–113.

McCormack, Eric. "Coyote Goes Slapstick." Rev. of *Green Grass, Running Water,* by Thomas King. *Books in Canada* 22.3 (1993): 40–41.

McGuire, P. C. *Speechless Dialect: Shakespeare's Open Silences.* Berkeley: U of California P, 1985.

McGrath, Robin. "Oral Influences in Contemporary Inuit Literature." *The Native in Literature.* Eds. Thomas King, Cheryl Calver, and Helen Hoy. Oakville: ECW, 1987. 159–73.

——. "Reassessing Traditional Inuit Poetry." *Native Writers and Canadian Writing. Canadian Literature: Special Issue.* Ed. W. H. New. Vancouver: U of British Columbia P, 1990. 19–32.

McKague, Ormond, gen. ed. *Racism in Canada.* Saskatoon: Fifth House, 1991.

Memmi, Albert. *The Colonizer and the Colonized.* Trans. Howard Greenfeld. Boston: Beacon, 1967. Originally published as *Portrait du Colonisé précédé du Portrait du Colonisateur* by Editions Buchet/Chastel, Corrêa, 1957.

Miller, David R., Carl Beal, James Dempsey, and R. Wesley Heber, eds. *The First Ones: Readings in Indian/Native Studies.* Piapot Reserve #75: Saskatchewan Indian Federated College, 1992.

Miller, Susan. *The Shame Experience.* Hillsdale: Analytic, 1985.

"Mimicry." *The Compact Edition of the Oxford English Dictionary.* Vol. I. Oxford: Oxford UP, 1971. 1799.

Minh-ha, Trinh T. *Woman, Native, Other: Writing Postcoloniality and Feminism.* Bloomington: Indiana UP, 1989.

Momaday, N. Scott. "The Native Voice." *The Columbia Literary History of the United States.* Ed. Emory Elliot. New York: Columbia UP, 1988. 5–15.

Monkman, Leslie. *A Native Heritage: Images of the Indian in English-Canadian Literature.* Toronto: U of Toronto P, 1981.

Monture-Angus, Patricia. *Thunder in My Soul: A Mohawk Woman*

Speaks. Halifax: Fernwood, 1995.

Moore, David L. "Myth, History, and Identity in Silko and Young Bear: Postcolonial Praxis." *New Voices in Native American Literary Criticism*. Ed. Arnold Krupat. Washington, DC: Smithsonian Institution Press, 1993.

Moraga, Cherríe, and Gloria Anzaldúa, eds. *This Bridge Called My Back: Writings by Radical Women of Color*. New York: Kitchen Table, 1981.

Morrison, Toni. *Beloved*. New York: Alfred A. Knopf, 1987.

——. "Unspeakable Things Unspoken: The Afro-American Presence in American Literature." *Michigan Quarterly Review* 28.1 (1989): 1–34.

Morson, Gary Saul, and Caryl Emerson, eds. *Rethinking Bakhtin: Extensions and Challenges*. Evanston: Northwestern UP, 1989.

Moses, Daniel David, and Terry Goldie, eds. *An Anthology of Canadian Native Literature in English*. Toronto: Oxford UP, 1992.

Mulhern, Francis. "English Reading." *Nation and Narration*. Ed. Homi K. Bhabha. London: Routledge, 1990. 250–64.

Naipaul, V. S. *The Mimic Men*. London: Andre Deutsch, 1974. New York: Penguin, 1967.

Nelson, Robert M. *Place and Vision: The Function of Landscape in Native American Fiction*. American Indian Studies. 1. New York: Peter Lang, 1993.

New, W. H., ed. *Native Writers and Canadian Writing*. Vancouver: U of British Columbia P, 1990.

Neuman, Shirley, and Smaro Kamboureli, eds. *A Mazing Space: Writing Canadian Women Writing*. Edmonton: Longspoon, 1986.

O'Brien, Susie. "'Please Eunice, Don't Be Ignorant': The White Reader as Trickster in Lee Maracle's Fiction." *Canadian Literature* 144 (1995): 82–96.

Olsen, Tillie. *Silences*. New York: Delacorte, 1965.

Ong, Walter J. *Orality and Literacy: The Technologizing of the Word*. Methuen, 1982. London: Routledge, 1988.

Ortega y Gasset. *Man and People*. Trans. Willard R. Trask. New

York: Norton, 1957.

Owens, Louis. *Other Destinies: Understanding the American Indian Novel.* Norman: U of Oklahoma P, 1992.

Perreault, Jeanne, and Sylvia Vance, eds. *Writing the Circle: Native Women of Western Canada.* Edmonton: NeWest, 1990.

Petrone, Penny, ed. *First People, First Voices.* Toronto: U of Toronto P, 1991.

——. *Native Literature in Canada: From the Oral Tradition to the Present.* Toronto: Oxford UP, 1990.

Philips, S. U. "Interaction Structured Through Talk and Interaction Structured Through 'Silence.'" *Perspectives on Silence.* Eds. Deborah Tannen and Muriel Saville-Troike. Norwood: Ablex, 1985. 205–13.

Ponting, Rick, ed. *Arduous Journey: Canadian Indians and Decolonization.* Toronto: McClelland & Stewart, 1986.

Pratt, Mary Louise. *Imperial Eyes: Travel Writing and Transculturation.* London: Routledge, 1992.

Pueblo Lands Act of 1924. Pub. L. No. 253. 7 June 1924. Stat. XLIII, Part 1, Chap. 331.

Radin, Paul. *The Trickster: A Study in American Indian Mythology.* New York: Greenwood, 1956.

Rajchman, John, ed. *The Identity in Question.* London: Routledge, 1995.

Redbird, Duke. "From We Are Métis." *An Anthology of Canadian Native Literature in English.* Eds. Daniel David Moses and Terry Goldie. Toronto: Oxford UP, 1992. 121–29.

Ridington, Robin. "Cultures in Conflict: The Problem of Discourse." *Native Writers and Canadian Writing. Canadian Literature: Special Issue.* Ed. W. H. New. Vancouver: U of British Columbia P, 1990. 273–91.

Rigal-Cellard, Bernadette. "Vizenor's *Griever*: A Post-Maodernist Little Red Book of Cocks, Tricksters, and Colonists." *New Voices in Native American Literary Criticism.* Ed. Arnold Krupat. Washington, DC: Smithsonian Institute, 1993. 317–43.

Robinson, Harry. *Write It On Your Heart: The Epic World of an Okanagan Storyteller.* Comp. and ed. Wendy Wickwire.

Vancouver: Talon/Theytus, 1989.

Robinson, Sally. *Engendering the Subject: Gender and Self-Representation in Contemporary Women's Fiction*. Albany: SUNY P, 1991.

Rooke, Constance. "Interview with Tom King." *World Literature Written in English* 30.2 (1990): 62–76.

Rose, Margaret. *Parody: Ancient, Modern, and Post-Modern*. Cambridge: Cambridge UP, 1993.

Rose, Wendy. "The Great Pretenders: Further Reflections on White Shamanism." *The State of Native America: Genocide, Colonization, and Resistance*. Ed. M. Annette Jaimes. Boston: South End, 1992. 403–21.

Ross, Rupert. *Dancing with a Ghost: Exploring Indian Reality*. Markham: Octopus, 1992.

Ruoff, A. LaVonne Brown. *American Indian Literatures: An Introduction, Bibliographic Review, and Selected Bibliography*. New York: MLA, 1990.

——, and Jerry W. Ward, Jr. *Redefining American Literary History*. New York: MLA, 1990.

Rupert, James. *Mediation in Contemporary Native American Fiction*. Norman: U of Oklahoma P, 1995.

Said, Edward. *Culture and Imperialism*. New York: Knopf, 1993.

——. "An Ideology of Difference." *"Race," Writing and Difference*. Ed. Henry Louis Gates, Jr. Chicago: U of Chicago P, 1985. 38–58.

——. *Orientalism*. New York: Vintage, 1979.

——. "Orientalism Reconsidered." *Race and Class* 27 (1985): 1–15.

——. *The World, The Text and The Critic*. Cambridge: Harvard UP, 1983.

Sartre, Jean-Paul. *Being and Nothingness: An Essay on Phenomenological Ontology*. Trans. Hazel E. Barnes. New York: Philosophical Library, 1956.

Scheff, Thomas J. *Microsociology: Discourse, Emotion, and Social Structure*. Chicago: U of Chicago P, 1990.

Schneider, Carl D. *Shame, Exposure and Privacy*. New York: Norton, 1977.

Scholes, Robert, and Robert Kellogg. *The Nature of Narrative*. Oxford: Oxford UP, 1966.

Shohat, Ella, and Robert Stam. *Unthinking Eurocentricism: Multiculturalism and the Media*. London: Routledge, 1994.

Silko, Leslie Marmon. *Ceremony*. New York: Penguin, 1977.

———. "Language and Literature from a Pueblo Indian Perspective." *Critical Fictions: The Politics of Imaginative Writing*. Ed. Philomena Mariani. Seattle: Bay, 1991. 83–93.

Silman, Janet. *Enough Is Enough: Aboriginal Women Speak Out*. Toronto: Women's Press, 1987.

Slemon, Stephen, and Helen Tiffin, eds. *After Europe: Critical Theory and Post-Colonial Writing*. Sydney: Dangaroo, 1989.

Slipperjack, Ruby. *Honour the Sun*. Winnipeg: Pemmican, 1987. (Extracted and revised from the diary of the Owl).

———. *Silent Words*. Saskatoon: Fifth House, 1992.

Sperber, D., and D. Wilson. *Relevance: Communication and Cognition*. Oxford: Blackwell, 1986.

Spivak, Gayatri Chakravorty. "Can the Subaltern Speak?" *Marxism and the Interpretation of Culture*. Eds. Cary Nelson and Lawrence Grossberg. Chicago: U of Illinois P, 1988. 271–313.

———. *In Other Worlds: Essays in Cultural Politics*. New York: Methuen, 1987. London: Routledge, 1988.

———. *The Post-Colonial Critic: Interviews, Strategies, Dialogues*. Ed. Sarah Harasym. London: Routledge, 1990.

———. 'Subaltern Studies: Deconstructing Historiography.' *In Other Worlds: Essays in Cultural Politics*. 197–221.

———. "Three Women's Texts and a Critique of Imperialism." In *"Race," Writing, and Difference*. Ed. Henry Louis Gates, Jr. Chicago: Chicago UP, 1986. 262–80.

Srivastava, Aruna. "'The Empire Writes Back': Language and History in 'Shame' and 'Midnight's Children.'" *Ariel* 20.4 (1989): 62–78.

Steiner, George. "The Retreat from the Word." *Language and Silence: Essays on Language, Literature, and the Inhuman*. New York: Atheneum, 1976. 12–36.

Stephan, Walter G., and Cookie White Stephan. "Cognition and

Affect in Stereotyping: Parallel Interactive Networks." *Affect, Cognition, and Stereotyping: Interactive Processes in Group Perception.* Eds. Diane M. Mackie and David L. Hamilton. San Diego: Academic, 1993. 111–37.

Stern, Kenneth S. *Loud Hawk: The United States versus the American Indian Movement.* Norman: U of Oklahoma P, 1994.

Swann, Brian, ed. *Coming to Light: Contemporary Translations of the Native Literatures of North America.* New York: Random, 1994.

——, ed. *Smoothing the Ground: Essays on Native American Oral Literature.* Berkeley: U of California P, 1983.

Tannen, Deborah. *You Just Don't Understand: Women and Men in Conversation.* New York: Morrow, 1990.

——. *That's Not What I Meant: How Conversational Style Makes or Breaks Your Relations with Others.* New York: Ballantine, 1986.

——. "What's in a Frame?" *New Directions in Discourse Processing.* Ed. R. O. Freedle. Norwood: Ablex, 1979. 137–81.

——, and Muriel Saville-Troike, eds. *Perspectives on Silence.* Norwood: Ablex, 1985.

Taussig, Michael. *Mimesis and Alterity: A Particular History of the Senses.* London: Routledge, 1993.

Tedlock, Dennis. "On the Translation of Style in Oral Narrative." *Smoothing the Ground.* Ed. Brian Swann. Berkeley: U of California P, 1983. 57–77.

——, and Barbara Tedlock, eds. *Teachings from the American Earth: Indian Religion and Philosophy.* New York: Liveright, 1975.

Tennant, Paul. *Aboriginal Peoples and Politics: The Indian Land Question in British Columbia, 1849–1989.* Vancouver: U of British Columbia P, 1990.

Terdiman, Richard. *Discourse/Counter-Discourse: The Theory and Practice of Symbolic Resistance in Nineteenth-Century France.* Ithaca and London: Cornell UP, 1985.

The Telling It Book Collective, eds. *Telling It: Women and Language Across Cultures: The Transformation of a Conference.* Vancouver: Press Gang, 1990.

Thiong'o, Ngugi wa. *Decolonising the Mind: The Politics of Language in African Literature.* London: Currey, 1986.

——. *Moving the Centre: The Struggle for Cultural Freedoms.* London: Currey, 1993.

Tiffin, Helen. "Postcolonial Literatures and Counter-Discourse." *Kunapipi* 9.3 (1987): 17–34.

Todorov, Tzvetan. *The Conquest of America: The Question of the Other.* Trans. Richard Howard. New York: Harper and Row, 1982.

Tomlinson, John. *Cultural Imperialism.* Baltimore: Johns Hopkins UP, 1991.

Usmiani, Renate. "The Bingocentric Worlds of Michel Tremblay and Tomson Highway: 'Les Belles-Soeurs' vs. 'The Rez Sisters.'" *Canadian Literature* 144 (1995): 126–40.

Vangen, Kate. "Making Faces: Defiance and Humor in Campbell's 'Halfbreed' and Welch's 'Winter in the Blood.'" *The Native in Literature.* Eds. Thomas King, Cheryl Calver, and Helen Hoy. Oakville: ECW, 1987. 188–205.

Vanman, Eric J., and Norman Miller. "Applications of Emotion Theory and Research to Stereotyping and Intergroup Relations." *Affect, Cognition, and Stereotyping: Interactive Processes in Group Perception.* Eds. Diane M. Mackie and David L. Hamilton. San Diego: Academic, 1993. 213–39.

Velie, Alan R., ed. *Native American Perspectives on Literature and History.* Norman: U of Oklahoma P, 1994.

Vizenor, Gerald. *Bearheart: The Heirship Chronicles.* Minneapolis: U of Minnesota P, 1978.

——. *Griever: An American Monkey King in China.* Minneapolis: U of Minnesota P, 1987.

——, ed. *Narrative Chance: Postmodern Discourse on Native American Indian Literature.* Albuquerque: U of New Mexico P, 1989. Norman: U of Oklahoma P, 1993.

Walcott, Derek "The Muse of History." *Is Massa Day Dead? Black Moods in the Caribbean.* Ed. Orde Coombes. New York: Doubleday, 1974.

——. "The Schooner Flight." *The Star-Apple Kingdom.* London: Cape, 1977.

Walton, Percy. "'Tell Our Own Stories': Politics and the Fiction of Thomas King." *World Literature Written in English* 30.2 (1990):

77–84.

Waring, Wendy, ed. *By, For & About: Feminist Cultural Politics.* Toronto: Women's Press, 1994.

Warrior, Robert Allen. *Tribal Secrets: Recovering American Indian Intellectual Traditions.* Minneapolis: U of Minnesota P, 1995.

Webber, Jean, and the En'owkin Centre, eds. *Okanagan Sources.* Penticton: Theytus, 1990.

Whorf, Benjamin Lee. *Language, Thought, and Reality: Selected Writings of Benjamin Lee Whorf.* Ed. John B. Carroll. Cambridge: MIT, 1956.

Wiget, Andrew. "His Life in His Tail: The Native American Trickster and the Literature of Possibility." In *Redefining American Literary History.* Eds. A. LaVonne Brown Ruoff and Jerry W. Ward, Jr. New York: MLA, 1990. 83–97.

Wigston, Nancy. "Nanabush in the City." *Books in Canada* 18.2 (March 1989): 7–9.

Wilder, David A. "The Role of Anxiety in Facilitating Stereotypic Judgments of Outgroup Behavior." *Affect, Cognition, and Stereotyping: Interactive Processes in Group Perception.* Eds. Diane M. Mackie and David L. Hamilton. San Diego: Academic, 1993. 87–111.

Williams, Patrick, and Laura Chrisman, eds. *Colonial Discourse and Post-Colonial Theory: A Reader.* New York: Columbia UP, 1994.

Williamson, Janice. *Sounding Differences: Conversations with Seventeen Canadian Women Writers.* Toronto: U of Toronto P, 1993.

Woolf, Virginia. *Between the Acts.* London: Hogarth, 1941. London: Granada, 1978.

Young, Robert J. C. *Colonial Desire: Hybridity in Theory, Culture and Race.* London: Routledge, 1995.

Index

insubordination, 127, 148,
175 (n21)
intentional hybrid, xviii
"interfusional literature," 30,
163 (n4)
"Interview with Tom King"
(Rooke), 27, 30–31, 103
Iron Eyes Screeching Eagles,
39
irony, xxii, 4, 20, 21, 33, 40,
42, 74, 80, 140, 145,
149, 151, 174 (n18)
Isabella, 43
Ishmael, 27, 28, 29, 35, 40,
44, 163 (n 8)

Jacob, Stacey's son, 125
Jacoby, Mario, 112, 114, 115,
116
JanMohamed, Abdul, 38, 93
Jaworski, Adam, 54, 55, 63,
67, 166 (n4)
"Jeannette Armstrong & The
Colonial Legacy"
(Currie), xxi
Jehovah, 33, 160 (n5), 164
(n10)
Jesus Christ, 28, 36
Jimmy, in *Slash*, 95–96, 105,
107
"Joe the Painter"
(King), 7, 20–23
John, 37
Johnson, Mr., 123, 124
Johnston, Basil
"One Generation from
Extinction," xxi
Joseph Hovaugh, 33, 37, 43,

46, 160 (n5), 163 (n8),
164 (n10, n13)
Judy, 116

Karen, 39, 44
"keeper of the ways," 88, 108
Kelasket, Mr., 92, 94, 107
Kelasket, Mrs., 99
King, Thomas, 70, 131
"A Seat in the Garden," 7,
164 (n10)
"Godzilla vs. Post-
Colonial," 26, 30, 31, 70,
163 (n4), 167 (n11)
Green Grass, Running Water,
xvi, 7, 26–49
title of, 32, 163 (n5)
"Joe the Painter," 7, 20–23
Medicine River, 27, 165
(n23)
"The One about Coyote
Going West," xvii, 144–
52
"Totem Poles," 8–9
Kitty Wells, 142
Krupat, Arnold, xx
The Turn to the Native, 27,
30

Laclau, Ernesto, 14–15, 84
Laguna, 16, 18
Lakoff, George
*Women, Fire, and Dangerous
Things*, 73, 168 (n3)
Metaphors We Live By, 63
land, 17, 21, 41, 42, 62, 63,
64, 85, 93, 99, 100, 115,

American Indian Studies

Elizabeth Hoffman Nelson and Malcolm A. Nelson, General Editors

The American Indian Studies series represents a growing group of important books on the literatures and cultures of America's indigenous peoples. The series is inclusive and open to a wide variety of approaches. We welcome scholarly literary studies and interdisciplinary studies of languages and cultures by American Indians, First Nations writers, and non-American Indians.

Original primary texts by American Indian and First Nations authors, thinkers, and religious and political leaders are especially encouraged.

For the submission of manuscripts, contact:

Heidi Burns, Senior Editor
Peter Lang Publishing, Inc.
516 N. Charles St., 2nd Fl.
Baltimore, MD 21201
(410) 385-5362
e-mail: hburnsplp@aol.com